DATE DUE

JA 28 03			

DEMCO 38-296

HUCK FINN

Major Literary Characters

CHELSEA HOUSE PUBLISHERS

Major Literary Characters

DAVID COPPERFIELD
Charles Dickens, *David Copperfield*

ROBINSON CRUSOE
Daniel Defoe, *Robinson Crusoe*

DON JUAN
Molière, *Don Juan*
Lord Byron, *Don Juan*

HUCK FINN
Mark Twain, *The Adventures of Tom Sawyer, Adventures of Huckleberry Finn*

CLARISSA HARLOWE
Samuel Richardson, *Clarissa*

HEATHCLIFF
Emily Brontë, *Wuthering Heights*

ANNA KARENINA
Leo Tolstoy, *Anna Karenina*

MR. PICKWICK
Charles Dickens, *The Pickwick Papers*

HESTER PRYNNE
Nathaniel Hawthorne, *The Scarlet Letter*

BECKY SHARP
William Makepeace Thackeray, *Vanity Fair*

LAMBERT STRETHER
Henry James, *The Ambassadors*

EUSTACIA VYE
Thomas Hardy, *The Return of the Native*

TWENTIETH CENTURY

ÁNTONIA
Willa Cather, *My Ántonia*

BRETT ASHLEY
Ernest Hemingway, *The Sun Also Rises*

HANS CASTORP
Thomas Mann, *The Magic Mountain*

HOLDEN CAULFIELD
J. D. Salinger, *The Catcher in the Rye*

CADDY COMPSON
William Faulkner, *The Sound and the Fury*

JANIE CRAWFORD
Zora Neale Hurston, *Their Eyes Were Watching God*

CLARISSA DALLOWAY
Virginia Woolf, *Mrs. Dalloway*

DILSEY
William Faulkner, *The Sound and the Fury*

GATSBY
F. Scott Fitzgerald, *The Great Gatsby*

HERZOG
Saul Bellow, *Herzog*

JOAN OF ARC
William Shakespeare, *Henry VI*
George Bernard Shaw, *Saint Joan*

LOLITA
Vladimir Nabokov, *Lolita*

WILLY LOMAN
Arthur Miller, *Death of a Salesman*

MARLOW
Joseph Conrad, *Lord Jim, Heart of Darkness, Youth, Chance*

PORTNOY
Philip Roth, *Portnoy's Complaint*

BIGGER THOMAS
Richard Wright, *Native Son*

CHELSEA HOUSE PUBLISHERS

Major Literary Characters

HUCK FINN

Edited and with an introduction by
HAROLD BLOOM

CHELSEA HOUSE PUBLISHERS
New York ◇ Philadelphia

[...] illustration by E. W. Kemble for [...] entures of Huckleberry Finn (1885). [...] Congress. *Inset:* Title page from the [...] ures of Huckleberry Finn. Courtesy of The Library of Congress.

Chelsea House Publishers

Editor-in-Chief   Nancy Toff
Executive Editor   Remmel T. Nunn
Managing Editor   Karyn Gullen Browne
Picture Editor   Adrian G. Allen
Art Director   Maria Epes
Manufacturing Manager   Gerald Levine

Major Literary Characters

Managing Editor   S. T. Joshi
Copy Chief   Richard Fumosa
Designer   Maria Epes

Staff for HUCK FINN

Researcher   Mary Lawlor
Editorial Assistant   Anne Knepler
Picture Researcher   Sue Biederman
Assistant Art Director   Loraine Machlin
Production Coordinator   Joseph Romano
Production Assistant   Leslie D'Acri

7   9   8

Library of Congress Cataloging-in-Publication Data

Huck Finn / edited and with an introduction by Harold Bloom.
p.   cm.—(Major literary characters)
Bibliography: p.
Includes index.
ISBN 0-7910-0940-9.—ISBN 0-7910-0995-5 (pbk.)
1. Twain, Mark, 1835–1910. Adventures of Huckleberry Finn.
2. Finn, Huckleberry (Fictitious character). I. Bloom, Harold.
II. Series.
PS1305.H827   1990
813'.4—dc19
89—31352
CIP

CONTENTS

CONTENTS

HAROLD BLOOM

The Analysis of Character

"Character," according to our dictionaries, still has as a primary meaning a graphic symbol, such as a letter of the alphabet. This meaning reflects the word's apparent origin in the ancient Greek *charactēr*, a sharp stylus. *Charactēr* also meant the mark of the stylus' incisions. Recent fashions in literary criticism have reduced "character" in literature to a matter of marks upon a page. But our word "character" also has a very different meaning, matching that of the ancient Greek *ēthos*, "habitual way of life." Shall we say then that literary character is an imitation of human character, or is it just a grouping of marks? The issue is between a critic like Dr. Samuel Johnson, for whom words were as much like people as like things, and a critic like the late Roland Barthes, who told us that "the fact can only exist linguistically, as a term of discourse." Who is closer to our experience of reading literature, Johnson or Barthes? What difference does it make, if we side with one critic rather than the other?

Barthes is famous, like Foucault and other recent French theorists, for having added to Nietzsche's proclamation of the death of God a subsidiary demise, that of the literary author. If there are no authors, then there are no fictional personages, presumably because literature does not refer to a world outside language. Words indeed necessarily refer to other words in the first place, but the impact of words ultimately is drawn from a universe of fact. Stories, poems, and plays are recognizable as such because they are human utterances within traditions of utterance, and traditions, by achieving authority, become a kind of fact, or at least the sense of a fact. Our sense that literary characters, within the context of a fictive cosmos, indeed are fictional personages is also a kind of fact. The meaning and value of every character in a successful work of literary representation depend upon our ideas of persons in the factual reality of our lives.

Literary character is always an invention, and inventions generally are indebted to prior inventions. Shakespeare is the inventor of literary character as we know it; he reformed the universal human expectations for the verbal imitation of personality, and the reformation appears now to be permanent and uncannily inevitable. Remarkable as the Bible and Homer are at representing personages, their characters are relatively unchanging. They age within their stories, but their habitual modes of being do not develop. Jacob and Achilles unfold before us, but without metamorphoses. Lear and Macbeth, Hamlet, and Othello severely modify themselves not only by their actions, but by their utterances, and most of all through *overhearing themselves,* whether they speak to themselves or to others. Pondering what they themselves have said, they will to change, and actually do change, sometimes extravagantly yet always persuasively. Or else they suffer change, without willing it, but in reaction not so much to their language as to their relation to that language.

I do not think it useful to say that Shakespeare successfully imitated elements in our characters. Rather, it could be argued that he compelled aspects of character to appear that previously were concealed, or not available to representation. This is not to say that Shakespeare is God, but to remind us that language is not God either. The mimesis of character in Shakespeare's dramas now seems to us normative, and indeed became the accepted mode almost immediately, as Ben Jonson shrewdly and somewhat grudgingly implied. And yet, Shakespearean representation has surprisingly little in common with the imitation of reality in Jonson or in Christopher Marlowe. The origins of Shakespeare's originality in the portrayal of men and women are to be found in the *Canterbury Tales* of Geoffrey Chaucer, insofar as they can be located anywhere before Shakespeare himself. Chaucer's savage and superb Pardoner overhears his own tale-telling, as well as his mocking rehearsal of his own spiel, and through this overhearing he is emboldened to forget himself, and enthusiastically urges all his fellow-pilgrims to come forward to be fleeced by him. His self-awareness, and apocalyptically rancid sense of spiritual fall, are preludes to the even grander abysses of the perverted will in Iago and in Edmund. What might be called the character trait of a negative charisma may be Chaucer's invention, but came to its perfection in Shakespearean mimesis.

The analysis of character is as much Shakespeare's invention as the representation of character is, since Iago and Edmund are adepts at analyzing both themselves and their victims. Hamlet, whose overwhelming charisma has many negative components, is certainly the most comprehensive of all literary characters, and so necessarily prophesies the labyrinthine complexities of the will in Iago and Edmund. Charisma, according to Max Weber, its first codifier, is primarily a natural endowment, and implies a primordial and idiosyncratic power over nature, and so finally over death. Hamlet's uncanniness is at its most suggestive in the scene of his long dying, where the audience, through the mediation of Horatio, itself is compelled to meditate upon suicide, if only because outliving the prince of Denmark scarcely seems an option.

Shakespearean representation has usurped not only our sense of literary character, but our sense of ourselves as characters, with Hamlet playing the part of the largest of these usurpations. Insofar as we have an idea of human disinterestedness, we tend to derive it from the Hamlet of Act V, whose quietism has about it a ghostly authority. Oscar Wilde, in his profound and profoundly witty dialogue, "The Decay of Lying," expressed a permanent insight when he insisted that art shaped every era, far more than any age formed art. Life imitates art, we imitate Shakespeare, because without Shakespeare we would perish for lack of images. Wilde's grandest audacity demystifies Shakespearean mimesis with a Shakespearean vivaciousness: "This unfortunate aphorism about art holding the mirror up to Nature is deliberately said by Hamlet in order to convince the bystanders of his absolute insanity in all art-matters." Of *Hamlet*'s influence upon the ages Wilde remarked that: "The world has grown sad because a puppet was once melancholy." "Puppet" is Wilde's own deconstruction, a brilliant reminder that Shakespeare's artistry of illusion has so mastered reality as to have changed reality, evidently forever.

The analysis of character, as a critical pursuit, seems to me as much a Shakespearean invention as literary character was, since much of what we know about how to analyze character necessarily follows Shakespearean procedures. His hero-villains, from Richard III through Iago, Edmund, and Macbeth, are shrewd and endless questers into their own self-motivations. If we could bear to see Hamlet, in his unwearied negations, as another hero-villain, then we would judge him the supreme analyst of the darker recalcitrances in the selfhood. Freud followed the pre-Socratic Empedocles, in arguing that character is fate, a frightening doctrine that maintains the fear that there are no accidents, that overdetermination rules us all of our lives. Hamlet assumes the same, yet adds to this argument the terrible passivity he manifests in Act V. Throughout Shakespeare's tragedies, the most interesting personages seem doom-eager, reminding us again that a Shakespearean reading of Freud would be more illuminating than a Freudian exegesis of Shakespeare. We learn more when we discover Hamlet in the Freudian Death Drive, than when we read *Beyond the Pleasure Principle* into *Hamlet*.

In Shakespearean comedy, character achieves its true literary apotheosis, which is the representation of the inner freedom that can be created by great wit alone. Rosalind and Falstaff, perhaps alone among Shakespeare's personages, match Hamlet in wit, though hardly in the metaphysics of consciousness. Whether in the comic or the modern mode, Shakespeare has set the standard of measurement in the balance between character and passion.

In Shakespeare the self is more dramatized than theatricalized, which is why a Shakespearean reading of Freud works out so well. Character-formation after the passing of the Oedipal stage takes the place of fetishistic fragmentings of the self. Critics who now call literary character into question, and who proclaim also the death of the author, invariably also regard all notions, literary and human, of a stable character as being mere reductions of deeper pre-Oedipal desires. It becomes clear that the fortunes of literary character rise and fall with the prestige of normative conceptions of the ego. Shakespeare's Iago, who wars against being, may be the first deconstructionist of the self, with his proclamation of "I am not what I am." This constitutes the necessary prologue to any view that would regard a fixed ego as a virtual abnormality. But deconstructions of the self are no more modern than Modernism is. Like literary modernism, the decentered ego came out of the Hellenistic culture of ancient Alexandria. The Gnostic heretics believed that the psyche, like the body, was a fallen entity, mechanically fashioned by the Demiurge or false creator. They held however that each of us possessed also a spark or pneuma, which was a fragment of the original Abyss or true, alien God. The soul or psyche within every one of us was thus at war with the self or pneuma, and only that sparklike self could be saved.

Shakespeare, following after Chaucer in this respect, was the first and remains still the greatest master of representing character both as a stable soul and a wavering self. There is a substance that endures in Shakespeare's figures, and there is also a quicksilver rendition of the unsettling sparks. Racine and Tolstoy, Balzac and Dickens, follow in Shakespeare's wake by giving us some sense of pre-Oedipal sparks or drives, and considerably more sense of post-Oedipal character and personality, stabilizations or sublimations of the fetish-seeking drives. Critics like Leo Bersani and René Girard argue eloquently against our taking this mimesis as the only proper work of literature. I would suggest that strong fictions of the self, from the Bible through Samuel Beckett, necessarily participate in both modes, the sublimation of desire, and the persistence of a primordial desire. The mystery of Hamlet or of Lear is intimately invested in the tangled mixture of the two modes of representation.

Psychic mobility is proposed by Bersani as the ideal to which deconstructions of the literary self may yet guide us. The ideal has its pathos, but the realities of literary representation seem to me very different, perhaps destructively so. When a novelist like D. H. Lawrence sought to reduce his characters to Eros and the Death Drive, he still had to persuade us of his authority at mimesis by lavishing upon the figures of *The Rainbow* and *Women in Love* all of the vivid stigmata of normative personality. Birkin and Ursula may represent antithetical and uncanny drives, but they develop and change as characters pondering their own pronouncements and reactions to self and others. The cost of a non-Shakespearean representation is enormous. Pynchon, in *The Crying of Lot 49* and *Gravity's Rainbow,* evades the burden of the normative by resorting to something like Christopher Marlowe's art of caricature in *The Jew of Malta.* Marlowe's Barabas is a marvelous rhetorician, yet he is a cartoon alongside the troublingly equivocal Shylock. Pynchon's personages are deliberate cartoons also, as flat as comic strips. Marlowe's achievement, and Pynchon's, are beyond dispute, yet they are like the prelude and the postlude to Shakespearean reality. They do not wish to engage with our hunger for the empirical world and so they enter the problematic cosmos of literary fantasy.

No writer, not even Shakespeare or Proust, alters the available stock that we agree to call reality, but Shakespeare, more than any other, does show us how much of reality we could encounter if only we retained adequate desire. The strong literary representation of character is already an analysis of character, and is part of the healing work of a literary culture, which implicitly seeks to cure violence through a normative mimesis of ego, *as if it were stable,* whether in actuality it is or is not. I do not believe that this is a social quest taken on by literary culture, but rather that we confront here the aesthetic essence of what makes a culture *literary,* rather than metaphysical or ethical or religious. A culture becomes literary when its conceptual modes have failed it, which means when religion, philosophy, and science have begun to lose their authority. If they cannot heal violence, then literature attempts to do so, which may be only a turning inside out of the critical arguments of Girard and Bersani.

I conclude by offering a particular instance or special case as a paradigm for the healing enterprise that is at once the representation and the analysis of literary character. Let us call it the aesthetics of being outraged, or rather of successfully representing the state of being outraged. W. C. Fields was one modern master of such representation, and Nathanael West was another, as was Faulkner before him. Here also the greatest master remains Shakespeare, whose Macbeth, himself a bloody outrage, yet retains our imaginative sympathy precisely because he grows increasingly outraged as he experiences the equivocation of the fiend that lies like truth. The double-natured promises and the prophecies of the weird sisters finally induce in Macbeth an apocalyptic version of the stage actor's anxiety at missing cues, the horror of a phantasmagoric stage fright of missing one's time, of always reacting too late. Macbeth, a veritable monster of solipsistic inwardness but no intellectual, counters his dilemma by fresh murders, that prolong him in time yet provoke him only to a perpetually freshened sense of being outraged, as all his expectations become still worse confounded. We are moved by Macbeth, however estrangedly, because his terrible inwardness is a paradigm for our own solipsism, but also because none of us can resist a strong and successful representation of the human in a state of being outraged.

The ultimate outrage is the necessity of dying, an outrage concealed in a multitude of masks, including the tyrannical ambitions of Macbeth. I suspect that our outrage at being outraged is the most difficult of all our affects for us to represent to ourselves, which is why we are so inclined to imaginative sympathy for a character who strongly conveys that affect to us. The Shrike of West's *Miss Lonelyhearts* or Faulkner's Joe Christmas of *Light in August* are crucial modern instances, but such figures can be located in many other works, since the ability to represent this extreme emotion is one of the tests that strong writers are driven to set for themselves.

However a reader seeks to reduce literary character to a question of marks on a page, she will come at last to the impasse constituted by the thought of death, her death, and before that to all the stations of being outraged that memorialize her own drive towards death. In reading, she quests for evidences that are strong representations, whether of her desire or her despair. Such questings constitute the necessary basis for the analysis of literary character, an enterprise that always will survive every vagary of critical fashion.

EDITOR'S NOTE

This book gathers together a representative selection of the best criticism of Mark Twain's Huck Finn as a literary character. I am grateful to Mary Lawlor for her skill as a researcher in helping edit this volume.

My introduction seeks to apply the principles of my series essay on "The Analysis of Character" to the senses in which Huck incarnates freedom while suggesting also an earlier mode of being than any now available to us.

A chronological series of critical excerpts begins with Twain himself and his friend, the novelist William Dean Howells, while continuing with such eminent writers as Sherwood Anderson, Carl Van Doren, F. Scott Fitzgerald, Ernest Hemingway, William Faulkner, and Lionel Trilling, all of whom emphasize the ways in which Huck Finn is perhaps the greatest of American originals.

Leo Marx begins another sequence by criticizing the views of T. S. Eliot and Lionel Trilling that defended the aesthetic adequacy of Huck's behavior in the novel's conclusion. The great African-American novelist, Ralph Ellison, questions that moral adequacy even more severely, as does Leslie A. Fiedler in a more Freudian mode, while James M. Cox defends it as appropriate to the comic mode, a defense joined in by Kenneth S. Lynn. Jesse Bier attempts to bring Fiedler up to date, while Neil Schmitz renews our awareness of the American centrality of Huck's humor. Esoteric grace notes are provided by Albert Waldinger and Hana Wirth-Nesher. David R. Sewell returns us to the fascinating triumphs of Huck's highly individual language.

The full-scale essays begin with Richard Poirier's celebrated demonstration as to Huck's immersion in the conventions he seeks to escape. Alan Trachtenberg emphasizes the paradoxes involved in Huck's quest for freedom, while Warwick Wadlington shows how class structures also are entangled in Huck's approaches to others. In the discussion by Susan K. Harris, Huck's relation to the river is seen as encompassing some of the same dilemmas.

R. J. Fertel traces the problematic process of maturation in Huck, after which Roger Asselineau investigates Emersonian elements in Twain's hero. In Millicent Bell's analysis of Huck's own imagination, as in Lee Clark Mitchell's examination of

Huck's language, we are given fresh modes for perceiving the American vagabond.

Nancy Walker contemplates Huck's attitudes towards women, while John S. Whitley examines Huck in the context of a world of boys. Patterns of evasion and deception in Huck's character are analyzed by Forrest G. Robinson, while in this volume's final essay Harold Beaver centers upon Huck's relation to his murderous father.

INTRODUCTION

Huck Finn seeks freedom; that is the judgment of Leo Marx and of most good critics of *Adventures of Huckleberry Finn.* What critics disagree about is the nature of Huck's longed-for freedom. Is it freedom *for* something, or primarily freedom *from* many things—society, family, respectability, daily reality, growing up, and ultimately dying?

Huck's family consists of a dangerous, indeed murderous father, who might always turn up again, somehow. Obviously, freedom in the first place must mean freedom from such a deathly father, and continuous motion, like that of the great river, is the best way of evading the father, and so the very best place to be is on the raft. But freedom for Huck does not mean solitude—Huck is neither a god nor a beast, and he is afraid of being alone, as most of us are. That must be why Jim is the perfect companion for him, particularly when Jim is in flight, a flight that in itself already is as much freedom as Jim so far has known.

But Huck is not a Kerouac beatnik on the road, just going for the sake of going. Huck is not a drifter, but more accurately a shrewd and kindly observer, who does not value his own freedom above the reality of other people, as say Thoreau did. Indeed, one accurate way of seeing Huck is to ponder the difference between Huck and Jim on the raft and Thoreau at Walden Pond. Thoreau's greatest pride is in economic freedom above all things, and so in getting his values right. He will not pay a jot more for anything than what it is worth. But Huck is always willing to overpay—up to a point—and with the currency of his leisure and his concern, including his capacity for compassion and affection.

Huck overpays for the friendship of Tom Sawyer, which is one way of explaining why the book ends so lamely, and perhaps he overpays also for most of his adventures, since he is morally superior to everyone he encounters, except for Jim. If the theme of the book is the search for freedom, and the book's major image is the river, then the theme and the image only superficially fit one another. The river is not in itself free, anymore than Walden Pond is—the river *must* move, and the pond *must* stay fixed in place. Perhaps the book after all is not just about freedom, but about the limits of freedom as well.

Yet that is the book, and not the literary character, Huck Finn. Huck's central dilemma defines the spiritual uniqueness of our country, for if Huck fears solitude, nevertheless he is driven to crave it. There are two crucial tenets in what I think must be called *the* American Religion, of which Emerson was the theologian, and Mark Twain the authorized Fool, or national storyteller. One is that no American feels free if she is not alone; the other is that every American passionately believes that she is no part of the Creation. Huck, no theologian, implicitly identifies himself with what preceded Creation, and so with what must regard all Creation, however beautiful, as a kind of Fall, since Creation introduces death and time into a Fullness beyond them. The superstitions that govern Huck, and his teacher, Jim, ultimately take their authority from the river, itself not free and yet somehow an emblem of freedom. It is as though the Fullness of the original Abyss takes its final representation in the river, and in those whom the river instructs.

Huck's superstitions (and Jim's, and Twain's, for that matter) are not at all African-American, but go back to the Thracian, shamanistic origins of Western folk-religion, to what can be regarded as Orphic traditions. As befits an American Orphic, Huck's Orphism bears a marked difference from the ancient variety. The emphasis is not upon the survival of an occult self, but upon survival plain and simple, upon the continuity of the self. That is the burden of the justly famous final paragraph of the book:

> Tom's most well, now, and got his bullet around his neck on a watch-guard, for a watch, and is always seeing what time it is, and so there ain't nothing more to write about, and I am rotten glad of it, because if I'd a knowed what a trouble it was to make a book I wouldn't a tackled it and ain't agoing to no more. But I reckon I got to light out for the Territory ahead of the rest, because Aunt Sally she's going to adopt me and sivilize me and I can't stand it. I been there before.

The bullet indeed is rightly a timepiece, in Huck's vision, and the identity of bullet and watch is part of our discomfort with culture, our discontent with supposed civilization. It is one of the poems of our climate, Walt Whitman's, that Huck joins in reckoning that he must light out for the Territory ahead of the rest of us. Lighting out upon the open road is the largest American lie against time, and Huck is the grandest of our deliberate liars, lying always, as he says, even just to keep in practice. Nietzsche warned that incessant lying is the most exhausting of modes, and one of the darknesses of Huck's character is how exhausted he so perpetually impresses us as having become. Unlike Twain, Huck is neither a humorist nor a misanthrope, as T. S. Eliot sensibly noted. Unlike Eliot, Huck does not aver that mankind cannot bear very much reality. I cannot recall many major literary characters who resign themselves to bearing as much reality as Huck does, since his capacity for fellow-feeling is well-nigh infinite.

Some critics have interpreted Huck's quest as being not for freedom, but for family. We can smile at the prospect of a fully domesticated Huck, while granting that the boy's fierce loneliness generates much of his marvelous pathos. Yet Huck's lies defend him against all fixed identity, because identity is not to be trusted. As the son of a murderous father, Huck evades identity and loves without trust, and so without expecting to be loved in return. The trope of fatherhood is allied for Huck with the murderousness of time, the universe of death. In turning to the river, and to Jim, Huck abandons any quest for family and chooses instead an origin that will also be an end, a fullness that has little to do with nature, and has much in common with Whitman's retrievements out of the night.

V. S. Pritchett once observed that Tom Sawyer was imaginative, but that Huck was not: "Huck never imagines anything except fears." Empirically, Pritchett may have been right, yet Huck's anxieties are considerably more impressive and moving than Tom's imaginary adventures, and Huck is clearly the more imaginative creation. He is like Whitman's Real Me or Me Myself, "both in and out of the game, and watching and wondering at it." His status as observer may be the product of estrangement or repression, but his observations have the curious authority of an anxiety that nevertheless does not seek to appropriate for itself. A good-hearted anxiety ought to be an oxymoron, but is not when we consider the character of Huck. That in turn leads to the question most central to judging Huck as a character: do we think of him as a boy, or as an ageless consciousness?

I cannot conceive of Huck Finn other than as he is, and aging could not change him. He need neither unfold nor develop, for there is nothing immature in him. His affections are fully formed, and would never abandon him. The Hamlet of Act I and of Act V are different men, yet we do not feel a contradiction between them, because the later Hamlet is the severely purged and purified form of the earlier. Huck is already his final self, even as a boy. What cannot alter in Huck is his will, which is both relatively unconditioned and wholly benign. One sees why Hemingway found his Nick Adams in Huck, and why Jake Barnes and the other major Hemingway protagonists are versions of Huck. Like their vagabond precursor, they are too pure in will to be violated by any experience. Huck will not sour or darken, even though he will never trust anyone, with the single and saving exception of Jim, and the more dubious instance of Tom Sawyer.

A wholly secular being, Huck nevertheless incarnates the American religion of reliance upon what is best and oldest in the self. History falls away before that spark of the best and oldest, because the spark takes no stock in dead people, which was Huck's reaction to Moses. Huck's concern is with the living, and with what is alive within the living. He is more Hemingway than Hemingway could be, because he begins with what Hemingway studies as nostalgia, and recovers only by the *ascesis* of his style. Huck is the image of freedom most central to American literary culture. The image represents loneliness and wildness, as well as freedom, and how could Huck not be lonely, being as he is a kind of originary *daemon?* A dead mother and a murderous father are less central to Huck than we can imagine. At his center there is a spark of an earlier Orphic existence, and he incarnates ancient truths that he himself cannot know, and that as Americans we relearn from him.

—H. B.

CRITICAL EXTRACTS

MARK TWAIN

⟨Twain:⟩ "I don't believe an author, good, bad or indifferent, ever lived, who created a character. It was always drawn from his recollection of someone he had known. Sometimes, like a composite photograph, an author's presentation of a character may possibly be from the blending of more than two or more real characters in his recollection. But, even when he is making no attempt to draw his character from life, when he is striving to create something different, even then, however ideal his drawing, he is yet unconsciously drawing from memory. It is like a star so far away that the eye cannot discover it through the most powerful telescope, yet if a camera is placed in proper position under that telescope and left for a few hours, a photograph of the star will be the result. So, it's the same way with the mind; a character one has known some time in life may have become so deeply buried within the recollection that the lens of the first effort will not bring it to view. But by continued application the author will find when he is done, that he has etched a likeness of some one he has known before.

"In attempting to represent some character which he cannot recall, which he draws from what he thinks is his imagination, an author may often fall into the error of copying in part a character already drawn by another, a character which impressed itself upon his memory from some book. So he has but made a picture of a picture with all his pains. We mortals can't create, we can only copy. Some copies are good and some are bad."

—Cited in LUKE PEASE, "The Famous Story-Teller Discusses Characters,"
Portland Oregonian, August 11, 1895, p. 10

W. D. HOWELLS

The story ⟨*The Adventures of Tom Sawyer*⟩ is a wonderful study of the boy-mind, which inhabits a world quite distinct from that in which he is bodily present with his elders, and in this lies its great charm and its universality, for boy nature, however human nature varies, is the same everywhere.

The tale is very dramatically wrought, and the subordinate characters are treated with the same graphic force that sets Tom alive before us. The worthless vagabond, Huck Finn, is entirely delightful throughout, and in his promised reform his identity is respected: he will lead a decent life in order that he may one day be thought worthy to become a member of that gang of robbers which Tom is to organize. Tom's aunt is excellent, with her kind heart's sorrow and secret pride in Tom; and so is his sister Mary, one of those good girls who are born to usefulness and charity and forbearance and unvarying rectitude. Many village people and local notables are introduced in well-conceived character; the whole little town lives in the reader's sense, with its religiousness, its lawlessness, its droll social distinctions, its civilization qualified by its slaveholding, and its traditions of the wilder West which has passed away. The picture will be instructive to those who have fancied the whole Southwest a sort of vast Pike County, and have not conceived of a sober and serious and orderly contrast to the sort of life that has come to represent the Southwest in literature.

—W. D. HOWELLS, *"The Adventures of Tom Sawyer"* [1875], *My Mark Twain* (New York: Harper & Brothers, 1910), p. 127

R. E. PHILLIPS

In both ⟨*Tom Sawyer* and *Huckleberry Finn*⟩, there is something more than humor and the delineation of humorous character. In the character of Huck Finn, the outcast and son of the village drunkard, is summed up in some sort the entire spirit of justice and equality—democracy in its broadest sense—of the Southwest of half a century ago. He is more than the Lazarillo of the picaresque novel; more, even, than Hugo's Gavroche, the immortal ragamuffin of fiction. For they were only gamins, the outcasts of the lowest round of society. Huck Finn is the equal not only of all the characters in the book, but of all readers. In spite of his birth, he is human; he has our sympathy; we must own him brother. It is the consummate art of the author that has brought this result to bear. But it is the broad spirit of equality, the result of actual experience and long familiarity with the ideas and ideals of that early Southwestern life that, in the first instance, made the conception of such a character possible.

—R. E. PHILLIPS, "Mark Twain: More Than Humorist," *Book Buyer* 22, No. 3 (April 1901): 199

SHERWOOD ANDERSON

Dear Brooks: I am glad you are going to get at Twain. It is absurd that he should have been translated as an artist by a man like Howells or that fellow ⟨Albert

Bigelow) Paine. There is something about him no one has got hold of. He belonged out here in the Middle West and was only incidentally a writer.

I've a notion that after Twain passed under the influence of Howells and others of the East he began to think of himself as a writer and lost something of his innocence. Should not one go to *Huck Finn* for the real man, working out of a real people?

Several years ago I tried to write a story concerning Twain. It never got to anything, but I have a copy of the attempt in my desk. There is a character in the story, the old cheese maker from Indiana, that I will sometime make the central figure in a real story. He is Twain's type of man.

It is odd what literary connections one makes. In my own mind I have always coupled Mark Twain with George Borrow. I get the same quality of honesty in them, the same wholesome disregard of literary precedent.

—SHERWOOD ANDERSON, Letter to Van Wyck Brooks (early April 1918), *Letters of Sherwood Anderson,* ed. Howard Mumford Jones and Walter B. Rideout (Boston: Little, Brown, 1953), pp. 30–31

SHERWOOD ANDERSON

My dear Brooks: Your letter has stirred up a world of thought in me. It isn't Twain I'm thinking of, but the profound truth of some of your own observations.

As far as Twain is concerned, we have to remember the influences about him. Remember how he came into literature—the crude buffoon of the early days in the mining camp, the terrible cheap and second-rate humor of much of *Innocents Abroad.* It seems to me that when he began he addressed an audience that gets a big laugh out of the braying of a jackass, and without a doubt Mark often brayed at them. He knew that later. There was tenderness and subtlety in Mark when he grew older.

You get the picture of him, Brooks—the river man who could write going East and getting in with that New England crowd, the fellows from barren hills and barren towns. The best he got out of the bunch was Howells, and Howells did Twain no good.

There's another point, Brooks. I can't help wishing Twain hadn't married such a good woman. There was such a universal inclination to tame the man—to save his soul, as it were. Left alone, I fancy Mark might have been willing to throw his soul overboard and then—ye gods, what a fellow he might have been, what poetry might have come from him.

⟨. . .⟩ The cultural fellows got hold of Mark. They couldn't hold him. He was too big and too strong. He brushed their hands aside.

But their words got into his mind. In the effort to get out beyond that he became a pessimist.

Now, Brooks, you know a man cannot be a pessimist who lives near a brook or a cornfield. When the brook chatters or at night when the moon comes up and the wind plays in the corn, a man hears the whispering of the gods.

Mark got to that once—when he wrote *Huck Finn*. He forgot Howells and the good wife and everyone. Again he was the half-savage, tender, god-worshiping, believing boy. He had proud, conscious innocence.

I believe he wrote that book in a little hut on a hill on his farm. It poured out of him. I fancy that at night he came down from his hill stepping like a king, a splendid playboy playing with rivers and men, riding on the Mississippi, on the broad river that is the great artery flowing out of the heart of the land.

Well, Brooks, I'm alone in a boat on that stream sometimes. The rhythm and swing of it is in some of my songs that are to be published next month. It sometimes gets into some of the Winesburg things. I'll ride it some more, perhaps. It depends on whether or not I can avoid taking myself serious[ly]. Whom the gods wish to destroy they first make drunk with the notion of being a writer.

—SHERWOOD ANDERSON, Letter to Van Wyck Brooks (early April 1918), *Letters of Sherwood Anderson,* ed. Howard Mumford Jones and Walter B. Rideout (Boston: Little, Brown, 1953), pp. 32–33

CARL VAN DOREN

A restless traveler, ⟨Twain⟩ wandered over America and Europe, and he lectured around the earth. Enough of a reader to find out what he wanted to know about the past, he went through it exactly as he went through the present. He saw everything with the eye of innocence. An American Adam, he did not know or care that the beasts in the garden had been named by earlier Adams and had traditional reputations for goodness and badness, ugliness or beauty. Mark Twain spoke like a new Adam, calling new names. The world, sluggish with opinions held by rote, heard him, suddenly perceived how right he was, and laughed.

No man of genius could find so much to laugh at without finding also much to hate. Mark Twain's hatred of cruelty and stupidity, of oppression and superstition and hypocrisy, lengthened the thrust of his ridicule. His burlesque of knightly life under King Arthur and his tender chronicle of Joan of Arc were at the same time savage forays against ancient wrongs. Many of his comments on contemporary life were stern and bitter. Yet the solid body of his work rose from his own memory of his real or imagined adventures. The older the memory the better the story.

In *Huckleberry Finn,* the high point of his achievement, he reached back to the Mississippi of his boyhood, when the great river had bounded his life and flowed through his imagination. He took Huck Finn from his native village to drift, as the actual Mark Twain had not been allowed to do, to freedom on the Mississippi. With a fugitive slave for his companion, Huck must not be seen. He must travel most of the time by night and lie and steal his way. The river is his universe of comedy and tragedy. Telling Huck's story, Mark Twain had small need of exaggeration. The

Mississippi, as he remembered it and his boyish idea of it, was more than any man could make up. The truth would do.

Perhaps he scarcely noticed that his memory had been touched by grandeur during creative years. Nor did this grandeur put out wings and lose itself in a void like that which had hovered over Melville's Pacific. Ahab had been metaphysical and mad. Huck was green, sly, and sane. Mark Twain had to cut the river to fit the understanding of his hero. He could be eloquent about it only in words which Huck might have used. As Huck's dimensions gave the story its form, so his nature colored its materials. Seen through him, as narrator, the episodes have a double innocence and are doubly comic. Laughter springs from both the story and the story-teller.

Huckleberry Finn is Mark Twain in his simplest words. It is the folk-tale of the American people told in their language by their Man Laughing. It is the epic of America's happy memory as *Moby-Dick* is the epic of America's unquiet mind.

—CARL VAN DOREN, *What Is American Literature?* [1933] (New York: William Morrow, 1935), pp. 81–84

F. SCOTT FITZGERALD

Huckleberry Finn took the first journey *back*. He was the first to look *back* at the republic from the perspective of the West. His eyes were the first eyes that ever looked at us objectively that were not eyes from overseas. There were mountains at the frontier but he wanted more than mountains to look at with his restless eyes—he wanted to find out about men and how they lived together. And because he turned back we have him forever.

—F. SCOTT FITZGERALD, Letter to Cyril Clemens (c. November 30, 1935), *Correspondence of F. Scott Fitzgerald*, ed. Matthew J. Bruccoli and Margaret M. Duggan (New York: Random House, 1980), p. 424

ERNEST HEMINGWAY

"The good writers are Henry James, Stephen Crane, and Mark Twain. That's not the order they're good in. There is no order for good writers."

"Mark Twain is a humorist. The others I do not know."

"All modern American literature comes from one book by Mark Twain called *Huckleberry Finn*. If you read it you must stop where the Nigger Jim is stolen from the boys. That is the real end. The rest is just cheating. But it's the best book we've had. All American writing comes from that. There was nothing before. There has been nothing as good since."

—ERNEST HEMINGWAY, *Green Hills of Africa* (New York: Scribner's, 1935), p. 22

WILLIAM FAULKNER

On the day the ⟨new financial⟩ plan goes into effect, I will get at a novel. I think I have a good one; I intend to get at it soon anyway. It is a sort of Huck Finn—a normal boy of about twelve or thirteen, a big, warmhearted, courageous, honest, utterly unreliable white man with the mentality of a child, an old negro family servant, opinionated, querulous, selfish, fairly unscrupulous, and in his second childhood, and a prostitute not very young anymore and with a great deal of character and generosity and common sense, and a stolen race horse which none of them actually intended to steal. The story is how they travel for a thousand miles from hand to mouth trying to get away from the police long enough to return the horse. All of them save the white man think the police are after the horse. The white man knows the police have been put on his tail by his harridan of a wife whom he has fled from. Actually, the police are trying to return the boy to his parents to get the reward. The story lasts a matter of weeks. During that time the boy grows up, becomes a man, and a good man, mostly because of the influence of the whore. He goes through in miniature all the experiences of youth which mold the man's character.   They happen to be the very experiences which in his middle class parents' eyes stand for debauchery and degeneracy and actual criminality; through them he learned courage and honor and generosity and pride and pity. He has been absent only weeks, but as soon as his mother sees him again, she knows what has happened to him. She weeps, says, 'He is not my baby anymore.'

—WILLIAM FAULKNER, Letter to Robert K. Haas (May 3, 1940),
Selected Letters of William Faulkner, ed. Joseph Blotner (New York:
Random House, 1977), pp. 123–24

JUDITH BRYANT WITTENBERG

Faulkner called *The Reivers* his "Huck Finn" novel when he first began it, and shortly before returning to the work a final time he referred to Mark Twain as "the father of American literature"—a phrase which recalls Hemingway's famous judgment that all modern American literature is descended from one book by Mark Twain called *Huckleberry Finn.* As critics have often noted, there are many Twainian elements in *The Reivers*—the intertwining of physical and psychological journeys in the experiences of the boy protagonist, the comradeship of white boy and black man, the earthy humor, and the maintenance of the first-person narration from a child's point of view, albeit from a grandfatherly perspective—and since Faulkner's work became increasingly like Twain's as time went on, it seems appropriate that his final novel should be a modern version of *Huckleberry Finn.*

—JUDITH BRYANT WITTENBERG, *Faulkner: The Transfiguration of
Biography* (Lincoln: University of Nebraska Press, 1979), p. 239

LIONEL TRILLING

Perhaps the best clue to the greatness of *Huckleberry Finn* has been given to us by a writer who is as different from Mark Twain as it is possible for one Missourian to be from another. T. S. Eliot's poem, "The Dry Salvages," the third of his *Four Quartets,* begins with a meditation on the Mississippi, which Mr. Eliot knew in his St. Louis boyhood:

> I do not know much about gods; but I think that the river
> Is a strong brown god ...

And the meditation goes on to speak of the god as

>   almost forgotten
> By the dwellers in cities—ever, however, implacable,
> Keeping his seasons and rages, destroyer, reminder of
> What men choose to forget. Unhonoured, unpropitiated
> By worshippers of the machine, but waiting, watching and waiting.

Huckleberry Finn is a great book because it is about a god—about, that is, a power which seems to have a mind and will of its own, and which to men of moral imagination appears to embody a great moral idea.

Huck himself is the servant of the river-god, and he comes very close to being aware of the divine nature of the being he serves. The world he inhabits is perfectly equipped to accommodate a deity, for it is full of presences and meanings which it conveys by natural signs and also by preternatural omens and taboos: to look at the moon over the left shoulder, to shake the tablecloth after sundown, to handle a snakeskin, are ways of offending the obscure and prevalent spirits. Huck is at odds, on moral and aesthetic grounds, with the only form of established religion he knows, and his very intense moral life may be said to derive almost wholly from his love of the river. He lives in a perpetual adoration of the Mississippi's power and charm. Huck, of course, always expresses himself better than he can know, but nothing draws upon his gift of speech like his response to his deity. After every sally into the social life of the shore, he returns to the river with relief and thanksgiving; and at each return, regular and explicit as a chorus in a Greek tragedy, there is a hymn of praise to the god's beauty, mystery, and strength, and to his noble grandeur in contrast with the pettiness of men.

Generally the god is benign, a being of long sunny days and spacious nights. But, like any god, he is also dangerous and deceptive. He generates fogs which bewilder, and contrives echoes and false distances which confuse. His sand bars can ground and his hidden snags can mortally wound a great steamboat. He can cut away the solid earth from under a man's feet and take his house with it. The sense of the danger of the river is what saves the book from any touch of the sentimentality and moral ineptitude of most works which contrast the life of nature with the life of society.

The river itself is only divine; it is not ethical and good. But its nature seems to foster the goodness of those who love it and try to fit themselves to its ways. And we must observe that we cannot make—that Mark Twain does not make—an absolute opposition between the river and human society. To Huck much of the charm of the river life is human: it is the raft and the wigwam and Jim. He has not run away from Miss Watson and the Widow Douglas and his brutal father to a completely individualistic liberty, for in Jim he finds his true father, very much as Stephen Dedalus in James Joyce's *Ulysses* finds his true father in Leopold Bloom. (In Joyce's *Finnegans Wake* both Mark Twain and Huckleberry Finn appear frequently. The theme of rivers is, of course, dominant in the book; and Huck's name suits Joyce's purpose, for Finn is one of the many names of his hero. Mark Twain's love of and gift for the spoken language make another reason for Joyce's interest in him.) The boy and the Negro slave form a family, a primitive community—and it is a community of saints.

Huck's intense and even complex moral quality may possibly not appear on a first reading, for one may be caught and convinced by his own estimate of himself, by his brags about his lazy hedonism, his avowed preference for being alone, his dislike of civilization. The fact is, of course, that he is involved in civilization up to his ears. His escape from society is but his way of reaching what society ideally dreams of for itself. Responsibility is the very essence of his character, and it is perhaps to the point that the original of Huck, a boyhood companion of Mark Twain's named Tom Blenkenship, did, like Huck, "light out for the Territory," only to become a justice of the peace in Montana, "a good citizen and greatly respected."

Huck does indeed have all the capacities for simple happiness he says he has, but circumstances and his own moral nature make him the least carefree of boys—he is always "in a sweat" over the predicament of someone else. He has a great sense of the sadness of human life, and although he likes to be alone, the words "lonely" and "loneliness" are frequent with him. The note of his special sensibility is struck early in the story: "Well, when Tom and me got to the edge of the hilltop we looked away down into the village and could see three or four lights twinkling where there were sick folks, maybe; and the stars over us was sparkling ever so fine; and down by the village was the river, a whole mile broad, and awful still and grand." The identification of the lights as the lamps of sick-watches defines Huck's character.

His sympathy is quick and immediate. When the circus audience laughs at the supposedly drunken man who tries to ride the horse, Huck is only miserable: "It wasn't funny to me . . .; I was all of a tremble to see his danger." When he imprisons the intending murderers on the wrecked steamboat, his first thought is of how to get someone to rescue them, for he considers "how dreadful it was, even for murderers, to be in such a fix. I says to myself, there ain't no telling but I might come to be a murderer myself yet, and then how would I like it." But his sympathy is never sentimental. When at last he knows that the murderers are beyond help, he has no inclination to false pathos. "I felt a little bit heavy-hearted about the gang, but not much, for I reckoned that if they could stand it I could." His will is genuinely good and he has no need to torture himself with guilty second thoughts.

Not the least remarkable thing about Huck's feeling for people is that his tenderness goes along with the assumption that his fellow men are likely to be dangerous and wicked. He travels incognito, never telling the truth about himself and never twice telling the same lie, for he trusts no one and the lie comforts him even when it is not necessary. He instinctively knows that the best way to keep a party of men away from Jim on the raft is to beg them to come aboard to help his family stricken with smallpox. And if he had not already had the knowledge of human weakness and stupidity and cowardice, he would soon have acquired it, for all his encounters forcibly teach it to him—the insensate feud of the Graingerfords and Shepherdsons, the invasion of the raft by the Duke and the King, the murder of Boggs, the lynching party, and the speech of Colonel Sherburn. Yet his profound and bitter knowledge of human depravity never prevents him from being a friend to man.

No personal pride interferes with his well-doing. He knows what status is and on the whole he respects it—he is really a very *respectable* person and inclines to like "quality folks"—but he himself is unaffected by it. He himself has never had status, he has always been the lowest of the low, and the considerable fortune he had acquired in *The Adventures of Tom Sawyer* is never real to him. When the Duke suggests that Huck and Jim render him the personal service that accords with his rank, Huck's only comment is, "Well, that was easy so we done it." He is injured in every possible way by the Duke and the King, used and exploited and manipulated, yet when he hears that they are in danger from a mob, his natural impulse is to warn them. And when he fails of his purpose and the two men are tarred and feathered and ridden on a rail, his only thought is, "Well, it made me sick to see it; and I was sorry for them poor pitiful rascals, it seemed like I couldn't ever feel any hardness against them any more in the world."

And if Huck and Jim on the raft do indeed make a community of saints, it is because they do not have an ounce of pride between them. Yet this is not perfectly true, for the one disagreement they ever have is over a matter of pride. It is on the occasion when Jim and Huck have been separated by the fog. Jim has mourned Huck as dead, and then, exhausted, has fallen asleep. When he awakes and finds that Huck has returned, he is overjoyed, but Huck convinces him that he has only dreamed the incident, that there has been no fog, no separation, no chase, no reunion, and then allows him to make an elaborate "interpretation" of the dream he now believes he has had. Then the joke is sprung, and in the growing light of the dawn Huck points to the debris of leaves on the raft and the broken oar.

> Jim looked at the trash, and then looked at me, and back at the trash again. He had got the dream fixed so strong in his head that he couldn't seem to shake it loose and get the facts back into its place again right away. But when he did get the thing straightened around he looked at me steady without ever smiling, and says:

"What do dey stan' for? I'se gwyne to tell you. When I got all wore out wid work, en wid de callin' for you, en went to sleep, my heart wuz mos' broke bekase you wuz los', en I didn' k'yer no mo' what became er me en de raf'. En when I wake up en fine you back agin, all safe en soun', de tears come, en I could a got down on my knees en kiss yo' foot, I's so thankful. En all you wuz thinkin' 'bout wuz how you could make a fool uv ole Jim wid a lie. Dat truck dah is *trash;* en trash is what people is dat puts dirt on de head er dey fren's en makes 'em ashamed."

Then he got up slow and walked to the wigwam, and went in there without saying anything but that.

The pride of human affection has been touched, one of the few prides that has any true dignity. And at its utterance, Huck's one last dim vestige of pride of status, his sense of his position as a white man, wholly vanishes: "It was fifteen minutes before I could work myself up to go and humble myself to a nigger; but I done it, and I warn't sorry for it afterwards either."

This incident is the beginning of the moral testing and development which a character so morally sensitive as Huck's must inevitably undergo. And it becomes an heroic character when, on the urging of affection, Huck discards the moral code he has always taken for granted and resolves to help Jim in his escape from slavery. The intensity of his struggle over the act suggests how deeply he is involved in the society which he rejects. The satiric brilliance of the episode lies, of course, in Huck's solving his problem not by doing "right" but by doing "wrong." He has only to consult his conscience, the conscience of a Southern boy in the middle of the last century, to know that he ought to return Jim to slavery. And as soon as he makes the decision according to conscience and decides to inform on Jim, he has all the warmly gratifying emotions of conscious virtue. "Why, it was astonishing, the way I felt as light as a feather right straight off, and my troubles all gone. . . . I felt good and all washed clean of sin for the first time I had ever felt so in my life, and I knowed I could pray now." And when at last he finds that he cannot endure his decision but must sacrifice the comforts of the pure heart and help Jim in his escape, it is not because he has acquired any new ideas about slavery—he believes that he detests Abolitionists; he himself answers when he is asked if the explosion of a steamboat boiler had hurt anyone, "No'm, killed a nigger," and of course finds nothing wrong in the responsive comment, "Well, it's lucky because sometimes people do get hurt." Ideas and ideals can be of no help to him in his moral crisis. He no more condemns slavery than Tristram and Lancelot condemn marriage; he is as consciously *wicked* as any illicit lover of romance and he consents to be damned for a personal devotion, never questioning the justice of the punishment he has incurred.

Huckleberry Finn was once barred from certain libraries and schools for its alleged subversion of morality. The authorities had in mind the book's endemic lying, the petty thefts, the denigrations of respectability and religion, the bad language, and the bad grammar. We smile at that excessive care, yet in point of fact *Huckleberry Finn* is indeed a subversive book—no one who reads thoughtfully the dialectic of Huck's great moral crisis will ever again be wholly able to accept without some question and some irony the assumptions of the respectable morality by which he lives, nor will ever again be certain that what he considers the clear dictates of moral reason are not merely the engrained customary beliefs of his time and place.

—LIONEL TRILLING, *"Huckleberry Finn," The Liberal Imagination*
(New York: Viking Press, 1950), pp. 106–13

LEO MARX

From the electrifying moment when Huck comes back to Jackson's Island and rouses Jim with the news that a search party is on the way, we are meant to believe that Huck is enlisted in the cause of freedom. "Git up and hump yourself, Jim!" he cries. "There ain't a minute to lose. They're after us!" What particularly counts here is the *us*. No one is after Huck; no one but Jim knows he is alive. In that small word Clemens compresses the exhilarating power of Huck's instinctive humanity. His unpremeditated identification with Jim's flight from slavery is an unforgettable moment in American experience, and it may be said at once that any culmination of the journey which detracts from the urgency and dignity with which it begins will necessarily be unsatisfactory. Huck realizes this himself, and says so when, much later, he comes back to the raft after discovering that the Duke and the King have sold Jim:

> After all this long journey ... here it was all come to nothing, everything all busted up and ruined, because they could have the heart to serve Jim such a trick as that, and make him a slave again all his life, and amongst strangers, too, for forty dirty dollars.

Huck knows that the journey will have been a failure unless it takes Jim to freedom. It is true that we do discover, in the end, that Jim is free, but we also find out that the journey was not the means by which he finally reached freedom. ⟨. . .⟩

The conflict between what people think they stand for and what social pressure forces them to do is central to the novel. It is present to the mind of Huck and, indeed, accounts for his most serious inner conflicts. He knows how he feels about Jim, but he also knows what he is expected to do about Jim. This division within his mind corresponds to the division of the novel's moral terrain into the areas represented by the raft on the one hand and society on the other. His victory over his "yaller dog" conscience therefore assumes heroic size: it is a victory over the prevailing morality. But the last fifth of the novel has the effect of diminishing the importance and uniqueness of Huck's victory. We are asked to assume that somehow freedom can be achieved in spite of the crippling power of what I have called the social morality. Consequently the less importance we attach to that force as it operates in the novel, the more acceptable the ending becomes. ⟨. . .⟩

Should Clemens have made Huck a tragic hero? Both Mr. Eliot and Mr. Trilling argue that that would have been a mistake, and they are very probably correct. But between the ending as we have it and tragedy in the fullest sense, there was vast room for invention. Clemens might have contrived an action which left Jim's fate as much in doubt as Huck's. Such an ending would have allowed us to assume that the principals were defeated but alive, and the quest unsuccessful but not abandoned. This, after all, would have been consonant with the symbols, the characters, and the theme as Clemens had created them—and with history.

—LEO MARX, "Mr. Eliot, Mr. Trilling, and Huckleberry Finn," American Scholar 22, No. 4 (Autumn 1953): 425–26, 435–36, 439

RALPH ELLISON

Despite their billings as images of reality, ⟨the⟩ Negroes of fiction are counterfeits. They are projected aspects of an internal symbolic process through which, like a primitive tribesman dancing himself into the group frenzy necessary for battle, the white American prepares himself emotionally to perform a social role. These fictive Negroes are not, as sometimes interpreted, simple racial clichés introduced into society by a ruling class to control political and economic realities. For although they are manipulated to that end, such an externally one-sided interpretation relieves the individual of personal responsibility for the health of democracy. Not only does it forget that a democracy is a collectivity of *individuals,* but it never suspects that the tenacity of the stereotype springs exactly from the fact that its function is no less personal than political. Color prejudice springs not from the stereotype alone, but from an internal psychological state; not from misinformation alone, but from an inner need to believe. It thrives not only on the obscene witch-doctoring of men like Jimmy Byrnes and Malan, but upon an inner craving for symbolic magic. The prejudiced individual creates his own stereotypes, very often unconsciously, by reading into situations involving Negroes those stock meanings which justify his emotional and economic needs.

Hence whatever else the Negro stereotype might be as a social instrumentality, it is also a key figure in a magic rite by which the white American seeks to resolve the dilemma arising between his democratic beliefs and certain antidemocratic practices, between his acceptance of the sacred democratic belief that all men are created equal and his treatment of every tenth man as though he were not.

Thus on the moral level I propose that we view the whole of American life as a drama acted out upon the body of a Negro giant, who, lying trussed up like Gulliver, forms the stage and the scene upon which and within which the action unfolds. If we examine the beginning of the Colonies, the application of this view is not, in its economic connotations at least, too far-fetched or too difficult to see. For then the Negro's body was exploited as amorally as the soil and climate. It was later, when white men drew up a plan for a democratic way of life, that the Negro began slowly to exert an influence upon America's moral consciousness. Gradually he was recognized as the human factor placed outside the democratic master plan, a human "natural" resource who, so that white men could become more human, was elected to undergo a process of institutionalized dehumanization.

Until the Korean War this moral role had become obscured within the staggering growth of contemporary science and industry, but during the nineteenth century it flared nakedly in the American consciousness, only to be repressed after the Reconstruction. During periods of national crises, when the United States rounds a sudden curve on the pitch-black road of history, this moral awareness surges in the white American's conscience like a raging river revealed at his feet by a lightning flash. Only then is the veil of anti-Negro myths, symbols, stereotypes and taboos drawn somewhat aside. And when we look closely at our literature it is to be seen operating even when the Negro seems most patently the little man who isn't there. ⟨. . .⟩

For perspective let us begin with Mark Twain's great classic, *Huckleberry Finn*. Recall that Huckleberry has run away from his father, Miss Watson and the Widow Douglas (indeed the whole community, in relation to which he is a young outcast) and has with him as companion on the raft upon which they are sailing down the Mississippi the Widow Watson's runaway Negro slave, Jim. Recall, too, that Jim, during the critical moment of the novel, is stolen by two scoundrels and sold to another master, presenting Huck with the problem of freeing Jim once more. Two ways are open: he can rely upon his own ingenuity and "steal" Jim into freedom or he might write the Widow Watson and request reward money to have Jim returned to her. But there is a danger in this course, remember, since the angry widow might sell the slave down the river into a harsher slavery. It is this course which Huck starts to take, but as he composes the letter he wavers.

> "It was a close place." [he tells us] "I took it [the letter] up, and held it in my hand. I was trembling, because I'd got to decide, forever, 'twixt two things, and I knowed it. I studied a minute, sort of holding my breath, and then says to myself:
>
> " 'Alright, then, I'll *go* to hell'—and tore it up, . . . It was awful thoughts and awful words, but they was said . . . And I let them stay said, and never thought no more about reforming. I shoved the whole thing out of my head and said I would take up wickedness again, which was in my line, being brung up to it, and the other warn't. And for a starter I would . . . steal Jim out of slavery again. . . ."

And a little later, in defending his decision to Tom Sawyer, Huck comments, "I know you'll say it's dirty, low-down business but *I'm* low-down. And I'm going to steal him . . ."

We have arrived at a key point of the novel and, by an ironic reversal, of American fiction, a pivotal moment announcing a change of direction in the plot, a reversal as well as a recognition scene (like that in which Oedipus discovers his true identity) wherein a new definition of necessity is being formulated. Huck Finn has struggled with the problem poised by the clash between property rights and human rights, between what the community considered to be the proper attitude toward an escaped slave and his knowledge of Jim's humanity, gained through their adventures as fugitives together. He has made his decision on the side of humanity. In this passage Twain has stated the basic moral issue centering around Negroes and the white American's democratic ethics. It dramatizes as well the highest point of tension generated by the clash between the direct, human relationships of the frontier and the abstract, inhuman, market-dominated relationships fostered by the rising middle class—which in Twain's day was already compromising dangerously with the most inhuman aspects of the defeated slave system. And just as politically these forces reached their sharpest tension in the outbreak of the Civil War, in *Huckleberry Finn* (both the boy and the novel) their human implications come to sharpest focus around the figure of the Negro.

Huckleberry Finn knew, as did Mark Twain, that Jim was not only a slave but a human being, a man who in some ways was to be envied, and who expressed his essential humanity in his desire for freedom, his will to possess his own labor, in his loyalty and capacity for friendship and in his love for his wife and child. Yet Twain, though guilty of the sentimentality common to humorists, does not idealize the slave. Jim is drawn in all his ignorance and superstition, with his good traits and his bad. He, like all men, is ambiguous, limited in circumstance but not in possibility. And it will be noted that when Huck makes his decision he identifies himself with Jim and accepts the judgment of his superego—that internalized representative of the community—that his action is evil. Like Prometheus, who for mankind stole fire from the gods, he embraces the evil implicit in his act in order to affirm his belief in humanity. Jim, therefore, is not simply a slave, he is a symbol of humanity, and in freeing Jim, Huck makes a bid to free himself of the conventionalized evil taken for civilization by the town.

This conception of the Negro as a symbol of Man—the reversal of what he represents in most contemporary thought—was organic to nineteenth-century literature. It occurs not only in Twain but in Emerson, Thoreau, Whitman and Melville (whose symbol of evil, incidentally, was white), all of whom were men publicly involved in various forms of deeply personal rebellion. And while the Negro and the color black were associated with the concept of evil and ugliness far back in the Christian era, the Negro's emergence as a symbol of value came, I believe, with Rationalism and the rise of the romantic individual of the eighteenth century. This, perhaps, because the romantic was in revolt against the old moral authority, and if he suffered a sense of guilt, his passion for personal freedom was such that he was willing to accept evil (a tragic attitude) even to identifying himself with the "noble slave"—who symbolized the darker, unknown potential side of his personality, that underground side, turgid with possibility, which might, if given a chance, toss a fistful of mud into the sky and create a "shining star."

Even that prototype of the bourgeois, Robinson Crusoe, stopped to speculate as to his slave's humanity. And the rising American industrialists of the late nineteenth century were to rediscover what their European counterparts had learned a century before: that the good man Friday was as sound an investment for Crusoe morally as he was economically, for not only did Friday allow Crusoe to achieve himself by working for him, but by functioning as a living scapegoat to contain Crusoe's guilt over breaking with the institutions and authority of the past, he made it possible to exploit even his guilt economically. The man was one of the first missionaries.

Mark Twain was alive to this irony and refused such an easy (and dangerous) way out. Huck Finn's acceptance of the evil implicit in his "emancipation" of Jim represents Twain's acceptance of his personal responsibility in the condition of society. This was the tragic face behind his comic mask.

But by the twentieth century this attitude of tragic responsibility had disappeared from our literature along with that broad conception of democracy which vitalized the work of our greatest writers. After Twain's compelling image of black and white fraternity the Negro generally disappears from fiction as a rounded human being. And if already in Twain's time a novel which was optimistic concerning a democracy which would include all men could not escape being banned from public libraries, by our day his great drama of interracial fraternity had become, for most Americans at least, an amusing boy's story and nothing more. But, while a boy, Huck Finn has become by the somersault motion of what William Empson terms "pastoral," an embodiment of the heroic, and an exponent of humanism. Indeed, the historical and artistic justification for his adolescence lies in the fact that Twain was depicting a transitional period of American life; its artistic justification is that adolescence is the time of the "great confusion" during which both individuals and nations flounder between accepting and rejecting the responsibilities of adulthood. Accordingly, Huck's relationship to Jim, the river, and all they symbolize, is that of a humanist; in his relation to the community he is an individualist. He embodies the two major conflicting drives operating in nineteenth-century America. And if humanism is man's basic attitude toward a social order which he accepts, and individualism his basic attitude toward one he rejects, one might say that Twain, by allowing these two attitudes to argue dialectically in his work of art, was as highly moral an artist as he was a believer in democracy, and vice versa.

—RALPH ELLISON, "Twentieth-Century Fiction and the
Black Mask of Humanity" [1953], *Shadow and Act* (New York:
Random House, 1964), pp. 27–34

LESLIE A. FIEDLER

The Good Bad Boy is, of course, America's vision of itself, crude and unruly in his beginnings, but endowed by his creator with an instinctive sense of what is right.

Sexually as pure as any milky maiden, he is a roughneck all the same, at once potent and submissive, made to be reformed by the right woman. No wonder our greatest book is about a boy and that boy "bad"! The book is, of course, *Huckleberry Finn* (with its extension back into *Tom Sawyer*), an astonishingly complicated novel, containing not one image of the boy but a series of interlocking ones. Tom Sawyer exists as the projection of all that Sid Sawyer, pious Good Good Boy, presumably yearns for and denies; but Huck Finn in turn stands for what Tom is not quite rebel enough to represent; and Nigger Jim (remade from boy to adult between the two books) embodies a world of instinct and primal terror beyond what even the outcast white boy projects.

In our national imagination, two freckle-faced boys, arm in arm, fishing poles over their shoulders, walk toward the river; or one alone floats peacefully on its waters, a runaway Negro by his side. They are on the lam, we know, from Aunt Polly and Aunt Sally and the widow Douglas and Miss Watson, from golden-haired Becky Thatcher, too—from all the reduplicated female symbols of "sivilization." It is these images of boyhood which the popular imagination further debases step by step via Penrod and Sam or O. Henry's "Red Chief" to Henry Aldrich on the radio or the insufferable Archie of the teen-age comic books. Such figures become constantly more false in their naïveté, in their hostility to culture in general and schoolteachers in particular; and it scarcely matters whether they are kept in the traditional costume of overalls or are permitted jeans and sweaters decorated with high-school letters.

Twain is surely not responsible for all the vulgar metamorphoses of his images of boyhood; but in one respect he is a conscious accomplice of the genteel kidnapers of Huck and Jim. Since not only in his avowed children's books, but almost everywhere in his work, Twain writes as a boy for a world accustomed to regarding the relations of the sexes in terms of the tie that binds mother to son. Not only does he disavow physical passion, refusing the Don Juan role traditional for European writers; but he downgrades even the Faustian role incumbent on American authors. In him, the diabolic outcast becomes the "little devil," not only comical but cute, a child who will outgrow his mischief, or an imperfect adult male, who needs the "dusting off" of marriage to a good woman. It was in the fading '60's that Twain's typical fictional devices were contrived, in the '70's that they were perfected—at a time, that is to say, when everywhere in the popular American novel the archetypes were being reduced to juveniles. As Clarissa becomes a small girl in *The Wide, Wide World*, so Werther becomes a child in Twain's total work, turns into the boy-author Mark Twain; and not only the American women who made Susan Warner's book a best-seller approve, but their husbands, too, who laughed at their wives' taste—just as Twain had at his wife's before being challenged to write *The Gilded Age*. Even dirty, tired, adult Europe approves, finds no offense in *The Innocents Abroad* itself, since Twain was playing a role that European self-hatred and condescension to the United States demanded, acting the Good Bad Boy of Western culture. For everyone, male and female, European and

American, he represents the id subverting tired ego-ideals, not in terror and anarchy, but in horseplay, pranks, and irreverent jests.

—LESLIE A. FIEDLER, *Love and Death in the American Novel*
(New York: Criterion Books, 1960; rev. ed. New York:
Stein & Day, 1966), pp. 270–72

JAMES M. COX

The freeing of the vernacular from the conventions is the larger historical fact of form which provides an index to the action of the novel. For this vernacular language, which implies respectable language, is not only the form of the book; it is at one and the same time the character of Huckleberry Finn. To talk about the revolt of the one should be to talk about the revolt of the other. I say *should*, because Huck's revolt seems on the face of things a genuinely tame performance. He is involved in a subversive project which has the reader's complete approval— the freeing of a slave in the Old South, a world which, by virtue of the Civil War, has been declared morally reprehensible because of the slavery it condoned. Huck's rebellion is therefore being negotiated in a society which the reader's conscience indicts as morally wrong and which history has declared legally wrong. Moreover, Huck is a boy, a relatively harmless figure who drifts helplessly into his rebellion, making his subversion not only an act which the reader can approve but can indulge. His badness is inverted into goodness.

All this seems obvious, yet many readers never cease to celebrate the pluck of Huck's rebellion, when if this were all there was to it we would have nothing but the blandest sentimental action. What, after all, was courageous about writing in Hartford twenty years after the Civil War—or what is courageous about reading in a post–Civil War world—a book about a boy who was helping a slave to freedom? Such an act would be roughly equivalent to writing a novel in our time about a boy in Hitler's Germany helping a Jew to the border. Not that a great novel could not emerge from either of these subjects. In the case of *Huckleberry Finn* one did. Yet the boldness of the book—its exploration and discovery—does not reside in so tame a representation, but in the utilization of the action to gain the reader's assent to make the voyage downstream. ⟨. . .⟩

And what of Huck? As Nick Carraway said of Gatsby, he came out all right. He went to the territory because he was true to himself and to his creator. He didn't go there to lead civilization either, but to play outside it. Refusing to grow up and tell the lie of the conscience, he left behind him a novel for all time. It was truly a novel of reconstruction. First, it had brought into fiction not the Old South but an entirely new one which the Northern conscience could welcome back into the Union. And in the process of its humor, it reconstructed the psyche, following the pleasure principle as far as it would go to discover in the southern reaches of the Great River the tyranny of the conscience which keeps the adult in chains and makes his pleasure the enactment of greater and greater cruelty. He had not reached childhood's end, but had disclosed the lie of the adult world. In his last moment he said, "so there ain't nothing more to write about, and I am rotten glad of it, because if I'd 'a'knowed what a trouble it was to make a book I wouldn't 'a'tackled it, and ain't a-going to no more." We of course constantly lecture Mark Twain about having turned away from his true vein of ore. The fact is, however, that he could not turn away but kept trying to do just what we want of him. He kept trying to call Huck back to tell another story. But Huck, though he came docilely, could never tell the truth. He had told all the truth he had to tell in one glorious lie.

—JAMES M. COX, *Mark Twain: The Fate of Humor* (Princeton: Princeton University Press, 1966), pp. 169–70, 183–84

KENNETH S. LYNN

Potentially, the Widow Douglas, "fair, smart, and forty," is the most interesting female character Mark Twain ever created. We meet her for the first time in *Tom Sawyer*. The house she occupies atop beautiful Cardiff Hill, "the only palace in town," symbolizes her social position in the St. Petersburg community. As hospitable as she is intelligent, this aristocratic lady gives parties that are "the most lavish ... that St. Petersburg could boast." Her generosities, furthermore, are not limited to her gentry friends or to people of her own age. So far as we know, the Widow herself is childless, but she likes and understands boys and girls all the same, and encourages them to come see her. It is only natural that Tom Sawyer should suggest to Becky Thatcher that they "climb right up the hill and stop at the Widow Douglas'. She'll have ice-cream! She has it most every day—dead loads of it. And she'll be awful glad to have us." Even Huckleberry Finn, the juvenile pariah of the village, son of the town drunkard and an illiterate woman long since dead, with whom the middle-class mothers of St. Petersburg have forbidden their children to associate, has "more than once" been befriended by the Widow. In all likelihood she has fed him when he was hungry, for Huck's principal complaint about the anarchic life he leads is that "I don't ever get enough to eat, gen'ally."

One dark night, on the edge of the Widow's estate, Huck overhears the dreaded Injun Joe vow to a criminal companion that before leaving St. Petersburg for good he is going to slit the Widow's nostrils and notch her ears like a sow, in revenge for being jugged as a vagrant and publicly horsewhipped by order of the Widow's late husband, who had been the town's justice of the peace. Although Huck fears he will be murdered if Injun Joe should discover who has informed on him, he immediately plunges down the hillside to warn a sturdy townsman and his sons that the Widow is in peril. All Huck asks for himself is that his own role in the affair be kept secret from everyone, including the Widow. "Please don't ever tell *I* told you," Huck begs the man. "Please don't—I'd be killed, sure—but the widow's been good friends to me sometimes, and I want to tell—I *will* tell if you'll promise you won't ever say it was me." The man promises, and Huck spills out his story.

Thus it is out of no special feeling of gratitude to Huck that the Widow Douglas volunteers to nurse the homeless boy when, a short time later, he falls deliriously ill with fever. Her willingness to take charge of him possibly saves his life, because all the doctors in town, along with all the other able-bodied men, are off at McDougal's cave looking for Tom Sawyer and Becky Thatcher, who are lost in its uncharted depths. In contrast to the disdainful attitudes of the other women of St. Petersburg, the Widow's feeling about Huck is that "whether he was good, bad, or indifferent, he was the Lord's, and nothing that was the Lord's was a thing to be neglected." Her Christianity, in other words, is a living faith, not an ossified piety.

In towns the size of St. Petersburg, secrets do not keep for long. Eventually, the Widow learns who had saved her from the Indian's revenge. From this revelation flows her decision "to give Huck a home under her roof and have him educated; and . . . when she could spare the money she would start him in business in a modest way." Huck accepts the Widow's offer—but with a deep sense of unease. After all, his only recollection of family life is an early childhood memory of the constant quarreling between his father and mother: "Fight! Why, they used to fight all the time." Since his mother's death, Huck's drunken father has simply let the boy run wild. The boy has worn the cast-off clothes of grown men, slept on doorsteps in fine weather and in empty hogsheads in wet, and avoided soap and water like the plague. He smokes and chews tobacco. He swears "wonderfully." He has never been to church or to school, and cannot recognize the letters of the alphabet.

In the last episode of *Tom Sawyer,* we witness this child being "introduced . . . no, dragged" into society. The Widow's servants keep him neat and clean. He has to eat with a knife and fork. He has to sleep in "unsympathetic sheets that had not one little spot or stain which he could press to his heart and know for a friend." He is required to go to church and to cut out swearing. Plans are afoot to send him to school, as soon as the new term begins. "Whithersoever he turned, the bars and shackles of civilization shut him in and bound him hand and foot." After three weeks of misery, he runs off. Finally Tom Sawyer locates him, stretched at ease in an empty hogshead down behind an abandoned slaughterhouse, smoking a pipe, clad in rags, and superbly uncombed. Tom understands the feelings of his friend—and yet loves him enough to give him advice he knows Huck doesn't want to hear. Go back to the Widow's, Tom urges him; "if you'll try this thing just a while longer you'll come to like it." Huck adamantly refuses.

In the long run, however, Huck is no match for the master manipulator who once had persuaded all the boys in St. Petersburg to whitewash a fence for him. Thinking fast, Tom tells Huck he is going to form a "high-toned" robber gang, of the sort that in most European countries is made of "dukes and such." In order to keep up the tone of his gang, Tom will restrict its membership to respectable boys. Returning to the Widow is the price Huck will have to pay for belonging. Upon hearing this, Huck's resistance collapses. "I'll stick to the widder till I rot," Huck declares, as *The Adventures of Tom Sawyer* draws to a close, "and if I git to be a reg'lar ripper of a robber, and everybody talking 'bout it, I reckon she'll be proud she snaked me in out of the wet."

With that sentence Mark Twain set the stage for a follow-up novel that could have become one of the most extraordinary studies of acculturation in modern literature, centering on a psychological contest between an emotionally deprived juvenile outcast and a smart, attractive, still youthful woman. Somewhere along the line, though, Mark Twain decided he had a better idea. The sequel to *Tom Sawyer* became a story about a runaway boy and a runaway slave, rafting down the big river on the June rise.

It was a marvelous idea. Yet by making Huck Finn his runaway hero, Mark Twain created certain problems for himself. The conventional wisdom about the *Adventures of Huckleberry Finn* is that the novel lets its readers down only in the long final episode at the Phelps plantation, when Tom Sawyer reenters the story and, with his romantic schemes, effectively destroys the emotional connection between Huck and Jim. Hemingway, for example, qualified his tribute to the novel by adding, "If you read it you must stop where the Nigger Jim is stolen from the boys. That is the real end. The rest is just cheating." As bad as cheating, however, are the incidents that occur at the outset of the story, in the chapters dealing with Huck's life at the Widow's.

The first problem Mark Twain confronted was how to blur his readers' awareness that Huck and the Widow are bound together by mutual feelings of gratitude, that they both are warmhearted, and that their experiment in living as symbolic son and mother has a chance of succeeding. Since *Huckleberry Finn* was to be a story of rafting on the river, the author had to spring Huck free from his ties to the Widow. Mark Twain solved this problem—if one can call a travesty a solution—by introducing, on page two, the cartoon character of Miss Watson. "A tolerable slim old maid with goggles on," Miss Watson is the Widow's sister, who has just recently—oh, yes, very recently!—come to live in the Douglas mansion. It is altogether incredible that the Widow would surrender the bulk of her parental responsibilities to this two-dimensional caricature of old-maid prissiness and henpecking tyranny, but that is exactly what Mark Twain was forced to ask us to believe. The richly interesting psychological drama that seemed to be promised to us at the end of *Tom Sawyer* is reduced in the first three chapters of *Huckleberry Finn* to a series of farcical confrontations between Huck and old Goggle Eyes, with the gentle, understanding Widow coming on stage only now and again.

As if embarrassed by the baldness of this strategem, Mark Twain admits at the beginning of chapter 4 that after four months in the same household Huck and the Widow have grown somewhat closer together, and that Huck is "getting sort of used" to her ways, albeit he still prefers his former habits. For her part, the Widow believes that Huck is coming along slowly but surely and is doing very satisfactorily, thank you. Almost immediately, however, the reason why Mark Twain could afford this outburst of literary candor is revealed: he had hit upon a legalistic means of removing Huck from the Widow's jurisdiction, once and for all. No matter that in the course of executing this maneuver the author would have to resort to a few "stretchers," as Huck would say.

Pap Finn has been missing from town for more than a year. Now, suddenly, he returns. He has heard about Huck's and Tom's discovery (in *Tom Sawyer*) of a buried treasure of golden coins. Huck's share, which comes to six thousand dollars, has been banked for him by the Widow at 6 percent interest. Pap claims that as Huck's father he should be given control of the six thousand dollars, and swears he will go to court about it. In the face of this threat, the Widow and the influential Judge Thatcher ask the court to take Huck away from his father and appoint one of them the boy's legal guardian. Confronted on one side of his courtroom by the Widow and Judge Thatcher, and on the other side by Pap Finn—"His hair was long and tangled and greasy, and hung down, and you could see his eyes shining through like he was behind vines. . . . There warn't no color in his face, where his face showed; it was white; not like another man's white, but a white to make a body sick, a white to make a body's flesh crawl"—what would any judge do?

But let us not ask the question only in moral terms. Let us also speak of clout. St. Petersburg is a small southern town, whose power structure stands before the judge in the persons of the Widow and Judge Thatcher. The power structure's adversary is the trashiest white for miles around, a man totally without influence. How will the judge rule? Mark Twain knows damned well, yet he has no choice but to lie to us. "It was a new judge," the novel lamely explains, "that had just come, and he didn't know. . . ." After ruling in favor of Huck's father, the judge invites Pap to his home, and persuades him to take a temperance pledge. The presumably reformed drunkard then goes to bed in the judge's guest room. Sometime during the night he sneaks out, buys a jug of forty-rod, sneaks back in, kills the jug," and towards daylight he crawled out again, drunk as a fiddler, and rolled off the porch and broke his left arm in two places and . . . when they come to look at that spare room, they had to take soundings before they could navigate it." Does the judge, first thing in the morning, grant the Widow a temporary injunction against the enforcement of his previous ruling, until a new trial on the guardianship question can be scheduled? Don't be silly.

Consequently, when Pap snatches Huck one day in the spring, takes him across the river to the Illinois shore, and locks him up in an old log hut, the Widow has no legal right to recover him. Some weeks later, Pap comes storming into the cabin on one of his irregular visits and reports that there are rumors floating around St. Petersburg that the Widow is about to make a second effort in the court. But by this time Huck has completely reverted to his old ways, and doesn't want to be "cramped up and sivilized" any more. He has also long since decided that he has no desire to go on living with his nightmarish Pap. Thus, on the day he breaks out of the cabin and makes for the river, Huck is fleeing first of all from his father, which is entirely understandable. But much less understandable is that he is also fleeing from all his boyhood friends, including the woman who had befriended him off and on throughout his childhood, had nursed him through a dangerous illness, had invested his money for him rather than mulcting him out of it, had supplied him with bed and board and loving understanding for four months, and had sent him to school so that he could learn to read and write. Can it be that we have been wrong in thinking that Huck Finn is a warmhearted boy—that in fact he is a cold-blooded little bastard who doesn't really care about the people who care about him? Of course not. It is simply that Mark Twain had to turn Huck into a runaway, and he could not do so without temporarily violating the consistency of his hero's character.

The point of this analysis is not to downgrade Mark Twain's literary reputation by exposing the social and psychological implausibilities in the early chapters of his masterpiece. Implausibilities, after all, were Mark Twain's stock in trade, in every book he ever wrote. The point, rather, is that teachers of *Huckleberry Finn* read every detail in the early chapters with a deadly literal-mindedness. Partly this is because a lot of professional interpreters of literature lack a sense of humor. But mainly they misread the beginning of *Huckleberry Finn* because of what appears to be their desire to denigrate American family life. Instead of showing students that the account of Huck's life at the Widow's is not to be taken seriously—that it is simply a series of chess moves designed to get Huck onto that raft with Nigger Jim as rapidly as possible, and that it most certainly does not reflect Mark Twain's real opinion of the Widow Douglas—they take the account at face value, in preparation for their Dropoutsville misreading of the novel's final sentences. In the last twenty years I have, as an observer, sat in on many classes that were discussing *Huckleberry Finn,* and in all but a handful the teacher has spoken of Miss Watson and the Widow Douglas in the same breath, as a double-headed symbol of familial suffocation.

Back in the 1950s, when this whole mess started, literary critics were moved to misread *Huckleberry Finn* for a variety of reasons. To its everlasting credit, American society in the postwar period gradually came to the conclusion—first in the area of sports, but raying out from there into other aspects of our national life—that the ancient pattern of discrimination against Negroes was morally and legally indefensible. This conclusion precipitated numerous misinterpretations of *Huckleberry Finn.* Critics wanted to believe that Huck was renouncing his membership in a society that condoned slavery because they themselves did not wish to live in a segregationist America. A less palatable concomitant of this truth is that some misreaders were as strongly motivated by a distaste for southern whites as by a sympathy for southern blacks. "Anti-southernism is the anti-Semitism of the liberals": the familiar wisecrack may have lost some of its force since last autumn's presidential election. Nevertheless a prejudice against the mores, the manners, and the drawling accents of white southerners still exists in this country, particularly among the highly educated; and a number of literary critics have always been pleased to think that Huck Finn is heading west for keeps because he can't stand all those funny-talking white folks who live along the banks of the southern half of the Mississippi. ⟨...⟩

⟨...⟩ Yet at the end of the book, ⟨Twain⟩ not only tried to tell us that Huck was planning to return to St. Petersburg, but he showed signs of feeling ashamed of himself for relegating the strong and admirable Widow Douglas to a minor role in her own household. In the final chapters, as the loose threads of the story are hastily being gathered up, we learn that Miss Watson, the erstwhile owner of Nigger Jim and persecutor of small white boys, is dead. We also learn that Pap Finn is dead. But what about the Widow Douglas? Amidst all the questions and answers that are flying about, she is never once mentioned. Even in the final sentences, in which Huck says he had tried being adopted and civilized once before, he does not pronounce the name of the woman who had done so much for him throughout his life.

—KENNETH S. LYNN, "Welcome Back from the Raft, Huck Honey!,"
American Scholar 46, No. 3 (Summer 1977): 340–47

JESSE BIER

It may be appropriate, now that *A Fiedler Reader* (Stein and Day) has been in circulation for a time, to recall the storms of protest his most notorious essay, the one on *Huckleberry Finn,* occasioned over thirty years ago. Fiedler is an old friend and former colleague of mine and, now that the critical dust has almost settled again, he may not mind a demurral from me as much as from downright hostile quarters. What follows is in the nature of an overdue and extended footnote— which may conceivably tramp down some of the new dust occasioned by the commemorative volume.

The central argument of "Come Back to the Raft Ag'in, Huck Honey" placed *Huckleberry Finn* with *Moby-Dick* especially as books that excluded—or avoided— heterosexual love, substituting a covert ideal of "chaste male love" as underlying theme. Fiedler's evidence in *Huckleberry Finn* was drawn from such homosexual suggestions as Jim's vocabulary of endearments, his dressing at one point in a woman's gown, and his general portrait throughout as a sort of unblemished bride. Further substantiation came from Twain's use of the watery setting, which suggested "the inviolable sea"—a sexually charged phrase. Finally, the crucial dream-like structure of the book, Fiedler thought, authorized certainly a partial release of inhibitions in the principal characters. And the cannily chosen age of fourteen-year-old Huck allowed or even forced Twain to treat at least latent adolescent homosexuality, while the concept of the outraged Negro fortified but also disguised the constant and highly affective tendencies of reconciliation. The "humbling" scene, therefore, took on far more sexual than racial import: for Fiedler it meant forgiveness begged from a wronged lover, in accordance with the only slightly repressed myth of the darkly beloved one.

Fiedler certainly could play fast and loose with selective evidence—don't we all, on occasion?—as in his convenient omission of Huck's own feminine disguise as Sarah Mary Williams. In some ways the article seems, at least in retrospect, a sort of facetious or parodic construction of ellipses, non-sequiturs and "stretchers" that might have tickled a scholarly avatar of Twain himself. Darkness and mist, for example, reinforce the dream-like structure of the novel, inevitably sponsoring the release of—whatever the essayist is looking for. If that indeed turns out to be homosexuality, then the great river becomes the mythic "sea," which is the historic and apparently exclusive escape route for homosexual sailors. And so on.

But from the first Fiedler was always more the critic, even the polemicist, than the scholar. One has to allow for that, especially in Fiedler's early Lawrentian phase. Few specialists, especially up and down the Eastern seaboard, were willing to make such allowances in 1948, heaping scorn in particular on his very title. It is true that, for his purposes, Fiedler simply ignored how universal the Southernism "honey" has always been. The particular tactic placed him in the very eye of a hurricane among experts in American literature and American studies, in Southern and Middle Atlantic universities especially. I think there was more indulgence—I had almost said, good-natured indulgence—out West, where his wider literary views, later formulated in *Love and Death in the American Novel*, were perhaps becoming apparent to disinvolved critics. By now, a generation later, I assume that all sections of the country can grant him his thesis about at least the slightly homosexual cast of a good deal of classic nineteenth-century American literature. He had to break through to that view as an *enfant terrible*, laying violent hold on what he wanted, wilfully ignoring the rest, obsessively following his own sequences of thought and prejudice, and even falsifying somewhat in the service of a larger hidden truth no one had even dared to mention.

Since the unmentionable is now mentionable, Fiedler on Twain might be able to stand some corrective. I have had the occasion myself, elsewhere, of pointing out the logical absurdity involved in extending Fiedler's racial/sexual parallels to, say, Joel Chandler Harris' Uncle Remus; between an elderly grandfather figure and a child in the stage of classic dormancy no sexuality of any kind can be inferred, whatever the sweetness of exchange. Furthermore, Maxwell Geismar reminds us of how easily Twain himself reverted to endearment when confronting father-figures in his own life. To the old tutorial pilot of *Life on the Mississippi*, Horace Bixby, Twain could write "Twenty years have not added a month to your age or taken a fraction of your loveliness. . . ." Likewise, there is the record of Twain's affectionate and unashamed veneration of the older Grant. Actually, it is Kenneth Lynn who has provided the specific and countervailing insight about the role of Jim in *Huckleberry Finn*—Jim's function as a substitute father rather than bride or lover. This is a view equally valuable for psychoanalytic interpretation, of course, though not the one Fiedler would prefer.

The fact is that the overview Kenneth Lynn suggested is the one that governs Twain's purposes and makes consistent structural and thematic sense. In the famous climactic scene of the smallpox imposture (Chapter 16), for example, while Huck is paddling the runaway hunters to the raft, he refers spontaneously to concealed Jim as his sick "Pap." The lie contains the central theme or truth of the book. The search for a father pervades the novel, motivating Huck in his pranksterism, serious mischief and deep emotions. There is an infinite or eternal dimension to the question since the boy is even willing to "go to hell" in his ultimate allegiance to the older Negro and friend. It is, at bottom, more important to find an affectionate father, from whom one's true identity takes rise, than to find one's lover—which belongs to another later and transcendent stage. In any event the two protagonists—one questing for a father, the other actually separated from his own children and adopting the hero as substitute son—are locked in a filial and paternal, not sexual, relationship.

Recall that even before any real action begins Huck consults Jim and his "hair-ball oracle" (Chapter 4) about Pap Finn's possible threatening return, a narrative device that conjoins the three and already shifts Huck's confidentiality from one parental figure to the other. The primary narrative itself, once the main action starts, involves Huck's faking his own murder to escape captivity at the older Finn's place and then traces Huck's—as well as Jim's—flight to freedom. That prime narrative theme paradoxically requires a sustaining human attachment. Twain, therefore, has Huck proceed directly from Pap Finn to Jim (Chapter 8).

And Twain takes pains to contrast Jim with Pap Finn. After being bitten by a rattlesnake (because Huck had not followed his fatherly advice about snakes), Jim drinks whiskey as an antidote (Chapter 10)—not for its own besotting sake, as Pap would do. It is actually whiskey from Pap's own whiskey jug, so that a symbolical transformation occurs from pure rotgut to a metaphoric aqua vitae—as from death to life. Incidentally, Jim keeps his knowledge of Pap's corpse from Huck until the very end, protecting Huck from the burden of untimely knowledge instead of "riling" him up as Pap himself always did. Both Pap's unregenerate equivocations about "borrowing" what you need and the Widow's strictures on stealing are succeeded by Jim's more selective and practical advice in the matter (Chapter 12), wise paternal counsel in unhypocritical survival. For all of his own ignorance, Jim is, in general, a helpful, sage, sober, self-respecting, affectionate and unbigoted human being—and at thirty-four, chronologically quite capable of having sired Huck—a true father-figure throughout the story. The noblest character in the book, his portrait is to be contrasted with both the phony nobility of the Duke and Dauphin and the fraudulent ignoble paternalism of Pap. He is the genuine spiritual father, into whom Huck virtually collides, as he runs off from his merely accidental and repudiated father, ultimately discovering the condition of mutual caring any child needs. Indeed, the crucial memory that precedes Huck's decision to go to hell for Jim is his remembrance of Jim's fatherly sacrifices and steady affection for him.

> I'd see him standing my watch on top of his'n, 'stead of calling me, so I could go on sleeping; and see how glad he was when I come back out of the fog.

Nothing else can prevail against this familial and binding experience.

Therefore, alongside of the spurious tag-line "Come back to the raft ag'in, Huck Honey" must be placed the truly governing sentiment of Jim: "Laws bless you, chile, I'uz right down sho' you's dead agin" (p. 340). It is easy enough, even in the context of Twain's book, to dispute at least the ambiguousness of "honey." The endearment is regularly and sometimes patronizingly used by any and all adults toward the younger Huck. Here is Mrs. Loftus, for instance, catching up the disguised Huck: "Honey, I thought you said it was Sarah when you first came in" (p. 259). But, of course, people are just as inclined to say "child" as "honey." Thus Aunt Sally:

> "Who'd you give the baggage to?"
> "Nobody."
> "Why, child, it'll be stole!"

Jim, himself, will put the interchangeable terms together:

> "But lawsy, how you did fool 'em, Huck! Dat wuz de smartes' dodge! I tell you, chile, I 'spec it save' ole Jim—ole Jim ain't gwyne to forgit you for dat, honey."

Even the punctuating illustration with which Fiedler's essay ended contains the key paternal equation, Fiedler's excerpt strategically cutting it short:

> "It's too good for true, honey, it's too good for true. Lemme look at you, chile...."

We must remember that Jim almost always has his children on his mind and in one magnificently ironic exchange "most froze" the backsliding Huck with his talk of one day stealing his own children out of slavery (Chapter 16). Similarly the burlesque dialogue about Solomon's alleged wisdom (Chapter 14) turns momentarily serious when Jim focuses his rebuttal on the question of a whole not a "half a chile." Like Huck, Jim also has separation and death obsessively on his mind, and he is always concerned with loved ones; but he is too old ever to joke about these matters and, instead, upbraids and counter-instructs his surrogate son.

It is no mere caveat to add that, in lengthening perspective on *Huckleberry Finn,* almost all readers are coming to appreciate the motif of death in the book, the presence of it (Philip Young has counted thirteen corpses), the fear of it and, often on Huck's part, the longing for it. Time and again Huck says, "I wish I was dead," no mere locution. The proof of how deep the impulse really is comes in the remarkable start of Chapter 23, where there is no immediate crisis to account for the ultimate escapism and no objective correlative at all; in fact, the day is bright, though felt as lugubrious, and the mood is peaceful, though registered through Huck's inner depression as deathful.

> When I got there it was all still and Sunday-like, and hot and sunshiny; the hands was gone to the fields; and there was them kind of faint dronings of bugs

and flies in the air that makes it seem so lonesome and like everybody's dead and gone; and if a breeze fans along and quivers the leaves it makes you feel mournful because you feel like it's spirits whispering—spirits that's been dead ever so many years—and you always think they're talking about *you*. As a general thing it makes a body wish *he* was dead, too, and done with it all.

Disconnection and melancholy are starkly signaled by that word "lonesome," probably the key to Huck's psychology here and elsewhere. All the more, Jim's greeting to Huck—

"... bless you chile, I'uz right down sho' you's dead again"—

echoes with reverberant thematic force throughout the book.

I shall not invest these suggestions with extravagant support equal and opposite to what Fiedler offered thirty years ago. There is nothing irrefutable in reminding everybody that the dominant feature of the setting is the great river itself, the Father of waters. Nor is there anything to be gained in, say, citing Jim, there in the all-embracive womb-like tent on board the raft that floats on the flowing waters, as a presiding mother-image, adding a mythopeic bisexual parental figure to repudiate his narrower case.

—JESSE BIER, " 'Bless You, Chile': Fiedler and 'Huck Honey' a Generation
Later," *Mississippi Quarterly* 34, No. 4 (Fall 1981): 456–62

NEIL SCHMITZ

The River is Huck's source: he is "snaked in out of the wet" at the end of *Tom Sawyer* and his first lesson in *Huckleberry Finn* is the story about Moses and the Bulrushers, the story of being landed, being born into an identity, the wrong one, a story he contemptuously rejects as being about "dead people." Huck's name, after all, is Finn. Others have said as much: Huck is a fin in a waste of water, and by the story's end, having assumed other names, he will be Finn again. The River is his source; it is the site where he enjoys Being, where his experience is fluent. There is only the interposition of the raft, which the River idly bestows upon him, and this is his craft, his conveyance, clumsily guided, foolishly risked, almost lost, seemingly destroyed, but always reappearing, and then at last forgotten. We barely notice the raft, its changes, its transformations, this refuge which becomes a prison. It is the type of Huck's style, its unseen trope, the craft of his craft, elemental discourse simply functioning to signify, never calling attention to itself, just there, used, instrumental, and finally abandoned, used up. The raft, which means one thing to Jim, another to Huck, makes possible the playing forth of their drama. It is a material they work on, fix up, enhance (a lantern, an extra steering oar), and it is a way of life, liberating and confining, that becomes increasingly absurd. ⟨...⟩

Rift, raft, reef. Huck is happiest when he is afloat, going nowhere. That is, when the river dissolves into a pure plenitude, when it is quiescent, simply the field or flow in which he exists. Only the raft, so given over to the river, can render this feeling. Only a writing, so given over to speech, can represent this feeling. The river that passes through "Old Times" is always problematical, reefstruck, clamorous, and what makes it so different, so distant, is the steamboat. On the raft, in his idiomatic prose, Huck feels the river. These instances always mark his regression toward finnytude, Huck's return to the primal lap, and they are, as we shall see, beautiful delusions only briefly sustained.

—NEIL SCHMITZ, *Of Huck and Alice: Humorous Writing in American Literature* (Minneapolis: University of Minnesota Press, 1983), pp. 82–84

ALBERT WALDINGER

Yehuda Karni's Hebrew translation of *The Adventures of Huckleberry Finn* (*Hameorot Huklberi Fin,* Tel Aviv: Omanut, 1928?) appeared at approximately the same time as Shalom Spiegel's *Hebrew Reborn* (New York: The Macmillan Co., 1930) and in many ways celebrated the same rebirth. Thus, although both the translation and its original stress renewal, only the translation points up rejuvenation as a fact realized in the Old Testament as well as in modern Israeli statehood. In this way, Karni's world, the "little Tel Aviv" of the 1920's, a kind of Jewish Greenwich Village, was filled with "reborn" and neo-Biblical poetry in addition to everyday coinages based on literary, linguistic, and cultural tradition. Passover—and the Exodus—expressed the desire for freedom and fulfillment in this past.

Thus, in the much maligned ending of Twain's book, Karni subheaded Jim's career as going from "Slavery to Freedom" in the same terms as the Passover Ritual; Mark Twain, on the other hand, could do no more than hint at the gospel song in his own capsule subtitle, "Out of Bondage." In addition, Huck gives little linguistic or stylistic attention to the "free States" and the hope that this emancipation may come quickly; on the other hand, the Passover Narration expresses the full wish that "Next year we may be free men" (*beney khorin*), and the translation uses the same expression carrying the same hope.

Such a traditional spirit is an important part of authentically Jewish translation, which is a cultural as well as narrowly linguistic act, and Karni had the necessary past for such a task. He was born in 1884 in Pinsk, Russia, an Eastern European Jewish "heartland," and until his death in 1949, one year after Israeli Independence, was on the editorial board of *Haarets* ("The Land"), an especially rich Hebrew newspaper, both in style and content. During this time, he became a well-known national poet who lovingly confessed to writing in the style of "zealots and liturgists," with the "scorch of fire and the bite of ice" and treating of "angels and devils."

Such "fundamentalism" is perfectly suited to the characterization of Jim, who is at once unlearned and the bearer of a learned tradition. Thus, what may be sneered at as the Southern Negro's easy "knack of 'terpretin' " takes on in Karni's rendering the full dignity of Joseph's gift in Genesis 40:16, 18: this is no mere necromancy but the redemptive talent for "finding solutions" (ptirat pitronot). Moreover, the humble "nigger name' Balum" is actually Balaam, the graced minor prophet of Num. 22, 23, and 24 to whom "the Lord manifested Himself" (Num. 23:16). Suiting this dialectic with Biblical tradition, it is Balaam who leaves the primitive world of such omens as Jim's hairy chest and hair ball in order to "turn his face toward the wilderness" (Num. 24:1), toward a Sinai (and Western Territory?) from which deliverance is to come.

Significantly, the fog that enwraps Chapter 15 of *Huckleberry Finn* is literally equivalent in Karni to the "clouds and thick darkness" of Deut. 4:11 which were remembered to have covered Mt. Horeb (or Sinai) when the Ten Commandments were given. The source of Jim's journey is thus ultimately the miracle of theophany far above Miss Watson's Hannibal. In this way, Jim's slavery becomes like the fog impeding justice. However, as the translation words it, Jim hopes that "our end will be to come out of the dark and dense cloud," a hope with much more import than the mere "pulling through" plotted by Tom Sawyer. Jim's freeing becomes—and is—a major moral deliverance.

The outcome of the hope is "coming to a great and broad river" ("big clear river" in Twain). Thus, the Mississippi becomes equated with the rivers of providential Near Eastern history and with the idea of "divine inheritance": "Unto thy seed have I given this land, from the river of Egypt unto the great river, the river Euphrates" (Gen. 15:18). Against this background, Jim definitely becomes the rightful owner not only of himself but also of an elevated past, and the Mississippi is interpreted as restoring his "inheritance" to him.

As one scholar (W. Stuart McCullough) has pointed out, parallelism and synonymous repetition typify the Hebrew Biblical line. Accordingly, in place of Twain's and Huck's natural and prosaic "wouldn't have no more trouble," Karni has a neo-Biblical meditation on "the end [which] will come to all of our *affliction and misery*" in precise reminiscence of Lam. 1:7 in which an "Exiled Jerusalem" is seen as captive and captivated by "the pleasant things that she had in the days of old." Moreover, the Huck of the translation not only regrets his "meanness" to Jim; he actually feels "ashamed and confounded" in the style of Ezek. 36:32 and not only wants to "eat his words," but is "contrite unto contrition."

Likewise, there is religiously motivated elevation in the translation of Jim's view of Huck's "foolin'," expressed by him as the treatment accorded to "trash." In Karni, through association with the Old Testament, the slangy denigration becomes the "dunghill" (*ashpa*) from which God redeems man. Thus, Ps. 113:7 asserts, using typically repetitive parallelism, "He raiseth up the poor out of the dust, and lifteth the needy out of the dunghill." In this way, Huck becomes a misunderstood—and even blamed—deliverer.

In sum, the translation views Jim in the same way that traditional Jewish literature viewed all oppressed, even up to Mark Twain's own day. Thus, Mendele Mocher Serforim (1836–1917) created late nineteenth century "boys books" for

Jewish children as did Twain for American—and was himself a major influence on Sholem Aleichem (1859–1916), often compared to Twain—while in such Hebrew fiction as "Fathers and Sons" (*Haavot vehabanim*, 1868), he saw the Jewish people in "Captivity" as a "prince" in the dress of a "slave."

—ALBERT WALDINGER, "Interpreting the Passover Dream: Jim in Traditional Hebrew," *American Notes & Queries* 22, Nos. 3/4 (November–December 1983): 43–45

HANA WIRTH-NESHER

Let us begin with the recognition that Pip and Huck are both orphans occupying a low rung on the social ladder and bearing names that reinforce their insignificance. The name Pip is a palindrome with several meanings, one of which is the small seed of fruit, something to be discarded but also the source of another generation of fruit. In Twain's time a "huckleberry" was a slang expression meaning someone of no consequence but, similarly, it could also mean precisely the right person for a particular purpose. Both names share the connotation of low esteem. Huckleberries, incidentally, resisted attempts at domestication and could not be transported to the city successfully.

Pip and Huck are born into a tradition of literary orphans who, by virtue of their not being limited by the rules and constraints of parents and kin, are free to seek spiritual surrogate parents and moral codes. The rise of the novel is in part a response to the newly found freedom of such individuals in the wake of feudalism. In a new society of shifting social classes, the roving orphan or picaro could create a past that suited his aspirations rather than his blood ties, and Dickens and Twain are both drawing on this literary heritage of either voluntary or involuntary disinheritance. *Great Expectations* begins with Pip at the gravesite of his parents, where an ogre seems to rise from his father's tomb, an ogre who eventually becomes his spiritual parent. Huck, enslaved by a parent who abuses him, chooses to stage his own death, so that he can be free to follow his own course.

The loner, cut loose from family responsibilities, is an inherent part of the romance of America, of the myth of eternal fresh starts. Huck's predecessors are Natty Bumpo and Ishmael; his successors are numerous, from Isabel Archer and Milly Theale, orphan heiresses of the ages, Sister Carrie, and Jay Gatsby springing from "his Platonic conception of himself," to Frederick Henry walking off into the rain, Vag making his way across the *U.S.A.*, the Lone Ranger, and Humphrey Bogart. Orphanhood in American literature is a clean slate, self-reliance, and often enchanted solitude that veers dangerously close to real loneliness. Huck's actual orphaning occurs long after his pretended death out of society and is revealed to him only at the book's end. Huck chose orphanhood for himself, and reality simply caught up with his wishes.

—HANA WIRTH-NESHER, "The Literary Orphan as National Hero: Huck and Pip," *Dickens Studies Annual* 15 (1986): 260–61

DAVID R. SEWELL

The first major text to exemplify "absurd" misunderstanding, *Tom Sawyer Abroad* (1893), suggests why it is so easy to see the last two decades of Twain's writing career as a desperate, misguided retreat from realism. Although characters called Tom, Huck, and Jim appear in *Tom Sawyer Abroad,* they are disappointingly unlike the trio in *Huckleberry Finn.* The plot Twain cribs from Jules Verne is painfully fantastic. (An evil balloonist kidnaps the heroes but is lost when he falls overboard during a scuffle with Tom. The three sail over the Sahara and have adventures with lions and tigers, caravans, and bands of thieves. The tale ends abruptly when Jim returns home to fetch Tom a corncob pipe and is caught by Aunt Polly, who demands that Tom come back at once.) It is wrong, however, to evaluate the novel as if it were a continuation of *Huckleberry Finn.* Although it presumes to depict real characters in real settings, it is in fact a precursor of the dream voyages Twain would write over the next few years. The distinguishing feature of Twain's dream tales is that characters in them do not share the same reality. As a fragment of Heraclitus has it, "They that are awake have one world in common, but of the sleeping each turns aside into a world of his own." *Tom Sawyer Abroad* is one of Twain's first works to suggest that all of us may be "sleepers" in this sense, with languages that express different subjective worlds. I read it as a philosophical fable not with any desire to elevate its position in the Twain canon but to clarify its continuity with the line of development that leads to the Mysterious Stranger stories.

"In *Huckleberry Finn,*" according to William Lyon Phelps, "we have three characters who are so different that they live in three different worlds, and really speak different languages, Tom, Huck, and Jim." This is even more radically the case in *Tom Sawyer Abroad.* In *Huckleberry Finn,* the three "languages," although stylized, were motivated by each character's social background. In *Tom Sawyer Abroad* the original tendencies of the characters are exaggerated, so that each represents a myopic vision of semiosis. Tom, as in *Huckleberry Finn,* is the most sophisticated, meaning both that he understands vocabulary, references, and figures of speech beyond the others' grasp and that he is slippery and protean—able to shift from one semantic category or mode of evaluation to another, whereas his friends commonly apply a single standard. Huck is more than ever the literalist, whose special idée fixe is that representations must be identical with represented objects. Jim takes over Huck's previous role as a linguistic innocent suspicious of figurative language.

In the story's first chapter incomprehension still has the satiric bite it had in *Huckleberry Finn.* Tom is trying to stir up the other two to undertake a crusade, explaining that "a crusade is a war to recover the Holy Land from the paynim." Huck offers moral objections: if he owned a farm and another man wanted it, would it be right for that man to take it? An indignant Tom clarifies: "It ain't a farm, it's entirely different. . . . They own the land, just the mere land, and that's all they *do* own; but it was our folks, our Jews and Christians, that made it holy." In this case, he goes on, it is "religious" to take land away from someone. Now Jim objects: "I knows plenty religious people, but I hain't run acrost none dat acts like dat." After more discussion in this vein, Tom gives up in disgust: "I don't want to argue no more with people like you and Huck Finn ... [that] ain't got any more sense than to try to reason out a thing that's pure theology by the laws that protects real estate." The misunderstanding here has less to do with differing vocabularies than with incompatible uses of words like "crusade" and "war." Semantic representations of these words as Tom understands them would each have some such component as

[+ morally sanctioned   ]

that would be lacking in Huck and Jim's versions. As in *Huckleberry Finn*, the reader is meant to sympathize with the naive view that the meaning of killing and theft cannot be changed by a label, no matter how widely that label is accepted. Yet this is the first of a series of arguments that undermine faith in the workings of dialectic. More radically than in the "King Solomon" debate of *Huckleberry Finn*, Twain implies that Socratic reasoning accomplishes nothing when disputants are divided by dissimilar languages or conceptual systems.

Social satire has nothing to do with Huck's naive belief that the states they fly over in the balloon should be colored differently:

"Huck Finn [Tom cries], did you reckon the States was the same color out doors that they are on the map?"
"Tom Sawyer, what's a map for? Ain't it to learn you facts?"
"Of course."
"Well, then, how is it going to do that if it tells lies?—that's what I want to know."
"Shucks, you muggins, it *don't* tell lies.". . .
"All right then; if it don't, there ain't no two States the same color. You git around *that* if you can, Tom Sawyer."

(Later on Twain repeats the joke when he has Huck suggest that to discover where they are, they keep a lookout for the meridians of longitude on the ground.) Like some of the paradoxes in Lewis Carroll's work, Huck's error plays with fundamental categories of logic and symbolization. One critic (Jack Matthews) has analyzed Huck's mistake as an instance of "confusing the map with the territory." The problem, however, is more complex. Huck knows that a map is a symbolic representation that is meant to translate geographical facts into two dimensions. In most respects a map is a formal diagram in which each component corresponds precisely to either a geophysical or a political reality. But the use of different colors to keep the states distinct violates the nonarbitrary one-to-one correspondence that rules the map in all other respects. Tom explains, "It ain't to deceive you, it's to keep you from deceiving yourself." But Huck, like Jim, remains steadfastly suspicious of multiply layered semiotic systems.

The story abounds in instances of humor or confusion arising from the discrepancy between signs and referents. For Huck and Jim there is no distinction between natural and artificial signs—both are supposed to correspond to their referents without ambiguity. Jim cannot bring himself to imagine how time can vary according to a difference in longitude, refusing to admit that hours and days are arbitrary demarcations of an undifferentiated continuum. Tom, scanning the horizon, announces that he sees camels through the telescope. Huck takes up a glass and is disappointed: "Camels your granny, they're spiders"; he has not learned the rules for translating small objects seen through a telescope into features of the landscape. Huck and Jim are terrified by a mirage and even more scandalized by Tom's insistence that it "ain't anything but imagination." A naive realist, Jim believes that the lake they see *must* be there one way or another; if it can disappear, it is the ghost of a lake, and the desert is haunted. Tom, as usual, is able to jump from one form of validation to another without difficulty, becoming confident that the third lake they see is real because the flock of birds heading toward it is a natural sign (or index) of the presence of water.

Metaphor, says Umberto Eco, is a "scandal" for any literalistic theory of language: "It is obvious that when someone creates metaphors, he is, literally speaking, *lying*—as everybody knows." "Everybody" does not include Jim, whom Twain allows to exhibit an incomprehension of metaphor unthinkable in a normal adult. Huck has just cornered Tom by forcing him to admit that he does not know what "welkin" means, even though Tom has just used the word. Tom counters that its meaning is irrelevant:

> "It's a word that people uses for—for—well, it's ornamental. They don't put ruffles on a shirt to help keep a person warm, do they? . . . All right, then; that letter I wrote is a shirt, and the welkin's the ruffle on it."
> I judged that that would gravel Jim, and it did. He says—
> "Now, Mars Tom, it ain't no use to talk like dat, en moreover it's sinful. *You* knows a letter ain't no shirt, en dey ain't no ruffles on it, nuther."

Protest as he will that his example was a "metaphor"—Tom himself uses the term ("that word kind of bricked us up for a minute," says Huck)—he cannot convince Jim that it is not "sinful" language. He pleads as precedent a saying whose truth he expects Jim to admit, that "birds of a feather flock together," but Jim observes that bluebirds and jays avoid each other despite their identical plumage. If Jim's incomprehension is polemical, it cannot be aimed at any particular social group, since figurative language is universal. We sympathize with his ignorance, because on some level we *do* believe both that metaphor is showy and that the deviation from ordinary language separating humans from one another results from our "sinful" human condition. Huck, Jim, and Tom are no longer characters tied to St. Petersburg, Missouri, but characters in a semantic morality play.

—DAVID R. SEWELL, "Toward a Chaos of Incomprehensibilities," *Mark Twain's Languages* (Berkeley: University of California Press, 1987), pp. 135–39

CRITICAL ESSAYS

Richard Poirier

TRANSATLANTIC CONFIGURATIONS: MARK TWAIN AND JANE AUSTEN

Like some of Hawthorne's better stories, *Huckleberry Finn* takes literary advantage of the complaints enunciated earlier by Emerson and Cooper: that not only American writing but also American social life was subservient to conventions, especially literary ones, that prevented the development of new human possibilities. A kindred awareness enters English fiction only with George Eliot and, with consequences for the shape of fiction, with Lawrence and Joyce. But in the nineteenth century, the note is most emphatically struck in American rather than in English fiction. The element in Cooper, Hawthorne, Melville, Mark Twain, and Henry James that anticipates *Ulysses* and *Women in Love* is the recognition that society provides an environment that in fact merely imitates the images provided by fiction. To accept what society calls "real" or "natural" thus became for American novelists such as these the equivalent of subscribing to the literary conventions from which they often claim to be liberating their readers. The problem provides the actual substance and meaning of Hawthorne's "The Maypole of Merrymount," where allegory and pastoral, in the forms of revelers and Puritans, are said to "contend for empire" and for control, by the way, of the destiny of the young lovers. Society in *Huckleberry Finn* is similarly a tissue of bookish assumptions and artificial forms that its members take for reality itself. ⟨...⟩

Mark Twain cannot imagine a society in which his hero has any choice, if he is to remain in society at all, but to be "of Tom Sawyer's party." The evidence for such a comparative limitation on the hero—and, indeed, a justification for making a comparison to the greater freedom allowed Emma ⟨in Jane Austen's *Emma*⟩—is in the similarity between the situations of the two characters at the central crisis in each book. Beside the famous picnic scene at Box Hill, when the heroine insults Miss Bates, can be placed the corresponding scene in *Huckleberry Finn* when, in Chapter xv, Huck also insults a social inferior who is at the same time a trusting friend. The process by which each of these insults comes about is roughly the same. Emma at

From *A World Elsewhere: The Place of Style in American Literature* (New York: Oxford University Press, 1966), pp. 144–45, 175–89, 204–6.

Box Hill gradually surrenders what is called her "self-command" to the theatrical urgings and flatteries of Frank Churchill, while Huck often acts in imitation of the "style" of Tom Sawyer even when it doesn't suit him. Emma literally forgets who she is and therefore the identity of Miss Bates in relation to her, and her witty retort to one of the older lady's simplicities expresses not her true relationship to Miss Bates so much as the theatrical and self-aggrandizing role which Churchill has encouraged her to play to the whole group. Her social and psychological situation—and the literary problem thus created—is much like Huck's at the similar moment when imitation of Tom's role has led to his violation of the bond between him and Jim. The central character in each novel has violated a social contract by being artificial. Both recognize what has happened and both make amends. But at this point there appears an important and essential difference between the situations of these two, and the difference is indicative of the problem in American nineteenth-century fiction of imagining personal relationships within the context of existent social environments. Huck's recognition cannot involve a choice, as can Emma's, against some forms of social expression in favor of others: against the Frank Churchills, Mrs. Eltons (and Tom Sawyers) of this world, and for the Mr. Knightleys. Mark Twain simply cannot provide Huck with an alternative to "games" that has any viability within the social organization which the novel provides. Huck's promise to do Jim "no more mean tricks" is, in effect, a rejection of the only modes of expression understood by his society. At a similar point Emma recognizes and rejects social artifice and is then in a position to accept her natural place in society as Knightley's wife.

Huck chooses at the end "to light out for the Territory ahead of the rest," while Emma, joined to Knightley in "the perfect happiness of the union," is both firmly within a social group and yet saved from all the false kinds of undiscriminating "amiability" practiced at Box Hill. The ceremony is witnessed, significantly, not by the whole community but by a "small band of true friends." "Marriageableness," as Emerson scornfully puts it, emphatically is Jane Austen's subject. Marriage represents for her what he chooses to slight—not merely the act of choice within society but, more importantly, the union of social and natural inclinations. Naturalness and social form are fused in her work in a way that I do not think Emerson, Mark Twain of *Huckleberry Finn,* or even Henry James were able sufficiently to value. It is no wonder that Mark Twain's difficulties begin at a comparable point where Jane Austen most brilliantly succeeds. *Huckleberry Finn* cannot dramatize the meanings accumulated at the moment of social crisis because the crisis itself reveals the inadequacy of the terms by which understandings can be expressed between the hero and other members of his society. There is no publicly accredited vocabulary which allows Huck to reveal his inner self to others.

The comparison between Huck and Emma offers at least a tentative answer to a question of some significance, not merely for *Huckleberry Finn,* but for other American novels of the century in which there is a limited view of the inclusiveness of social environments and of the language that holds them together. The question again is why, precisely at Box Hill, Jane Austen is able to see her way clear to a dramatic resolution of the meaning of her novel, while Mark Twain is stalled at a similar point to a degree that makes him observe, in a letter to Howells, that he liked his novel "only tolerably well, as far as I have got, and may possibly pigeonhole or burn the MS when it is done"? The threat, only partly in jest, was made in August 1876. In barely a month almost a third of the novel had been written. It was not to be finished for seven years. It had reached a point where Huck, having tricked and then apologized to Jim, decides that he can no longer exploit his Negro friend with tricks but will instead try to save him by tricking society. By his decision not to use the "style" of Tom on a runaway slave (Chapter XV), Huck gives up conformist for rebellious trickery. In Chapter XVI, at the point where the novel came to a halt in 1876, Huck, halfway between the raft and the shore, intends to betray his companion. Instead he saves him from capture by inventing an elaborate lie, persuading the two men in the skiff that the raft is occupied by the boy's contagiously sick father. Chapters XV and XVI constitute what I shall be calling the "reversal scenes": they bring about the dramatic crisis by which Huck decisively reverses, for a time, the Tom Sawyerish trend in his relationship to Jim; and they also reverse his efforts to belong imaginatively to society, as most attractively represented by that "respectable" boy Tom Sawyer.

My explanation of Mark Twain's difficulty at this point and of why, after it, his greatest novel goes to pieces will not, I hope, suggest that *Huckleberry Finn* is inferior to *Emma*, whatever that would mean. For one thing, I cannot imagine how *Huckleberry Finn* could have succeeded in resolving the issues that it creates. It makes nothing less than an absolute disavowal, after Huck lies to protect Jim, of any significant dramatic relationship between the hero and all the other characters, whose habitual forms of expression define what I mean by "society" in this novel. The failure is predictable and inescapable in view of the accomplishment, never adequately described by commentaries on the novel, of the first sixteen chapters. These chapters reveal an experimental mastery beyond anything that the author's other works would allow us to expect. Henry Nash Smith points out, perhaps forgetting *The Blithedale Romance,* that not even Henry James had ever dared, by 1885, when *Huckleberry Finn* was published as a book, to entrust the point of view so fully to a character of such evident individuality. My reservations about this judgment are mostly in the interest of pointing to accomplishments and complexities in excess merely of manipulating point of view. For one thing, it cannot be demonstrated that Huck's point of view is maintained with any success throughout the book. The novel is remarkable for the degree to which the hero's voice—from which his point of view is deduced—becomes increasingly inaudible. Even at the beginning, the author uses his narrator to create, all unknown to him and through what are made to seem the most natural habits of his mind—its tendency to verbal repetition—a metaphorical definition of society as no more than a fabrication of art and artifice. Thus, even while we are hearing in Huck's voice a desire for accommodation to this society, as exemplified in Tom, we are seeing in these repeated metaphors Mark Twain's own alienation from that society.

The Shakespearean use of language in the opening chapters allows Mark

Twain to blend immediacy and significance, pictorial entertainment and metaphoric implication, in a way that imperceptibly ties the destiny of the narrator to the destiny of the culture defined by Mark Twain's images. In a style that has the easy movement of a boy's story and a compactness usually found only in poetry of considerable density, these early pages reveal a society shaped entirely by fantasy and illusion and that depends for sanction primarily on literary authority. Unlike *Emma*, who is offered many ways of speaking and may choose even from among competitive definitions of words, Huck's language is rigidly controlled by people who are essentially alien to him. To both adults and companions he sounds like a "numb-skull" because he takes them at their word and finds that he is thereby taken in. By assuming that their statements have at least some literal meaning, he unintentionally discovers the actual self-interest or self-delusion behind their language. These are rather grim suggestions, when in fact the experience of reading the opening chapters is not grim at all and answers the objection, best phrased by Poe, that if allegory "ever established a fact, it is by dint of overturning a fiction." Poe's attack on Hawthorne includes a description of an alternative to allegorical simplicities that might be applied to the metaphoric structure I am about to examine:

> Where the suggested meaning runs through the obvious one in a *very* profound undercurrent, so as never to interfere with the upper one without our volition, so as never to show itself unless *called* to the surface, there only, for the proper uses of fictitious narrative, is it available at all.

The undercurrent has been indeed so "very profound" that it has never been clearly exposed beneath the surface of the first three chapters, which even some recent commentators have described as belonging to the tradition of *Tom Sawyer*. Such a reaction should not too quickly be dismissed, however. The narrative voice at the beginning does in fact lull our attention to implications lurking in it. The implications are contemptuous of the tradition of *Tom Sawyer,* even while the voice is not nearly so anxious to be separated from it. As early as the second paragraph there is a metaphoric equation which effectively condemns society as embodied in Tom Sawyer; yet the condemnation is so clearly the unintentional revelation of Huck's mind that it is as if Mark Twain himself is trying to exorcise it. Huck's voice is like a screen protecting the author from the abstractions implicit in his own metaphors:

> The Widow Douglas she took me for her son, and allowed she would sivilize me; but it was rough living in the house all the time, considering how dismal regular and decent the widow was in all her ways; and so when I couldn't stand it no longer, I lit out. I got into my old rags, and my sugar-hogshead again, and was free and satisfied. But Tom Sawyer, he hunted me up and said he was going to start a band of robbers, and I might join if I would go back to the widow and be respectable. So I went back.

Tom Sawyer's games are intimately related, it is implied, to the "respectable" aspects of adult society. The alternative to both is "freedom," with Huck caught between his impulsive need for it and his equally strong need for company: "so I went back." It is metaphorically suggested that Tom Sawyer and Widow Douglas are in tacit alliance, and both are indicted by the further suggestion that to be "respectable" in her terms is the necessary condition for membership in his gang. "Respectable" society as represented by the Widow is equivalent to a "band of robbers." The parallel is then advanced, with relevance to social artificiality of a specifically literary sort, by the account of Huck's training with the Widow. Evocations of "her book," her Biblical authority for believing things that are not true for Huck, anticipate the even more frequent references in the next and later chapters to Tom's "books," the romances which are also "authorities" for illusion. Before this equation is developed, however, Huck turns for the first time in the novel away from society, not by "lighting out" but by entering into a soliloquy which is in part a communion with nature and spirits. He turns, like Emerson at the opening of *Nature,* not only away from people but also away from "books," from the "study" which Emerson, in the first paragraph of his essay, also rejects for the "stars":

Miss Watson she kept pecking at me, and it got tiresome and lone-some. By-and-by they fetched the niggers in and had prayers, and then everybody was off to bed. I went up to my room with a piece of candle and put it on the table. Then I set down in a chair by the window and tried to think of something cheerful, but it warn't no use. I felt so lonesome I most wished I was dead. The stars were shining, and the leaves rustled in the woods ever so mournful; and I heard an owl, away off, who-whooing about somebody that was dead, and a whippowill and a dog crying about somebody that was going to die; and the wind was trying to whisper something to me and I couldn't make out what it was, and so it made the cold shivers run over me. Then away out in the woods I heard that kind of a sound that a ghost makes when it wants to tell about something that's on its mind and can't make itself understood, and so can't rest easy in its grave and has to go about that way everynight grieving. I got so downhearted and scared I did wish I had some company.

At the outset the reader might be so beguiled by Huck's narrative voice as to forget not only the metaphoric implications in his language but also that, except for his address to the reader, he is remarkably quiet. He speaks infrequently to anyone else; he is seldom heard in conversation, and he is always inconspicuous in company, even in the "gang." His loneliness, we might say, is a want of conversation, a lack, in terms of the literary problem raised by the book, of dramatic relationships. He listens for sounds from nature and interprets them more confidently than language, which tends to confuse or disturb him. "But I never said so," is one of his characteristic comments. The form of the book itself, an autobiography that is also a kind of interior monologue, testifies to the internalization of his feelings and reactions.

And yet, it is necessary to stress that any Emersonian detachment from society for the companionship of the "stars" would never satisfy Huck (or Mark Twain) for very long. His soliloquies are punctuated with the words "lonesome" and "lonely," ending in the present instance with the direct admission that "I did wish I had some company." Company is announced from below the window in the animal noises of Tom Sawyer, and the first chapter ends with tones of deep companionable satisfaction: "Then I slipped down to the ground and crawled among the trees, and, sure enough, there was Tom Sawyer waiting for me."

The organization of the chapter suggests, with pleasure and excitement, that by joining Tom Huck has escaped social entrapment and achieved a Laurentian kind of "freedom"—"freedom together." But Chapter ii, with Tom's incessant talk about rules, gangs, and especially books and authority, only confirms the early hint of an essential solidarity between Tom's world and the Widow's, despite her amused assurance that Tom will not qualify for her heaven. Tom's world is dominated by games and fantasies imitated from literature, just as hers is based on illusions derived from religion and the Bible. His tricks, the first of which is an exploitation of Jim in Chapter ii, are justified by the "authorities" of boys' games and, by extension, of religion and social respectability, which sanction Miss Watson's exploitation of Jim at still another level. Tom's question in Chapter ii when they are discussing the conduct of a game—"Do you want to go to doing different from what's in the books, and get things all muddled up?"—implies even at this point that an argument with the "authority" of boys' games is a disruption of accredited social procedures.

The alternatives promised in Chapter ii by Tom's gang and its games to the "civilized" confinements of Chapter i turn out, then, to be no alternatives at all. Offering confirmation of such a reading, Chapter iii puts into direct juxtaposition the activities of religious, conservative, respectable society, as embodied in Widow Douglas and Miss Watson, and the activities of children, based on the authorities of romantic literature as interpreted by Tom Sawyer. We have before us the creation in words of a whole society built on games, tricks, and illusions, and the adult version is only superficially different from the children's. You play the game without asking literal-minded questions, play as if it were "for real," or you're a "numb-skull."

The metaphorical equation of the world of adults and of children indicates the relative eccentricity of Huck. Thus while his treatment of Jim during the reversal scenes is a matter of playing one of Tom's tricks, of "playing the game" in the larger sense, his subsequent apology violates the rules of the game as observed both by children and adults. Implicit here, in the most placidly comic part of the book, is what Huck will most painfully discover later: that to give up "tricking" Jim means more than giving up Tom's games. It means, so closely are they imaginatively connected with adult forms of exploitation, that he must also believe himself damned to social ostracism and to Hell.

These significances are not declared nor are they derived merely from images. They are instead the result very often of the similarity of phrasing applied first to the Widow and Miss Watson and then to Tom. The unobtrusiveness by which a parallel is thus established results from the use of phrases having the sound merely of idiomatic repetitiousness, not uncommon in vernacular literature. For example, in the first half of Chapter ɪɪɪ, in which Huck is advised by Miss Watson about the advantages of prayer and the Bible, there is a sequence of phrases applied to religion and its promises ("it warn't so," "spiritual gifts," "I couldn't see no advantage to it") that in slightly varied form are applied in the second half to Tom's games and the romantic books which authorize them ("but only just pretended," "done by enchantment," "I couldn't see no profit in it"). In the first half, Huck's literalness, inseparable from a concern for human profit and loss, makes Miss Watson call him a "fool," just as in the second it leads Tom Sawyer to call him a "numb-skull." The list can be extended by anyone who turns to Chapter ɪɪɪ, and the implications are in fact summarized in the final sentence of the chapter by Huck himself: "So then I judged that all that stuff was only just one of Tom Sawyer's lies. I reckoned he believed in the A-rabs and the elephants, but as for me I think different. It had all the marks of a Sunday-school." These concluding remarks make the metaphoric intention of the opening chapters unmistakable. Each side of the comparison is modified by the other. Boys' games as Tom plays them are finally, so the comparisons seem to indicate, as genteel and proper as Miss Watson's religion (he always leaves payment for anything he "steals"), and the social respectability and religion which she represents are, like Tom's games, remote from the requirements of natural, literal, daily experience, from a concern for elementary human feelings that are revealed in Huck's "numb-skull" skepticism both about games and religion.

But it is time to remind ourselves again that as we read we are listening to a voice, not drawing metaphoric diagrams. The voice makes the reading of the metaphors and any effort to determine their weight within the total experience of these chapters extremely difficult. Even at this early point we are uncomfortably aware of a gap between Mark Twain's position, his view, expressed through these metaphors, of society merely as system, and the more socially engaged and eager position of the hero. The gap will ultimately mean that the novel becomes simpler later on than it is here. After the reversal scenes, personal drama is not allowed to intrude into a massive parade of social games and disguises. The sound of Huck's socially involved voice first wavers, then nearly disappears, then returns as a sickly version of what we find in these opening scenes. Here, though, it is heard distinctly enough to make the metaphors amusing and affectionate, however damaging they become if one isolates their implications.

The great difficulty for the reader in the opening chapters is that we feel no confidence in balancing the implications of style, its tendency to repudiate what is at the same time being affectionately rendered. It is no wonder that there are many differences of opinion about the structure of the book and about whether or not it expresses an ultimate surrender to the so-called genteel tradition or a final repudiation of it, and of Hannibal, the so-called Happy Valley of Mark Twain's youth. Those critics who respond weakly, or not at all, to the metaphoric implications of the early chapters ignore as a consequence the extent to which

Mark Twain has begun even here to isolate the consciousness he values from the society in which it seeks to express itself. Put simply, it is predictable from the outset that the book must elect to give its attention either to the development of the hero or to a review of the environment which forestalls that development. The two cannot be synchronized. This literary difficulty is what plagued the author in the summer of 1876, not any discovered contempt of his own, presumably released only by his trip to the Mississippi in 1882, for the environments of his youth. His criticisms are already evident enough in 1876. On the other hand, those who do stress the evidences of repudiation in the early chapters are apt to miss the complications brought about by the freedom Mark Twain allows to the more loving, socially agreeable expressions of his hero. The latter reading is best represented by Leo Marx, whose criticisms of T. S. Eliot and Lionel Trilling for approving of the later portions of the novel have been much admired. But I think the reading he himself offers in his essay confuses Huck Finn with Mark Twain in the opening chapters, not letting us see how much Huck's voice modifies the social criticism, and it then confuses Mark Twain with Huck in the concluding chapters, missing, it seems to me, the degree to which we can only respond to Huck within what has become by then the author's rigidly bitter and impersonal metaphoric design.

What happens to this novel is what happens to Huck at the hands of his creator. The problem for the author after the crucial scenes in Chapters xv and xvi is that the novel can no longer be the autobiography of Huck Finn. It must instead become a kind of documentation of why the consciousness of the hero cannot be developed in dramatic relations to any element of this society. ⟨. . .⟩

The style and design of any book trains us as we read to respond in some ways and not others to certain uses of language, to find some kinds of conversation artificial and others natural. It matters very little, therefore, that in some other book the author approves of certain kinds of behavior if in the one we are reading he has managed to make them ambiguously attractive or even reprehensible. *Huckleberry Finn* so insistently educates us to feelings of exasperation about tricks, games, and theatricality that we cannot have learned our lessons and want when we reach the last chapters still to be entertained by Tom's prolonged antics. The uncertainty that one feels, nevertheless, about the intended effect of the concluding scenes results from the fact that the weight of prejudice urged upon us by what precedes so brutally outbalances Tom's innocuous behavior.

Mark Twain's metaphoric rejection of society in this book saps the potential energy of any of the dramatic relationships within it. The effect is apparent in his lassitude and indifference at the end when he shows Huck Finn confronted by the representative members of this society, young or old. Mark Twain's distaste for Tom and Aunt Polly in their final conversation is directed at their characteristically seeing even one another as embodiments of style and as acting out stereotyped roles. What Aunt Polly really wants in Tom is a literary "good-bad boy," so long as his actions are "bad" only as a "good" boy's should be:

"Then what on earth did *you* want to set him free for, seeing he was already free?"

"Well, that is a question, I must say; and *just* like women! Why, I wanted the *adventure* of it; and I'd 'a'waded neck-deep in blood to—goodness alive, *Aunt Polly!*"

If she warn't standing right there, just inside the door, looking as sweet and contented as an angel half-full of pie, I wish I may never!

The cloying effect of this passage is obvious. And yet the reaction of the reader to it is strangely muffled by Huck's presentation. It is apparent that he does not respond in the way the book has prepared the reader to respond, and that he is here glaringly unlike the character we have loved and respected earlier in the book. What is most significant, however, is that Mark Twain does not seem to think it matters much that Huck be given any place in the scene at all. His unctuous "angel half-full of pie" and the effeminate exclamation "I wish I may never!" merely scan the scene in terms too abundantly provided by it already. He is merely *of* the scene, uncritically absorbed into it.

Huck is given back to us at the very end in his declaration of independence, but it is significant that he is re-created primarily in the image of flight, of "lighting out for the Territory ahead of the rest." He is a character who can exist at all only outside the society that the novel allows us to imagine, who can exist in our imagination, finally, only outside the novel itself. Understandably, Huckleberry Finn became for Mark Twain a kind of obsession, appearing in the years that followed in various sketches for stories and sequels to the novel. It is as if his creator wanted yet another chance to find a home, to build a world, to make a place for him. And yet each version only further disfigures the wondrous boy created in the first sixteen chapters of *Huckleberry Finn*.

Alan Trachtenberg

THE FORM OF FREEDOM
IN *HUCKLEBERRY FINN*

Certain literary works accumulate an aura which possesses the reader before he ventures into reading itself; it gives him a readiness to respond, and a set of expectations to guide his response. Who has come to *Adventures of Huckleberry Finn* free of associations, even of some intimacy with characters and episodes? An aura can be considered a mediation which situates the book and guides the reader toward an available interpretation. This is to say that books like *Huckleberry Finn* can be powerfully predetermined experiences; we encounter them, especially at certain stages of their career, from deep within the culture shared by reader, author, and work. How any book achieves an aura is a problem for the historian of culture: a book's career implicates the history of its readers. *Huckleberry Finn* became a cultural object of special intensity during a period after World War II when many Americans seized upon literary experiences as alternatives to an increasingly confining present. Mark Twain's idyll seemed to project an answerable image—an image of wise innocence in conflict with corruption, of natural man achieving independence of a depraved society. It seemed to project an image, in short, of freedom. But not freedom in the abstract; the values of the book were seen by readers as the precise negation of all the forces felt as oppressive in the 1950s. Common to the several major interpretations of the book was one absolute theme, that the book's most prominent meanings were, as Henry Nash Smith wrote, "against stupid conformity and for the autonomy of the individual." Autonomy vs. conformity: the terms condense a memorable passage of recent American history. The conception of freedom and individualism which pervades the criticism reveals as much of the subliminal concerns of the critics as it does the themes of the book, and should be understood in light of the political and social anxieties of the postwar period.

But does *Huckleberry Finn* deserve its celebration as a testimony to freedom? What exact place, in fact, does freedom have among the book's themes? To say that a theme does not exist apart from its verbal matrix may seem commonplace.

From *Southern Review* n.s. 6, No. 4 (October 1970): 954–71.

But criticism has often addressed itself to extractable elements in this novel such as imagery, symbol, and episode rather than to the total and continuous verbal performance. Granted, the book's susceptibility to a variety of readings—its ability to come apart into separate scenes and passages which affect us independent of the continuous narrative—is a mark of strength. But a firm grip upon the complete and total text is necessary to understand the form freedom takes in the book.

We want first to locate the problem implied by "autonomy" and "conformity," the problem of freedom, within the text, and if possible, to identify the thematic problem with a formal problem. In the broadest sense, the theme of freedom begins to engage us at the outset: Huck feels cramped and confined in his new condition as ward of Widow Douglas and closet neophyte of Miss Watson. The early episodes with Tom Sawyer add a complicating paradox: to enjoy the freedom of being "bad"—joining Tom's gang—Huck must submit himself to his adopted household and appear "respectable." With Pap's arrival the paradox is reversed; now he can enjoy his former freedom to lounge and choose his time, but the expense is a confinement even more threatening, a virtual imprisonment. The only release is escape, flight, and effacement of the identity through which both town and Pap oppress him; he can resume autonomy only by assuming "death" for his name.

In brief and general terms, such is the inner logic of the theme of freedom as we arrive at the Jackson Island episode. With Jim's appearance as a runaway slave a new and decisive development begins. We now have two runaways, and their conjunction generates the rest of the narrative, deepens the theme, and forces nuances to the surface. Jim's situation is both simpler and more urgent than Huck's. His freedom is no more or less than escape from bondage, escape to free territory. He expects there to assume what is denied him in slave society, his identity as an adult man, husband, and father. The fact that the reader is made to share this expectation with Jim, that the novel does not allow us to anticipate a reversal of hope if Jim reaches free territory, is important; as readers we are freed of normal historical ambiguities in order to accept as a powerful given the possibility of fulfilled freedom for Jim. Thus by confining the action to the area of slave society, Mark Twain compels us (at the expense of historical accuracy, perhaps) to imagine the boundary between "slave" and "free" as real and unequivocal, and to accept that boundary as the definition of Jim's plight: on one side, enslaved; on the other, free.

Jim presents himself, then, unencumbered by the paradoxes of Huck's problem: to be free, to possess himself, to reveal a firm identity—these will be equal consequences of the single act of crossing the border. The effect of such a simplifying and unambiguous presence in the book is, first, to bring into relief the more subtle forms of denial of freedom, forms which cannot be overcome by simple geographical relocation, and second, to force Huck, once the boy commits himself to the slave, into a personal contradiction. Jim can say, as soon as he escapes from Miss Watson, "I owns myself," while Huck is still "owned" by the official values supervised by his "conscience." Once Jim's freedom becomes Huck's problem, the boy finds himself at odds with what Mark Twain called his "deformed conscience." Huck's "sound heart" may respond to Jim's desire to recover his humanity at the border, but his conscience wants to repress that response.

In light of this conflict, implicit in Huck's words at the end of Chapter 11, "They're after us!" what would constitute freedom for Huck? Clearly, getting Jim to the free states would not be enough. He would need to free himself of moral deformity before he too can say "I owns myself." Just as clearly neither issue is resolved in the novel. And the book's indecision is reflected in criticism. The controversies regarding the "Evasion" at the Phelps farm need not be reviewed here, but it is useful to point out that the question of the ending eventually becomes a question of *form,* of judgment about the book's unity of tone and intention. Those who wish for Jim's release through a heroic act by Huck tend to feel the ending flawed, and those who wish for Huck's escape from all consciences, including a "good" abolitionist conscience, tend to accept the ending. In either case the burden of both meaning and form has fallen on the question of unity, of the wholeness of the narrative as a patterned action.

The question of unity is, however, only one of the formal problems of the book. If form is understood as the shape given to the reader's consciousness, as the unique engagement the text makes available, criticism might profit by an account of that engagement, of the reader's participation in the book's flow of words. And from this point of view the first fact we encounter is that the book is the speech of a single voice. At the outset we learn that Huck is teller as well as actor, that we are listeners as well as witnesses of action.

Reading begins by acceding to the demands of the voice. "You don't know about me," Huck begins, and his accents identify him immediately as a recognizable type, a western or frontier speaker whose vernacular diction and syntax stand for a typology which includes dress and posture along with characteristic verbal strategies. Huck asks to be heard, as if he faced a live audience from a stage. The first edition Frontispiece has him posing with a smile for the reader, in rags and tatters, the familiar long-barrelled rifle in hand; the bow and flourish in the concluding illustration confirm the quasi-theatrical stance. Huck appears before us, at least in part, within the conventions of an oral tradition. But if Huck is by convention a storyteller, Mark Twain is at the same time a novelist, a maker of a book which asks to be read as "literature" even if its mode is in some ways preliterary.

The book is born for us, in short, under the aegis of a dual tradition, a dual vision of art. The dualities are not always in accord with each other, and some tensions between an oral and a written, especially a "high" or sophisticated tradition, account for technical problems, problems which, I mean to show, bear on the theme of freedom. The book is marked by an uneasy accommodation between seriously differing modes of literary art. Before detailing some of these, it is worth commenting that the pressure to fuse a vernacular verbal style and its methods of narrative with an accepted form of "literature"—a book-length fiction—

characterized all of Mark Twain's mature work. As Justin Kaplan has made clear, Clemens' career contained many unresolved tensions and ambivalences, and none had more consequence for his work than his simultaneous though uneven commitment to two kinds of audience. On the one hand he saw himself as popular spokesman for a vast, nonliterary readership. "My audience is dumb," he wrote: "it has no voice in print." He claimed "the Belly and the Members" as his people, not the "thin top crust of humanity," and insisted, not without defensiveness, that it was unfair to judge his work by "the cultivated-class standard." At the same time that standard appealed to him, and even if his paranoia before it represented social as well as literary anxieties, he did bow toward the established conception of "literature" held by readers of the *Atlantic Monthly*. "*It* is the only audience that I sit down before in complete serenity," he confessed. Writing books which resemble novels is one capitulation to that audience, while marketing his books through the subscription system kept him in touch with his large "dumb" audience.

Even as an "author," however, Mark Twain clung to his root notion of literary art as a performance by a speaking character, usually a non-literary figure with a calculatedly vernacular voice. Such a figure—Simon Wheeler in "Jumping Frog" is a good instance—characteristically deflates expectations and values associated with the "cultivated-class standard." But he does so on behalf of a standard of "common sense," of common and humble humanity. Rather than pose one class standard against another, the vernacular tradition in American humor offers a universal standard, open to all, skeptical of hierarchies, self-evident in its truths. Through a fusion of vernacular values with "literature," Mark Twain strived to achieve exactly such a universal, classless appeal. "I can't stand George Eliot, & Hawthorne & those people," he wrote to Howells in 1885; their "labored & tedious analyses of feeling & motives" were suspiciously aristocratic. Instead he preferred Howells's own *Indian Summer:* "It is a beautiful story, & makes a body laugh all the time, & cry inside." This describes just the kind of response he wished from his own readers: direct and uncomplicated and moving.

What better means did he have toward this end than to create vernacular characters, unencumbered by analysis or excessive introspection, whose universality was obvious to every reader? Matching his manner of creation to his self-conception as a popular writer, Clemens seemed always more comfortable inventing such characters than filling out complete books or imagining narrative actions. He might even be better considered a maker of figures, like Huck and Tom and Jim, and "Mark Twain," who populate a general fictional realm unconfined by specific verbal contexts, than a maker of particular books. The tendency of his characters to live in the mind apart from their texts is a revealing feature of Clemens' talent.

But our aim is to hold the characters fast within their verbal settings. Transforming an oral art to a written one presented Mark Twain with difficulties apparent in almost all his long narratives. Consider the matter of filling out a book that wants to be the "adventures" of a vernacular voice. One difficulty is simply how to bring such a book to a close. The ending of *Huckleberry Finn* does, to be sure, bring the action to a point of general resolution: Jim is freed, masks are stripped away, misunderstandings cleared up, some sort of order restored. But the loose plot which calls for resolution has been kept out of sight during much of the narrative, and we cannot avoid feeling that the plain duration of the book has depended more upon the arbitrary postponement of any event (such as the recapture of Jim) which might end things too soon than upon an inner logic of plot. The only conclusive ending is the drop of the curtain, the final words, "The End. Yours Truly, Huck Finn," and silence. The performance of Huck's voice does not so much complete itself as exhaust itself.

To begin with, then, the problem of the ending is a technical problem of *an* ending. The source of the problem is the attempt to accommodate the opening convention of a vernacular storyteller, whose story simply unwinds, to the imperatives of a book-length written narrative. But the ending is a relatively minor matter. Of more consequence are the pressures upon the narrative voice through the entire course of its performance. An enormous burden is placed upon Huck, who must not only tell the story but enact it as the leading player. My discussion will focus on this double role, will attempt to assess Huck's role as the verbalizer of the narrative in order to assess his role as a character within the narrative. What freedom means in the book, and what form freedom takes, cannot be understood at all without such assessments.

What part of Huck's life in the book derives from the inner necessities of his "character," and what part derives from the outer necessities of his role as speaking voice? Huck has precisely the split identity this question implies. The consequent tensions within the narrative have been obscured in criticism by the great attention given to "identity" as a theme. The pervasive deployment of disguises, verbal and sartorial, through which Huck extricates himself from tight spots alerts the reader to the significance of hidden and revealed identities. When Huck is taken for Tom Sawyer in Chapter 32, he accepts the name with relief (it saves him the trouble of having to invent yet another name), "for it was like being born again, I was so glad to find out who I was." The line follows one of Huck's meditations on death, and some critics have been moved to discover a pattern of death and rebirth throughout, a pattern in which Huck's true name finds protection in the "death" of assumed identities. The motif is familiar in oral literature (see the excised "Raftsmen" passage), and the fact that Huck is legally dead through most of the book adds suggestive weight. At least as long as Pap lives, and as long as Huck is associated with Jim's escape, it seems impossible for the boy to own up to his true identity. The motif of disguise thus seems to harbor a dilemma directly related to the question of freedom: is it possible for Huck to both show and be his true self? To show himself as a runaway who has faked his own death and is aiding an escaped slave would invite disaster. This is a given of the narrative: to be himself Huck must hide himself.

What are the sources of this commanding paradox? Social reality, for one:

Miss Watson, Pap, slavery, general avariciousness, all constitute an environment of treachery. Some critics argue too that the need to hide derives from deep psychic needs, from the extreme vulnerability expressed in Huck's character, especially his recurrent feelings of guilt. In this view, colored by psychoanalytic rhetoric, Huck's disguises represent a shrewd reality principle which acts to protect the very shaky equilibrium of his inner life, the life of a "lost" boy who prefers the pleasure of a precivilized and precharacterological state of nature. This is a compelling and widely held view of Huck. "You feel mighty free and easy and comfortable on a raft." Pleasurable drift and unruffled harmony seem the conditions Huck demands for "free and easy" selfhood.

The issue is subtle and difficult. Do Huck's traits derive in fact from an inner life at odds with social necessity, or from, I want to add, imperatives of his role as narrator? Obviously we need not make an either/or choice. But the second alternative has been so little present in criticism it is worth considering at some length. The crux of the matter is whether Huck presents a consistent character, whether a sentient inner life is always present. Some critics have suggested not. Richard Poirier finds that after his reversal of attitude toward Jim in Chapter 15 (the "trash" episode) and the defeat of his "white" conscience in Chapter 16, Huck gradually disappears as an active agent in the narrative. Unable to continue the developing consciousness implicit in these scenes, Poirier argues, Mark Twain became absorbed in sheer "social panorama," to which Huck is a more or less passive witness. Henry Nash Smith makes a similar point. After losing Cairo in the fog, and losing the raft in Chapter 16, Mark Twain set aside the manuscript, and when he resumed several years later, he "now launched into a satiric description of the society of the prewar South." Huck becomes Mark Twain's satiric mask, which prevents him, Smith argues, from developing in his own right.

These are promising hints regarding Huck's status as a fictional character. Of course any criticism which charges Mark Twain with failing to continue a developing consciousness assumes such a development is a hallmark of fictional character. It might be countered that such a standard is inappropriate to this book, as Clemens himself may have suggested in his attack on the "cultivated-class standard," or that Huck's so-called disappearance in the middle section is actually another disguise, profoundly enforced by an increasingly hostile setting. His retreat, then, after the Grangerford episode, might be consistent with what had already developed as his character.

Even to begin to discuss this issue we need to understand what we mean by a "fictional character." Our expectations derive, in brief, from the novelistic tradition, in which character and action have a coextensive identity. Henry James insisted in "The Art of Fiction" (consider the differences implied by the title of Mark Twain's comparable essay, "How to Tell a Story") upon the inseparability of character and action by describing the novel as "a living thing, all one and continuous, like any other organism." "What is character," he wrote, "but the determination of incident? What is incident but the illustration of character?" The reciprocity of character and action implies, moreover, a process, a twofold development in which character fulfills itself just as it reveals itself to the reader. By development we expect a filling out, a discovery of possibilities and limitations. We also expect a certain degree of self-reflectiveness in character to register what is happening internally.

We need not remind ourselves that *Huckleberry Finn* is not a Jamesian novel. But it is important to know what sort of novel it is, to know what to expect of Huck as a character. What happens to Huck in the course of the narrative? Is he a changed being at the end from what he was at the beginning? In the opening scene Huck chafes at the "dismal regular and decent" routine of Widow Douglas, says he can't stand it "no longer," and "lights out" to his old rags and hogshead and "was free and satisfied." He returns only to qualify for Tom's gang. At the end of the book he again "lights out," this time for "howling adventures amongst the Injuns, over in the Territory." Has anything changed? The final words rejecting civilization, this time Aunt Sally's, do seem to register a difference: "I been there before." These are precious words for the reader; they confirm what he has discovered about civilization. But do they mean the same thing to Huck?

The difference we want to feel between the two rejections of civilization which frame the book parallels the indisputable difference between the two instances when Huck decides to go to hell rather than obey moral conscience. In Chapter 1, Miss Watson tries to frighten the child into sitting up straight by preaching about the bad place and what is in store for boys who don't behave. Huck retorts that he wishes he were there; if Miss Watson is heading for heaven, he would rather not try for it. In Chapter 31, in Huck's famous struggle with his conscience, this comedy of inverted values recurs, but with much expanded significance. In the first instance the preference for hell is expressed in a raffish, offhanded manner; it is a joke, not a serious commitment. In Chapter 31, in a much analyzed passage, we witness a genuine choice, preceded by an inward struggle. The language, first of self-condemnation ("here was the plain hand of Providence slapping me in the face"), then of self-reproach ("and he was so grateful, and said I was the best friend old Jim ever had in the world, and the *only* one he's got now"), externalizes the opposite perspectives of sound heart and deformed conscience. The feat of language itself convinces us that Huck has now earned a meaningful damnation on behalf of his friendship with Jim. This episode has a structure of modulated feeling entirely missing in the first case. Moreover the much deeper implications for Huck's freedom in the second instance are affected by the location of the moment in the narrative, after the exposure of greed, corruption, hypocrisy, and violence in the river society. If the Grangerfords and all the others name heaven as their goal, then hell is by far a better aspiration. Huck's decisive words, "All right, then, I'll *go* to hell," are a release for the reader, for he too has been in "a close place." The line affirms Huck's fundamental rightness.

In short, the deepened implications of "I'll go to hell" and "I been there before," implications which have led critics to impute to Huck a self-generated liberation from moral deformity, arise from the context of narrative action. But does Huck actually catch the same implications? Does he know and understand exactly what he is saying? Of course we might argue that the implications are finally comic precisely because Huck does not understand them. But if this is the case, can we also say that he is a conscious character? If we cannot believe that Huck shows himself just at the moment when we most approve of his words, then we necessarily claim we are superior to him. We fix him in an ironic relation to his own words: he says more than he knows. But then again, does he not by nature *feel* rather than think? If we say so, if we excuse him from an intellectual act we perform, then are we not exploiting our sense of superiority and condescending toward him? Of course Huck is clearly mindful of the seriousness of his impasse, that he is deciding "forever, betwixt two things." Even earlier in the narrative, however, Huck had settled moral dilemmas by choosing what to him is the easiest, most comfortable course; we approve his choices, and smile at his handy rationalizations (some of which he learns from Pap). A similar pattern finally emerges in Chapter 31; after his "awful thoughts, and awful words" about hell, he "shoved the whole thing out of my head; and said I would take up wickedness again, which was in my line, being brung up to it." A beautiful line; but beautiful because of its perfect ironic tone. Is Huck aware of the irony? Has he learned what we have learned as witnesses, overhearers, of his conflict? Can we be sure, here or at the end of the book, that we are not extrapolating from our own lessons in expecting Huck to share our recognitions?

In at least one episode Huck does achieve an unequivocal self-awareness, and the scene is the measure of Huck's behavior elsewhere in the book. I refer to the colloquy with Jim that concludes Chapter 15, after Huck had played his joke on Jim during the fog. The scene is unusual in the book, in part because of its realized tension between Huck and Jim, in part because of the completely unfettered, "free" and honest speech by Jim ("What do dey stan' for? I's gwyne to tell you.... Dat truck dah is *trash;* en trash is what people is dat puts dirt on de head er dey fren's en makes 'em ashamed"). Huck is forced by the speech to reckon with Jim as a person who has developed specific human expectations regarding Huck. By reckoning with such expectations Huck must reckon with, must confront himself, as a social being whose acts make a difference. He experiences himself through the sense compelled by Jim's speech of how another person experiences him. Huck once more wins our approval, but more important, he wins a self-conception which issues into an action—his apology "to a nigger."

The implications of a deepening human relation between Huck and Jim fail to materialize in the book; they have no other dramatic conflicts of this sort. But perhaps one confrontation is sufficient; perhaps the implications are buried in order to return in Huck's comparably "free" speech in Chapter 31, which recalls the circumstances of his friendship with Jim on the raft. It is curious, however, in light of the growing consciousness of these moments of mutual perception and self-perception, that the book, filled as it is with so many characters, is so barren of human relationships. The superficial quality of how people deal with each other (and themselves) is, of course, a deliberate element in Mark Twain's portrait of river society. It is also true that in Huck's experience people usually represent problems rather than possibilities, objects rather than subjects. His disguises are manipulative; he usually plays the role of the victimized orphan boy in order to exact enough sympathy to permit an escape. His many encounters leave him relatively untouched by memory (with a few notable exceptions); threads of meaning do not appear between episodes. Pap, Miss Watson, Tom, cannot be said to exist for Huck as subjectivities in their own right: if Tom were here he would do this or that, Miss Watson is a nuisance, Pap is a threat.

The scarcity of complicating relations, of *dramatic* encounters, does in fact qualify the reader's relation to Huck. To repeat what I propose is the critical issue at stake, we want to learn if these features of the narrative follow from Huck's "character," the demanding needs of his inner being, or if they in some way reflect the double role he plays, as a narrator who tells a story and a character who has a story. We need to look more closely at Huck's technical and dramatic roles.

The absence of serious complications helps account for the book's universal appeal. Compared to the "analytic" works Mark Twain condemned, *Huckleberry Finn* seems "easy" reading. Mark Twain could rely upon a readership already trained to recognize and "read" a comic vernacular speaker, to place him within its verbal universe; Huck appears within the guise of local color conventions (dialect, regional dress, essential "goodness" of heart). As a storyteller he intervenes very little between the events and the reader; he rarely projects a mind that calls attention to itself apart from the immediate experiences it records. Verbally, Huck displays a prepositional exactness in defining himself in space, but more or less imprecision in regard to time; his language is keyed more to geography than to the clock—as befits a mind with little active memory. The intervals between episodes, which themselves have fairly concrete temporal structures, are filled usually with drift: "So we would put in the day, lazying around, listening to the stillness." The mythic force of many separate passages in the book arises from the absence of an obtruding sense of historical time. In the drift, one thing follows another without more relation than sequence: "Two or three days and nights went by"; "Soon as it was night"; "One morning."

But if sequential time matters little in the narrative structure, "timing," the arch device of the oral storyteller, does. In "How to Tell a Story" Mark Twain speaks of the importance of a studied nonchalance, an appearance of rambling purposeless-ness, and of the strategic pause. The storyteller holds his listener in a relation which has a strict temporal order of its own. Within that order, generated by the verbal posture of casualness, the placement or the withholding of details is of first importance. Thus the comic story tends to appear within longer narratives as a set piece, such as Huck's account of the Grangerford household, or his colloquy with Jim about "Sollermun." Within these pieces, Huck's role follows what Clemens called "the first virtue of a comedian"—to "do humorous things with grave decorum and without seeming to know they are funny." Grave decorum and seeming humorlessness well describe Huck's appearance. But is he so guileful as to dissemble his appearance for the reader? Who is the controlling comedian of the book, Huck or Mark Twain? Is humorlessness, the dead pan, Huck's trick on us, or Mark Twain's? Is grave decorum a feature of Huck's own character, or of Mark Twain's deployed mask?

We need to consider dead pan, not only as a mode operative in specific passages, but as the dominant mode of the entire narrative, even when it does not lead to a punch line or reversal. The mode is based on a form of trickery, of saying less than one means. As such it can be taken as a form of insincerity, benign though it may be. "I never seen anybody but lied, one time or another," says Huck in the fifth sentence of the book. The comment disarms in several ways. It evokes a village world where the highest premium is placed upon "telling the truth." To admit that the official value of truth telling is often violated by everyone, including Miss Watson and Widow Douglas, requires either the courage of an iconoclast, which Huck is not, or a personal station outside the official values. As a vernacular character, Huck is free to speak this way; his manner is not aggressive nor muckraking, but grave, decorous, and deadpan. (Contrast, for example, the tone of Colonel Sherburn's speech.) At the same time, the offhanded, flat manner of the admission hides the fact that the statement is of more than passing importance in the book. Lying, indeed, is a major and complex theme. The reader will eventually recognize instance after instance of lies passing as truths, deceptions sanctioned by the social order. Moreover, liars often believe their own lies, are unable to distinguish truth from appearance. On a level of considerable abstraction, the book offers as a basic deception the notion that Jim is "worth" $800, or that money can be traded for human value. Tom seems to think so when he pays Jim forty dollars "for being prisoner for us so patient"; Jim's being "pleased most to death" is one of the jarring notes in the Phelps conclusion. Another variation of the theme belongs to the Duke and the King, perhaps the supreme liars of the book. Cynicism liberates them to purvey appearance as truth without qualms. For this reason they are among the abstractly "free" characters; without thoughts of heaven, without conscience, they menace not only the social order but the fragile harmony of the raft. They represent an ultimate freedom in which the "other" is entirely an object, a freedom Huck ostensibly has overcome in himself after his elaborate lie to Jim after the fog in Chapter 15.

Dead pan exists in a complex relation to lies. It too is a falsehood, a manipulated appearance. But it is a lie in the service of truth or "reality," an honest lie whose effect as humor is based on our ultimate recognition of its falseness. As James Cox writes of the tall tale—a variant of dead pan—it "is true in that it is the only lie in a world of lies which reveals itself to be a lie." Commonly the procedure is to dramatize in the comic voice an apparently unrecognized discrepancy between what is perceived (the awful gimcrackery of the Grangerford sitting room) and what is felt (Huck's sentimental approval). The reader is allowed to accept the feelings as provisionally his own, only to be thwarted by the details which normally arouse a contrary response; he is released from the false feelings by recognizing their cause to be ludicrously inadequate. The reader is initially taken in by Huck's manner so that he may, so to speak, be saved from Huck's foolish approval.

But does Huck really approve? If so, he is indeed a fool, and we laugh at him as well as the complacent Grangerfords. In the convention of dead pan the teller is only apparently a fool. We permit him to practice deception on us because in the end some absurdity will be exposed to the light of universal common sense; we will gain an advantage over the world. The teller's manner is a mask which steadily, deliberately, misleads us, until at the critical moment the mask falls. Behind the mask we might expect to find the real Huck, sharing our laughter, perhaps laughing at us for being momentarily taken in. The revealed comedian becomes at least our equal. But is this model at work here? Again we face Huck's paradoxical situation, as teller and as character. If we say that Huck's manner is a deliberate guise on his part, what happens to his gravity, his solemnity, his innocence, which we have normally taken as traits of character? Apart from depriving, or freeing, him of these elements of personality, such a reading would seriously upset the balance established between reader and narrative voice established at the outset. The voice presents itself as genuinely literal-minded; it presents itself as inferior in its own mind to the civilization of Widow Douglas and Tom Sawyer. We quickly make the judgment Huck seems unable to make for himself, that literal-mindedness is notably superior to the respectable lies of the town. The obvious superiority of Huck's frankness frees the reader from the deceptions of a world where respectability is the qualification for membership in a gang of robbers. To assign duplicity to Huck (by claiming he knows more than he is saying) would disturb this effect. To serve as our liberator Huck must remain ignorant and solemn. He must remain so in order to serve as Mark Twain's comic mask. In short, Mark Twain may have removed himself from the frame of the book, as the guileful, controlling voice, but the control remains in force, internalized and sublimated. The outside speaker who in earlier versions of vernacular presentation appeared, as in the Sut Lovingood stories, as a colloquist, now hides in the mask, a secret character in the book.

Dead pan predominates, and with it, Mark Twain's use of Huck's surface manner to reach the reader on a level of common values. But Huck's speech periodically escapes studied solemnity to become either lyrical, as in the sunrise passage which opens Chapter 19, or dramatic, as when he faces up to himself after Jim's "trash" speech. Such moments usually occur after actions which begin within the comic mode. Dead pan in part neutralizes the world, holds it at bay, seems to remove the threat of harm. But genuine harm frequently springs up to threaten the comic mode itself. One of many instances occurs in Chapter 18; the deadpan technique exposes Huck's explanation of the feud as absurd (the scene parallels the exposure of Tom's absurdities in trying to enforce an oath upon his fellow robbers in Chapter 2). Before long the slaughter begins and we hear "Kill them, kill them!" The sunrise passage and the idyllic account of the raft follow in Chapter 19. Huck's lyric-dramatic voice seems to require a violation of his surface deadpan manner for release. The book alternates between a voice given over to deadpan trickery and narrative, and undisguised, direct feeling. The second voice generates needs for dramatic realization the author does not accommodate. Mark Twain's own needs, perhaps for some revenge against Southern river society, seemed to require a Huck Finn who is ignorant, half-deformed, and permanently humorless. To put the case strongly, we might say that Huck's character is stunted by his creator's need for him to serve as a technical device. The same devices of irony which liberate the reader by instructing him about civilization and human nature also repress Huck by using him; they prevent his coming into his own.

Huck's freedom, I want finally to argue, requires that he achieve a conscious moral identity. Huck cannot be free in this sense unless Mark Twain permits him a credible and articulate inner being, with dramatic opportunities to realize his self. Of course this is to make perhaps impossible and therefore inappropriate demands upon this novel. But I think Mark Twain came close enough to such a realization for us to judge the book by its own best moments. Consider, for example, the raft, often taken as the symbol of freedom. The ethic of the raft is stated eloquently: "You feel mighty free and easy and comfortable on a raft." Yes; but this mood is possible because Huck had earlier humbled himself before Jim and decided to give up the pleasure of playing tricks. The raft has a tacit code, what we might call its own conscience. When the Duke and King arrive, that code bends to accommodate the rascals, for, as Huck tells himself as justification for not letting on to Jim that the men are frauds, "what you want, above all things, on a raft, is for everybody to be satisfied, and feel right and kind towards the others . . . it's the best way; then you don't have no quarrels, and don't get into no trouble." "Free and easy" of the first passage has become "satisfied" and "no quarrels . . . no trouble." The difference is subtle but crucial. The raft is no longer free. Dissembling has returned. Huck decides in the name of "peace in the family" not to share with Jim his insights into the intruders: "it warn't no use to tell Jim." No one but the wary reader recognizes that trickery and deception have returned for the sake of the comedy Mark Twain can wring from Jim's ignorant wisdom about kings. True, Jim plays a pastoral role in his discussions about royalty with Huck, but his stature is reduced. Long before the Phelps episode he is required to submit to being tied up and left alone in the wigwam, or to donning "King Lear's outfit" to play a "Sick Arab." No one protests, and "Jim was satisfied."

The raft cannot defend itself against imposture. In the end imposture itself seems the only resort for Huck and Jim. From this point of view the elaborate theatricals at the Phelps farm seem an appropriate conclusion: how else might the two fugitives be returned to a possible world without real harm, without damaging the comic expectations of the novel? But what then can we say about freedom? Are we to judge the vulnerability of the raft, the necessity of a concluding "Evasion" (necessary to have any conclusion at all), to mean that by *its nature* the difficult freedom of owning oneself is impossible? Are we too hard with this book to blame it for failing to sustain the self-consciousness and process of self-discovery implicit in several scenes? Or more to the point, is that failure part of Mark Twain's design, or a result of technical limitations? Does the book project a fully realized vision, or is the vision blocked by the author's inability to sustain a novelistic development? These questions characterize the critic's dilemma in assessing the book.

Of course a vision and the verbal means of its realization and execution are virtually inseparable. Mark Twain saw the world the best he was able to, given his special verbal resources. My argument has meant to say that the formal problems which proceed from the initial conception of a book-length narrative in a mainly deadpan vernacular voice themselves enforce a certain vision. Mark Twain's work as a whole suggests that he seriously doubted the possibilities of personal freedom within a social setting. He seems to have taken freedom as true only when absolute and abstract, outside time. The imagery of drift in this novel is invested with such longing perhaps because it represents a condition already lost and insubstantial the moment it is imagined. The other side of the image reveals the fully invulnerable trickster, whose cynicism releases him from the control of any conscience. The dream voyages and mysterious strangers which obsessed Mark Twain's later years are anticipated in *Huckleberry Finn*.

The book is finally more persuasive as a document of enslavement, of the variety of imprisonments within verbal styles and fictions than as a testimony to freedom. Of course its negativity implies an ideal. I would like to identify that ideal with the "free" speech of Huck and Jim at the moments of engagement. I have tried to explain why such speech breaks out so rarely, why moral identity was so difficult to attain given the technical resources of the book. But we should recognize that the limits placed upon Huck's character are also forceful imperatives from the society within which Mark Twain portrays him. Moral character requires that social roles be credible to young people about to assume them. The society rendered in *Huckleberry Finn* deprives all roles of credibility when viewed from a literal-minded vernacular perspective. Rationalization and improvisation have convincing survival value, and virtuosity of disguise earns our admiration. Pap, after all, did bequeath a fatherly heritage by teaching Huck how to cheat and get away with no more than a bruised conscience. Perhaps the book's Americanness is most profoundly revealed in this heritage of eluding fixed definitions, in the corrosive decreation of established roles. Jim's presence reminds us, however, of the cost history has exacted from a society which drives its children to negativity. The cost is charged most heavily against Huck; he pays with his chance to grow up.

Warwick Wadlington

BUT I NEVER SAID NOTHING

I

Huckleberry Finn is a story of pure courtship first in the important respect that Huck admires "from afar": he admires what he is convinced he can never be a part of, and does not even desire for himself since it is not for the likes of him, not "being brung up to it." The fact that Twain has us frequently view with disenchantment the objects of Huck's appreciation, summed up in the respectable Tom Sawyer, who follows the best authorities, only confirms the purity of Huck's motive per se. Huck's affectionate tolerance of the ways of the "quality" is the more impressive because often they exasperate him personally. And his mistaken admirations seem the more courtly-gallant because of their innocent misdirections of focus, just as his famous decision to go to hell rhetorically purifies his moral choice of aiding Jim—that is, offers Twain's dramatic assurance to us that Huck's intent is as purely selfless as is imaginable. This is the significant point that Huck's deference to Tom in the concluding section reemphasizes: with whatever comic demurs, Huck defers to a socially superior respectability that he does not altogether understand and finds personally inappropriate. The weight that the essential motivation carries with Huck is explicit in his concern that Tom would be injuring his respectability by helping Jim escape, combined with an acquiescence to Tom's authoritative statement that he generally knows what he's about.

But the controversial Phelps section is unsettling largely because Twain insists on Huck's unchanging submission to Tom after two important effects climax in the moral decision Huck has just made. Huck has drawn our affectionate esteem because of his very humility, his certainty that he is inferior to the aristocratic class of Widow Douglas and the Grangerfords that keeps wanting to adopt him, whose

From *The Confidence Game in American Literature* (Princeton: Princeton University Press, 1975), pp. 244–49, 257–61, 272–81.

God he is sure he offends. However, this same decorously expressed admiring humility has also been used to make us increasingly impatient of much that Huck feels to be superior. As a result, at the end we want Huck to cease being the humble courtier of Tom Sawyer and all that Tom represents, although it is this very disposition that has given Huck fictive stature and the book's social criticism its powerful and moving ironic edge. In effect, I wish to argue, the novel leads us à rebours to want Huck Finn to cease being Huck Finn; we unconsciously want a fundamental egalitarian or aristocratic transformation in a fiction whose profoundest logic denies such a possibility. ⟨. . .⟩

Huck, otherwise evidently the paragon of utilitarianism, admires and defers on principle, disinterestedly. It is as if—to begin with an ultimate model—the perfection of homage were dramatized by showing the damned in hell worshiping God. (In fact, it is characteristic of Huck that immediately after deciding that he will go to hell and live a life of wickedness, he announces as he approaches the Phelps farm that he will trust in Providence to put words in his mouth.) This supposititious model would evidence the more forcefully the human need for some form of courtly behavior if at the same time the Deity were shown as venial and unworthy. For then the hierarchical motive per se is unmodified by circumstance and is therefore capable of being felt in its purity: this ironic, or negative, model would show a courtship unaffected by the unworthiness of the entities occupying the hierarchical positions or by any hope of individual advancement up the scale. The principle of the scale is seen as suasive in itself; the hierarchical motive, thus ironically uncircumstanced, would be felt in its inevitability and perfect reality as a constituent of human action.

This model is intended to be illustrative, but it is approached in the book's treatment of Providence, prayer, and cognate matters. Students of *Huckleberry Finn* have dealt with these ideas almost wholly in thematic terms that neglect Huck's persuasive habits both as protagonist and narrator. The connection is a key one, for the book marshals rank upon rank of persuasive order—including magic, prayer, confidence trickery, and personal-social "style"—in which the *adventures* of the book's title take their complete meaning.

Huck's introduction to the rites of civilizing in the first several chapters has a strongly religious complexion, but the definitive religious act, prayer, is set within the context of a practical rhetoric, magic, identified with socially inferior status. When Huck is first introduced to prayer, he regards it as if it were magic, of a piece with the prophylactic and coercive actions one performs when one has killed a spider or wishes to make a hairball prophesy. Thus Huck is quickly disappointed in his attempts at praying when "nothing come of it."[1] But "superstitious" magic is also given a broader frame of analogy. From the first, Huck has impressed upon him the near-magical properties attributed by everyone to correct "style," a word recurrently on the lips of Tom Sawyer as well as Huck. The world portrayed in the first scenes is charged with manneristic significance: Huck's gaping and stretching is interpreted by Miss Watson as stylistic misbehavior to be countered by threats of hell; his unintentional killing of the spider is particularly terrifying because he feels stylistically helpless, knowing no specific ritual counter to ward off bad luck, and so "hadn't no confidence"; the juvenile gang and its games are established according to a detailed outlaw style determined by the mysterious ordinances of Tom's precious books; Tom's genie must be summoned in the correct way; Jim's hairball only reveals its secrets if properly approached; Pap Finn is as outraged by his son's new upperclass dress and behavior, and by the style of an educated Black, as any punctilious guardian of the social ladder would be; and so on through Jim's lessons in folk magic on Jackson Island.

In short, each social class is carefully identified with the style in which it has confidence and in terms of which it understands its own persuasive authority, properly circumscribed in relation to that of classes above and below. This is the fictive world of summoning, coercing, blandishing, and threatening in which the fittingly named Duke and King will make their way by mimicry of pertinent manners, and in which the ribald Royal Nonesuch is tailor-made by the Duke: "So the duke said these Arkansaw lunkheads couldn't come up to Shakespeare. . . . He said he could size their style" (p. 200). Given the cultural obsession with degree and appropriate and impressive sets of decorum, "style" threatens to become solely constitutive of act, subsuming all considerations of will and intention into graduated performances acceptable according to certain conventions. *Huckleberry Finn* is in its own way a symbolic investigation of the classical courtly dilemma, represented in the Renaissance for example by the machiavel type: in a community where stylistic decorum and hierarchical suasions are predominant values, what will keep Iago and those who smile and smile from making everything subservient to empty shows? The problem is only exacerbated in a democratic, ostensibly egalitarian society, for "Degree being vizarded, / Th' unworthiest shows as fairly in the mask" (*Troilus and Cressida*). Pap's redneck version of this fear is manifest in his double-edged complaint that he is a wealthy man ("worth six thousand dollars and upwards") brought low by the "govment" while a mulatto professor walks freely about with fine clothes. From here the path is plain to the Duke's lament about being "fetched . . . so low, when I was so high" (p. 167) and the steps the two confidence operators take to right this hierarchical injustice, nonetheless real for being only rhetorically alleged. In part, Twain's reply to the dilemma is traditional, as in aristocratic Colonel Sherburn's coordination of style and the courage to back it up. But this particular answer raises more problems for Twain than it solves. Another reply, also troublesome, is Huck Finn himself, with his "good heart" and his calm assertion as he first assumes the role of our narrator: "I never seen anybody but lied." ⟨. . .⟩

II

Huck's consciousness, then, from first to last remains hierarchically motivated, and in the novel's action it is refined increasingly regarding trust and its abuses within this psychosocial order: regarding what is owed others and, inseparably, oneself. But a modern confusion of liberty and fraternity with equality has influenced many readers either to deny that any real development takes place or to claim too much for Huck's growth. A largely unwitting preconception about what development must entail in a social bond has caused misconception about what development means in *this* novel. Even aside from humane or political habits of mind, one of two major tendencies in a hierarchy, particularly as it must be presented in a democratic environment, tempts to this confusion. In the ideal courtly dynamic stasis, there exists an ordination of degrees securely graduated, yet interpersuasive, to that extent interidentifying, and thus mobile in imagination. As against this ideal, the hierarchy may collapse in one of two similar but distinct ways. Either all the ranked terms may be imperiously summoned into the god-term (a providential Tom Sawyer), or there may be a thorough egalitarian leveling to some lower common denominator. Twain exploits both tendencies masterfully for purposes of purification: to make the basic courtly issues salient and to pretend simultaneously that they are not; thus the right hand can do vigorously what the left hand does not know. An examination of hierarchy's tendency to collapse in the direction of equality, because it requires primary consideration of Huck's development, calls for rather tenacious pursuit of ancillary ideas before the other tendency—the imperial summons—will again claim our attention. One investigation leads us to the novel's pivotal action, the other to its end.

I have in mind first, of course, Jim. Jim is the repeated focal point of Huck's internal struggle; and Huck's apparently callous relationship to him in the concluding section has usually either been explained away as Twain's blunder or as not meaning what it seems to, or else used as conclusive evidence that Huck's "growth" was nonexistent after all. The truth is, between themselves Jim and Huck achieve a comic and poignant kind of liberty and fraternity, but not equality. Huck's much-discussed statement that no one was killed in a steamboat accident (" 'No'm. Killed a nigger.' ") is not simply indicative of Huck's perhaps harmless failure to generalize from his earlier revelations about Jim. Nor is "nigger" when directly applied to Jim simply a term wholly neutralized by its common generic usage: " 'Ain't them old crippled picks and things in there good enough to dig a nigger out with?' " Huck incredulously asks Tom, who is intent on promoting Jim to State Prisoner (p. 314). Jim is, in fact, usually "my nigger" to Huck. Yet this is the proprietary air not of slave possession but of loyal *noblesse oblige* toward a friend who is nevertheless a social inferior and never has ceased to be after carefully attaching himself to Huck in exactly that combination of terms. When Huck apologizes to Jim for tricking him at the end of chapter xv, Huck is entirely aware that it is "a nigger" to whom he is apologizing. His apology does not alter his consciousness of relative status but if anything impresses it on him, because Huck despises above everything having to feel "low-down," "humble," and "mean," as he typically does whenever he is troubled.

The book tempts us to misread precisely by playing up such tensions and resolutions as those in the apology scene, as a condition for making the courtly motive manifest dramatically but hidden linguistically and socio-morally. (Even here, however, we will note a double effect.) As hierarchies create themselves by an endless structural drama of symbolic and actual transgressions, resistance, and resolution, so Twain depicts status-defining tests of authority accompanied by apology, praise, and demonstrations of loyal confidence. To understand both Huck's development and Twain's purifying equivocation, we can proceed at once to the major turning point of the novel, the trickster Huck Finn's remarkable assertion at the end of chapter xv: "I didn't do [Jim] no more mean tricks. . . ." The assertion has the rhetorical status of a promise, apparently foreclosing a trouble-some possibility. But it seems to be a true promise to the reader only if it is interpreted rather narrowly, since Huck subsequently engages in at least three contradictory actions commonly cited as showing that he has not really matured his perception of Jim: he does not tell Jim that the Duke and the King are frauds, he acquiesces in their binding Jim and dressing him in a comically demeaning "King Lear" costume, and he cooperates with Tom's similar exploitation of Jim on the Phelps farm. If we examine both the immediate and the general contexts, however, the matter appears in a different light, and in turn illumines the rest of the novel.

First, the remainder of the quoted sentence reads: "and I wouldn't done that one [i.e., trick] if I'd a knowed it would make him feel that way." Nothing in the three later actions indicates, either to Huck or the reader, that Jim's feelings are hurt by his treatment. Jim, like Huck, at last comically protests the physical inconveniences involved in Tom's proceedings, but there is no sign that his dignity or *amour propre* are touched, as they are in chapter xv by what might seem a much less significant transgression against him. Exactly like Huck, Jim yields to higher authority at the end: "Jim he couldn't see no sense in the most of it, but allowed we was white folks and knowed better than him; so he was satisfied . . ." (p. 321). Shortly after this, Jim farcically apologizes to Tom for briefly rebelling against the further burdens Tom sees as opportunities for glory.

Second, the sequence of events leading up to and away from chapter xv demonstrates that what is at stake when Jim does stand up for his dignity as an individual is the hierarchically appropriate area of stylistic authority that signifies his identity. Huck's trick climaxes a running battle over sovereignty in superstitious magic. Huck acknowledges Jim's lore ("Jim knowed all kinds of signs"), but he is also covetous of it and seeks to debunk it. Although the novel shows that there is an overlap of socially decorous stylistic power here between slaves and lower-class whites, and although there is a natural tension in Huck because of the ambiguous relationship of dependency between a white child and an adult runaway slave, the conflict of dominion also manifests Huck's stylistic hunger. By this I mean that Huck, existing on the margins of divergent classes, and concomitantly possessing a sensitive, frequently troubled consciousness, is exceptionally avid for stylistic devices that seem to have calmative power internally and externally. At the same time, his debunking habit not only is an attempt to neutralize and resist potentially threatening stylistic powers, but more importantly is a reflection of his intense disappointment at finding that the allegedly potent device is yet another lie, that his hunger has been teased and not fulfilled. ⟨. . .⟩

I I I

Huck's marginality accounts for both his sensitivity and his insensitivity. To be marginal is to be uncertain of where one's ties of obligation exist and, conversely, what responsibilities others owe oneself. In the largest perspective, it is to be anxious concerning the pertinence of events to the self and vice versa, and thus to be alert and perceptively vulnerable to them. Marginal acuteness thus covers the wide range indicated by these instances: Huck's fear of haunting night-sounds; his acute delight at a river sunrise scene, which nevertheless includes notation of a deceptive woodpile and rotting fish; and his singular concern for a circus rider. This consciousness is what Huck and Twain mean by "conscience," the free-floating scrutiny that, unconfident of any stable accountability, projects personal obligation when cruel suffering is perceived, although one's moral choice has not caused the pain. To recall the vocabulary instituted earlier: "conscience" is a property of consciousness like superstition, promoting deed into act, but without the ameliorative ritual. And we can now understand that this exaggerating consciousness is profoundly concordant, generally, with Huck's trickster talent for "stretching," and specifically, with his habitual self-portrayal as a waif beset by calamity, as a means of disarming others. All this is summed up when Huck says, as he sees the King and the Duke punished by being tarred-and-feathered and ridden on a rail, ". . . I warn't feeling so brash as I was before, but kind of ornery, and humble, and to blame, somehow—though *I* hadn't done nothing. But that's always the way; it don't make no difference whether you do right or wrong, a person's conscience ain't got no sense, and just goes for him *anyway*. If I had a yaller dog that didn't know no more than a person's conscience does, I would pison him. It takes up more room than all the rest of a person's insides, and yet ain't no good, nohow. Tom Sawyer he says the same" (p. 300).

What Tom Sawyer typically says comprises a way of hypnotizing the moral imagination. Tom's style is to make discomfort the obligatory, manneristic stuff of adventure. In a burlesque perversion of conscious ingenuity, Tom labors at the gold-leaf distinctions (Huck's term) that the literary authorities demand. By contrast, though Jim's presence is recurrently troubling to Huck, the trouble is transmuted by Jim's courtly descriptions and proscriptions into a clarifying stipulation of confidence. Yet Tom's systematizing of clear-cut but illusory obligation is so much more comprehensive in what it seemingly accounts for and confidently clinches in place that Huck finds it irresistible. The book ends by rescuing Huck with the frontier metaphor that embodies his cultural status. The novel breaks off, that is, with Huck's reestablishing his tense marginality, preparing to escape to the borders of civilization "ahead of the rest," but not before Twain has indeed almost collapsed everything into Tom and his aristocratic play. If we look ahead to clarify the implications of this tendency, we see that *A Connecticut Yankee in King Arthur's Court* does collapse all into one consciousness that reveals its psychosocial reality in a courtly dream-vision fictionally poising the objective and subjective. For the protagonist the dream-fact of identity is intolerable and is attacked and destroyed self-destructively. From here it is only a very short step to "Which Was the Dream?," "The Great Dark," and the confused manuscripts Paine palmed off as *The Mysterious Stranger*. This last pseudo-tale is broadly symptomatic, for it really exists as a dislocated ending that Twain, perhaps self-protectively, could not find creative ligatures for among several inadequate narrative alternatives: the solipsistic collapse of everything into a solitary ruling thought.

Huck's language works against this strongly seductive summons of the god-term. It is in Huck's language, after all, that we sense him most firmly; and it is in his language that many of the best readers of Twain have tried to discover the old true Huck amid his renewed marginal pullings and driftings. Huck's language resists a dangerous hierarchical mounting not only in a general vernacular lowness but in two features that can be isolated within his vernacular. One is the often-remarked negative flair of his vocabulary, his constructions, and his outlook, which also signifies in other related ways: as an attempt to flatly negate "trouble," for instance in the formula he uses to trick Jim with an alleged dream (" 'I hain't seen no fog, nor no islands, nor no troubles, nor nothing.' "); and as a reflection of the relatively unfixed identity that makes Huck, within his marginal boundaries, a protean, stylistically avid, trickster.

Huck's other linguistically resistant trait may be termed, to recall the prior discussion again, his anti-prayer. That is, Huck's narrative speech placidly digs in its heels against changing linguistic registers to comport with the dignity of its subject matter. On the opening page of the narrative, for example, the unwitting irreverence at once overtly acknowledges the social distinctions—Mr. Mark Twain, Judge Thatcher; and Aunt Polly and the Widow as possible exceptions to universal lying—and speaks of everyone and every action, high or low, in the only language Huck knows. The pleasure the language furnishes is precisely the fresh sense it gives of the hierarchical shibboleths by innocently failing to do them linguistic obeisance. Huck's anti-prayer effortlessly refuses to acknowledge that now the Judge, now the Widow's charitable adoption, now the investment of significant funds, is being treated. According to Huck's report, the Widow "allowed she would sivilize" him much as Jim Smiley allows he will train the best jumping frog in Calaveras County. Even when Huck clearly wants to praise, the language seems to go its own way, as in his enthusiastic pronouncement on the King's Shakespearean performance: "It seemed like he was just born for it; and when he had his hand in and was excited, it was perfectly lovely the way he would rip and tear and rair up behind when he was getting it off" (p. 185). "Perfectly lovely" tells us which way the speech seems to want to go by gesturing toward fragile upper-class locution; but the subsequent phrasing refuses to budge, in comic counterpoint to the sort of uplift it describes. Another, longer example, dealing with Mary Jane Wilks' promise to pray for Huck, can provide its own commentary in collocating ideas of prayer "for its own sake," flattery, and equivocal nonflattery ranging from the obvious to connotative nuances like "lays":

> Pray for me! I reckoned if she knowed me she'd take a job that was more nearer her size. But I bet she done it, just the same—she was just that kind. She had the grit to pray for Judas if she took the notion—there warn't no backdown to her, I judge. You may say what you want to, but in my opinion she had more sand in her than any girl I ever see; in my opinion she was just full of sand. It sounds like flattery, but it ain't no flattery. And when it comes to beauty—and goodness too—she lays over them all. I hain't ever seen her since that time that I see her go out of that door; no, I hain't ever seen her since, but I reckon I've thought of her a many and a many a million times, and of her saying she would pray for me; and if ever I'd a thought it would do any good for me to pray for *her,* blamed if I wouldn't done it or bust. (pp. 250–51)

Huck's admiration for Tom indicates a love of "style" for its own sake to which Huck blinds himself (as the Connecticut Yankee will do later) whenever he implies that he is totally pragmatic. This delusion helps to maintain the hierarchical distinction between what one admires and therefore to an extent identifies oneself with, and what one nevertheless resists becoming wholly. In this sense, Huck's language, in enacting Twain's purifying concealment, is also partly a self-concealment, or benign repression, for Huck. The language refuses to go the whole way with Huck's admirations. Like his grumbling even as he submits to Tom's domination, it is a form of foot-dragging to maintain the coherent continuity of one identity—a resistance to that with which Huck identifies himself and yet refuses to become identical.

Nevertheless, though the language is courtly resistant in its inability to change registers, within its register it is not deluded at all, but is characterized by such adjectives as *noble* and *grand* at one extreme, and *low-down* and *ornery* at the other. The result is a courtly tension of high and low in the set of hierarchically loaded terms, so that Huck can speak of a "noble good lot" of rats and yet provide this sort of verbal placing: "Well, when Tom and me got to the edge of the hill-top we looked away down into the village and could see three or four lights twinkling, where there was sick folks, maybe; and the stars over us was sparkling ever so fine; and down by the village was the river, a whole mile broad, and awful still and grand" (pp. 22–23). The effect is dependent not so much on the commonplace complimentary adjectives as on the simple stateliness of rhythm accompanying the discriminations of place. Another passage, eschewing all fine adjectives but instead employing language like "creeping" and "monstrous big," is even more elegant in its rhythm of placing:

I went up and set down on a log at the head of the island, and looked out on the big river and the black driftwood and away over to the town, three mile away, where there was three or four lights twinkling. A monstrous big lumber-raft was about a mile up stream, coming along down, with a lantern in the middle of it. I watched it come creeping down, and when it was most abreast of where I stood I heard a man say, "Stern oars, there! heave her head to starboard!" I heard that just as plain as if the man was by my side. (p. 60)

For all the economical effect of the passage, it allows for unobtrusive stylistic elaborations of location that are "inefficient" in the most courtly way, the sound and rhythm celebrating the easy release of intimate distance: "away over to the town, three mile away"; "coming along down"; "as if the man was by my side." With this kind of beguiling lucidity, it is difficult to notice that Huck is presented as both sitting and standing.

The excitement of Huck's language, as we begin to find out not very far into the novel, is that the slouching manner is a spell cast over a subsurface of insistent disturbances. Its defensive function for Huck in maintaining his distance from the upper and lower boundary terms, Tom and Jim, also appropriately gives his narrative speech its courtly circumspection, as in his habit of saying, "but I never let on," or "but I never said nothing," and his formulaic "no matter" and "no harm" regarding some apparent human failing. This is the rhetoric of comfort, more exactly the coziness that hearkens back to *Innocents Abroad* in creating the sensation of comfort sharpened by the threats encompassing it. As narrative action and rhetorical enactment proceed, comfort becomes not a negative state but an achievement that attracts our sympathy with Huck's restless escape toward rest. The opening pages negotiate a tacit understanding with the reader to the effect that Huck's discomfort, as it is stylistically transformed and shielded, will produce our own feeling of relaxation. It "ain't no matter" whether we know or not who Huck Finn is; there is "no harm" meant by Huck's behavior or the manners of his "dismal regular and decent" captors. "That is nothing," that Mark Twain lied in *Tom Sawyer;* we all lie, and it was mostly a true book anyway. And it does not matter how one talks, for the seemingly careless chaos of grammar appears to get the job done very competently, inviting us simply to enjoy the language's swift energy since the "matter" of just who and just how does not appear to demand much concern. This assurance of comfort, renewed periodically, acts as a buffer for every disturbing event that follows (modern critics have counted up the murders and other cruelties). Otherwise stated, this is an assurance that the title of the book is trustworthy, that we will be reading *the adventures of . . .* , with all this promises for the treatment of disturbance as excitement, and mayhem as challenge. Like Huck's promise of no more mean tricks, this rhetorical assurance must be understood as a definitively ambivalent statement.

The novel as a whole is formally designed to arouse and preserve the deliciously cozy feeling of Jim and Huck snug in their cave watching the storm. In the light of this conservation of feeling, which must renew a threat and turn it adventurously into something new and strange, we can elucidate the "problem of the ending." Or rather, we can observe how it elucidates itself. In the closing section, Huck feels "easy and comfortable" (p. 290) on finding that he is supposed to play Tom Sawyer once more. But we are now naggingly bothered because for the first time at any length the book presents us with an untransformed trouble that we sense the more sharply because the three major characters sweat and contrive before our eyes to make it into adventure, even as Twain also now labors to find his culminating, all-transforming "snapper" of an ending. Now it is apparent that not only alchemic adventures but base-metal difficulties themselves must be fabricated, as Tom strongly complains. Tom supplies the reason as well: the people are too trusting (see especially pp. 308, 343). This implicit denial that there is real trouble to be encountered and countered is, paradoxically, disturbing, because our comfort has been constructed on the basis of the very real troubles that the book's adventures disclose and buffer. We are like Huck and Jim in their cave, watching, instead of a storm, Tom/Twain doing an interminable rain dance. And the troubles that we have seen have arisen exactly because people are too trusting in one sense and treacherous in another. Thus at the very time that Tom complains of a lack of difficulties—the complaint itself partly an indication of difficulty—we increasingly recognize several: Huck's bowing to Tom; Jim's mistreatment; and, making both of these disturbing in a way they otherwise would not be, Twain's drastic diffusion of language and invention in a joke that goes on far too long as it strains to end itself satisfactorily.

Yet the near-collapse of the ending carries its own diagnosis in the play of the boys with Jim. The "failure" is more interesting than the successes of most writers, in analyzing the basic matter of the book by a pretended pretense that "it ain't no matter." The transformational labors that until now have been brilliantly successful unmask themselves. But retrospectively we can see that, throughout the work, a subsidiary theme has been the impossibility of fundamental transformations, reformations—as with Pap Finn and the new judge, the King at the camp meeting, and Huck's attempt to be a better boy by the prayer that would allow him to betray Jim. The attempts at making new by renaming are pretenses that are consequential in refining hierarchical perceptions, and in causing peace or discomfort for a time, but leave things unchanged in *essentials*. They are transformations, but they do not amount to transubstantiation. The redundancy of such attempts is summarized in Huck's exclamation near the end: "all that trouble and bother to set a free nigger free!"

This disclosure is also recapitulated in the repetitive adventure-structure of the book, signifying that Huck will always have "been there before" precisely by evading adoption to flee to the margins of society "ahead of the rest." Huck, in other words, is a genuinely marginal, not a liminal, figure—his interstitial existence is not temporary or probative, leading to a reconsolidation with a secure social order, but instead fundamentally constitutive of being. Nevertheless, though no essential change can take place, we have seen that Huck's consciousness does develop in a firmer awareness of the external and internal realities it embodies. His freedom is also his necessity: to evade between his bounds, and to refine his perception of what tricks and burdens they elicit. The farcical quality of the ending does not deny or negate this troubled understanding but seeks to manipulate it by an overt caricature, usurping its high power according to the book's operational logic, and thus making climactic adventure. The attempt is not to laugh it away but to make it, once and for all, gay. But at the same time, being true to itself, the novel must diagnose the impossibility of doing this in any final sense by verbal conjurations, the tricks of nomenclature.

The end is therefore predictably an attempted transmutation that laughs in part at its own failure to transubstantiate, inseparably from the effort Tom directs. Huck quits writing because he needs a rest, not because he has found an end. We are left with the fundamental trouble: as Huck says, the trouble it is to make a book; to purify a troubling motive by inventing both fictional difficulties and the ruses that convert them into adventures; to call into existence a court and a fantastic "democratic" set of kings, dukes, and other courtiers and turn it all into equivocal elucidation and concealment. Yet, besides this revelation of fundamental trouble, we are also left with Huck's reference to the adventures he anticipates with Tom and Jim in the Territory. The two components face each other in an unresolvable, but endlessly self-refining, dialectic of hierarchical consciousness: trouble and adventure, Jim and Tom; with Huck the mobile diacritical mark between them.

Everything ends in a game, but Twain has nearly had a king's immunity all along. Huck's disclosure of fundamental trouble is of course a revelation not of his, but of Twain's, basic efforts. Huck's final complaint of discomfort—the Author to His Book in an inverted envoy—is a self-dismissal and a last gesture of comfort toward us, making us smile in permissive affection at Huck's characteristic language. With this pleasure we consolidate conclusively a shared adult vision with the real fabricator of these adventures.

Like Twain's initial notice, the closing section is preemptive. Whereas initially he had equivocally forbidden investigation, now Twain outbids our diagnosis of "failure" by himself being diagnostic. This affective distinguishing is after all the function of the courtier. Indeed, as Henry Nash Smith has pointed out, it is primarily Twain's voice we hear over Huck's during the concluding episode,[2] though Twain had led up to this dominance in Huck's increasing sentimentality regarding the Wilks' girls. Turning a mirror on the novel, Twain shows how it has not only depicted but woven transformational spells that smuggle into our perception one self-refining, circular motive of action. By making this situation the theme of parodic adventures, Twain gets us to forgive everything in uneasy amusement at seeing the difficulties showing through the adventures. The mirror, however, is not one but many since what is revealed is a self-reflexive contraband communication. Twain's long-standing device of the concluding palinode is thus perfected, for the implied mirror-sequence endlessly retracts, and withdraws retractions. I have said we are left facing adventures and troubles. This also means we are left with the authority who put up the warning notice in the first place; and who preceded it in the original edition by setting his sternly aristocratic likeness, from the new bust by Karl Gerhardt, directly facing Kemble's pen illustration of a ragamuffin Huckleberry Finn.

Huck is Twain's greatest creation, one of the greatest in literature, and the greatest usurpation by Twain. The self-wrenching, book-wrenching diagnosis purifies Twain of his purifier. Thus retracting its prize palinode, Twain's art reaches its height and effectively ends there.

NOTES

[1] *The Writings of Mark Twain,* Author's National Edition (25 vols.; Harper, 1907–18), XIII, 28. Hereafter cited in the text by page number alone unless the volume identification is required for clarity.
[2] Henry Nash Smith, *Mark Twain: The Development of a Writer* (Cambridge, Mass.: Harvard University Press, 1962), pp. 130–34.

Susan K. Harris

HUCK FINN

You must become an ignorant man again
And see the sun again with an ignorant eye
And see it clearly in the idea of it.

—Wallace Stevens

The term *alienation* is used in this study to describe the uneasiness a character feels when he realizes that he cannot wholly share the value system of a given group. In the novels we have examined so far, narrative alienation was manifested consciously, either, as with Hank Morgan (in *A Connecticut Yankee in King Arthur's Court*), as an overt rejection of the values of an alien culture, or, as with Louis de Conte (in *Joan of Arc*), as a gradual process of psychological disengagement from one's own culture. Whether the narrators begin or end their narratives with indications that they are not comfortable in their social group, at some point they all do assume an antagonistic stance. All indicate the loneliness that their spiritual independence engenders, and all find respite from it through preferred images that enable them to feel that there is some ideal "place" where they can feel truly at "home," that is, unselfconsciously at ease.

It is rather more difficult to discuss Huckleberry Finn in terms of narrative alienation than it is to discuss de Conte, August (Feldner, in "No. 44, The Mysterious Stranger"), and Hank because, first, the concept strikes many readers as absurdly incongruous with Huck's naiveté and, second, Huck almost never makes a directly antagonistic statement about his society. Nevertheless, Huck does communicate a nervousness, a tension, that is central to his narrative stance. Huck's alienation is more complex than that of the other narrators because in part it is a result of class differences: as the town pariah, child of the town drunkard, he has developed an outsider's point of view because he has been treated like an outsider all his life. But Huck's tensions also spring from his moral consciousness. Like the other narrators we have examined, he imposes psychic distance between himself and others because he cannot tolerate the way they treat one another. Even though he shares many of the culture's assumptions, he is in fundamental—if largely unconscious— disagreement with the hypocrisy and cruelty that characterize the lives of his neighbors. Yet he has too weak a sense of his own moral rectitude to criticize others outright. When he finds himself in conflict, he assumes that he, rather than they, is wrong. Thus the famous "dramatic irony" of *Huckleberry Finn,* the narrative

From *Mark Twain's Escape from Time* (Columbia: University of Missouri Press, 1982), pp. 60–71.

strategy whereby the author forces the reader, more sophisticated than the narrator, to make judgments the narrator cannot. In *Adventures of Huckleberry Finn* the reader is an accomplice of the novel's didactic intent. The hermeneutical structure of the book mandates that we do Huck's moralizing for him.

By discussing *Adventures of Huckleberry Finn* (1884) last, I hope to show how the pattern of Huck's conflict with his society and his escape to the tranquillity of the river conform to the patterns of alienation and resolution in the other texts already examined. Clearly, in *Huckleberry Finn* the river is the place where Huck feels most comfortable; by analyzing his descriptions we will better understand how the timelessness of the river landscape is central to the ideal landscape of Mark Twain's preferred images. Prior to examining Huck's patterns of resolution, however, it will be useful to briefly review Huck's patterns of alienation, first, because they are similar to the distancing exhibited by de Conte and August (if not by Hank); second, because one of the effects of *Huckleberry Finn*'s unique narrative strategy is to make the reader experience Huck's ecstasies in the same way he or she experiences Huck's anxieties. By making us perceive as Huck does, the author pulls us into Huck's center of consciousness.

As in the other patterns of alienation we have examined, in *Huck Finn* literacy functions as a means of separating Huck from the people to whom he has the closest connections. In contrast to the society of the Middle Ages, Huck's society values literacy: on the American frontier it was regarded as one of the dividing lines between primitive and civilized men. In *Adventures of Huckleberry Finn* even the con men are marginally literate, gaining their livelihood in part through bringing makeshift scenes from Shakespeare's plays to the culture-starved inhabitants of the river towns, while Tom Sawyer, who is often seen as epitomizing the society, is not merely literate but widely read and an active thief of literary ideas for use in his adventures. Although Huck initially resists learning to read, once he realizes that education will make him different from Pap, he begins to regard education favorably. For all his resistance to "respectability" Huck is enough a product of his society not to want to be classed with its dregs. Thus, when Pap invades his room at the Widow's and insists that Huck stop going to school because "Your mother couldn't read, and she couldn't write, nuther, before she died. None of the family couldn't, before *they* died. *I* can't; and here you're a-swelling yourself up like this,"[1] Huck recalls that "I didn't want to go to school much, before, but I reckoned I'd go now to spite pap" (*HF*, p. 21). While on the one hand Huck's attitude can be seen simply as rebellion against his father, it is also his way of distancing himself. By rejecting Pap's values, he demonstrates that he is better than his drunken, thieving sire.

Literacy also helps Huck convince himself that even though he and Jim are friends, he is still different from the slave not only because he is white but also because he is smarter. Most of his conflict about their relationship comes from the fact that a "nigger lover" is rated a step below "trash" in his society, and while he never forgets their racial difference, as his intimacy with Jim progresses he runs the risk of forgetting that it matters. One of the ways in which he reminds himself that he and Jim are different and that he, being white, must be correct, is to read to Jim out of the books they salvage from the wreck of the *Walter Scott* and to stand by written authority even when Jim presents the commonsense objections to conventional wisdom that, in other contexts, Huck would usually have presented himself. As he realized that he could establish social distance from Pap by learning to read, so he also establishes intellectual and emotional distance from Jim by demonstrating the one skill he has that Jim—his superior in almost every other useful art—does not possess. In both cases literacy is a tool for him to define his difference from the two men with whom he has the most in common and who have the strongest legal and moral claims on him.

While he uses literacy to indicate his superiority to Pap and Jim, Huck uses his unworthiness to indicate his inferiority to others. His class consciousness, in other words, is a tool for him to establish distance. Even when he is approached by a person sincerely willing to grant him membership in society, he creates barriers by insisting that he is undeserving. Despite wanting to please the Widow by accepting her God, for example, he insists, "I couldn't make out how he [God] was agoing to be any better off than what he was before, seeing I was so ignorant and so kind of low-down and ornery" (*HF*, pp. 11–12). Throughout his sojourn with the Widow he tries to convince himself that, as Miss Watson claims, "I was a fool." In implying that he is unworthy to belong to civilized society he gives himself an excuse to leave it; in an almost Emersonian effort to preserve his independence, he defines all people he encounters as antitheses to himself.

Huck establishes distance from the more respectable members of the community less purposefully than he does from Pap or Jim, as an almost reflexive response to his intuition that their values differ from his own. His uneasiness about the community—the "special sensitivity" Thomas Blues sees as at the root of much of Huck's defensiveness—is marked by the same raw sensitivity to hypocrisy, cruelty, and violence demonstrated by de Conte, August, and Hank. As Twain uses the ideology of the Church in the three novels we have already examined, in *Huckleberry Finn* he uses the ideology of slavery as a means of showing how severely a web of false values can warp human morals and how keenly Huck's sensibility (if not his rationality) responds to moral decadence. It is generally recognized that in this novel Jim, as the representative victim of slavery, is the touchstone for morality; virtually every character is evaluated in regard to him or another slave, and only Huck and Mary Jane Wilks demonstrate any degree of sensitivity to his plight. But while slavery is the historically correct catalyst for the demonstration of human evil in *Huckleberry Finn*, it is not the only one. Humaneness is measured not only by the responses of white people to black ones but by their responses to each other as well; their lack of humaneness is proved to transcend racial categories and provides the implicit justification for Huck's nervousness whenever he encounters a new group.[2]

Huck's responses to the inhabitants of Bricksville, to the Grangerford and

Shepardson feud, and to the King and the Duke have been subjected to much critical analysis and do not need extensive review here.[3] Nevertheless, it is useful to note that his responses parallel de Conte's horror at Joan's execution, August's anguish at an old woman's being burned at the stake, and Hank's outrage over the plight of England's slaves. In fact, the difference between Huck and these later narrators lies not in their response to human evil, but, as we have already noted, in the way they express it. Conscious of their narrative duties, the later narrators try to evaluate the behavior of the people they portray; the result is that, horrified by what they perceive, they openly moralize about it. Huck, in contrast, is neither a chronicler of a major historical event, a writer revealing his journey to enlightenment, nor a student of the social organism; consequently, he rarely, if ever, moralizes openly.[4] Since his stream-of-consciousness method of recording his experiences makes him a transmitter rather than a translator of what he sees, however, one way of judging his response to experiences is to examine our own. As James Cox notes, "in turning the narration over to Huck, Mark Twain abandoned the explicit norms and risked making his vernacular force the reader to supply the implied norms."[5] Thus we see the "shackly dried-up frame concerns" that pass for houses in Bricksville, and the gardens that "didn't seem to raise anything in them but jimpson weeds, and sunflowers, and ash-piles, and old curled up boots" (HF, p. 117), and know that even though Huck never tells us that he thinks Bricksville is a decadent town, his description of a garden that only grows trash implicitly renders his evaluation. His metaphors tell us that Bricksville's residents are as worn-out morally as their environment is materially—they "roost" on dry-goods boxes and "lean" against awning posts. Even when he describes the delight the loafers take in "covering a dog with turpentine and seeing him run himself to death" (HF, p. 118), he avoids overt moralizing; nevertheless, by the standards of our culture the cruelty of the act is clear. Perhaps one reason Adventures of Huckleberry Finn is considered one of the most ethically concerned novels in our literature stems from the fact that Huck's narrative method elicits the reader's participation. By the time Huck, in one of his rare comments about the situation in which he is involved, remarks that "it was enough to make a body ashamed of the human race," readers have sufficiently participated in his experience to feel that he is reflecting their judgments rather than simply registering his own shock.

Not only do Huck's patterns of alienation demonstrate the same sensitivity to hypocrisy and cruelty that we have seen in the narratives of Louis de Conte, August Feldner, and Hank Morgan, his patterns of resolution are also familiar. The lyricism with which he records his experiences on the river alone with Jim echoes de Conte's paean to the fairy tree, Hank's to the institution of marriage, and August's dream-self's to his life in "general space"; most importantly, his portrayal of the experience indicates that for him it is an avenue to timelessness. Unlike the other narrators, however, Huck takes his readers with him through his escape from time. The narrative strategy of Huckleberry Finn permits us to share Huck's ecstasies much as it forces us to do his moralizing for him. Thus the same narrative precision that brings "pieces of bottles, and rags, and played-out tin ware" so vividly to our order-loving minds also brings "the branches . . . tossing their arms as if they was just wild" (*HF*, p. 42), or "the sky up there, all speckled with stars" (*HF*, p. 101) directly to our nature-starved sensibilities. Huck's preferred image is the river and the river landscape; as Richard Poirier notes, Huck's metaphors of the human landscape reflect the influence of Emerson's image of society as "a conspiracy . . . against the manhood of . . . its members," while Huck's metaphors of the natural landscape reflect the influence of Emerson's image of nature as the resting place for the self-reliant soul.[6]

One of the difficulties critics have always had in discussing Huck's narrative function stems from the fact that the very act of labeling it seems to distort Huck's posture. Most readers have settled for regarding him as a naif or new Adam; perhaps Poirier's perception that Huck's response to man and nature reflects Emersonian dualisms comes closest to the truth. In fact, Huck acts, in part, as a phenomenologist—a label that, in its pretensions to descriptive accuracy, is furthest from the boy's concept of himself. Yet Huck's inability to analyze, which implies that he has no sense of historical causation; his reluctance to moralize openly, which implies that he is not confident that he has a moral basis from which he can judge others; and, most importantly, his preference for precise physical details rather than for general statements, which implies that when he observes, he does so without the backlog of descriptive terminology that rules most verbal painters of landscapes, all function to bring him closer to the things he sees than any other of Twain's narrators. Consequently, in his stream-of-consciousness narration he functions phenomenologically, for in his extraordinarily precise descriptions, especially of the river landscape, he re-creates the objects of his perceptions with a sympathy that shows that he feels such an intimacy with the organic world that he virtually sees himself as part of it. Moreover, in rendering the river world as he perceives it he also re-creates—rather than simply recounts—his experience for the reader.[7]

Maurice Merleau-Ponty defines phenomenology, in part, as a philosophy that "places in abeyance the assertions arising out of the natural attitude, the better to understand them; but it is also a philosophy for which the world is always 'already there' before reflection begins—as an inalienable presence; and all its efforts are concentrated upon re-achieving a direct and primitive contact with the world and endowing that contact with a philosophical status."[8] The difference between a phenomenologist and a primitive is that the latter never arrives at the last step of Merleau-Ponty's formulation. Huck is a naif, not a philosopher; he certainly never endows his perceptions with any kind of status. Nevertheless—and the point, I think, is crucial—the last step in this phenomenological exercise is performed by the reader of *Adventures of Huckleberry Finn,* and any critic who comments on Huck's transcendental moments on the river has completed the philosophical task. When Huck portrays the landscape of the river he does not posit causes and effects (that is, he suspends the natural attitude); he merely describes the way it looks, feels, and sounds, and the reader is absorbed into the world he re-creates. When he describes how "the rain would thrash along so thick that the trees off a little ways looked dim and spider-webby" and how the thunder went "rumbling, grumbling, tumbling down the sky towards the other side of the world," we, too, hear and see the storm. Moreover, when he says that he "wouldn't want to be nowhere else but here," the nervousness he evinces in virtually all his contacts with others disappears. In these descriptions, he merges with, rather than distances himself from, the natural landscape. Consequently, when he reports that "days and nights swam by, they slid along so quiet and smooth and lovely" (*HF,* p. 99), he seems to speak from the timelessness of the diurnal cycle. Far from regarding nature as he regards society, as a "not-me" from which he seeks relief, he embraces the river landscape as his rightful home.

Thus in his lack of narrative consciousness, his *lack* of distance between himself and the objects of his perceptions, Huck Finn overcomes his sense of estrangement from the community and is fulfilled because he speaks from within the cycle of plenitude. His narrative strategy—his tendency to describe a scene so meticulously that the reader is absorbed in its detail and persuaded to do his or her own evaluation—re-creates in the reader not only Huck's moments of unease but also his moments of joy. On the river Huck communicates his contentment in the process of describing the components of the immediate, sensory world in which he lives and with which he interacts; the effect of his narrative is to make the reader also retrieve that life-world as he or she reads his book. Huck's descriptions of his ecstatic moments actually let us experience what it feels like to be on the river through the immediacy of reading, or activating, the text. Part of his narrative function is to remind us that the sensory world exists beyond the narrow conventions of the human community and that it is the place for the regeneration of the soul.

Huckleberry Finn, then, is the only one of the narrators we have examined to have overcome his sense of estrangement from his society by finding an actual environment in which he can live both physically and spiritually. He is able to find it precisely because he is a naif; unlike the other narrators we have examined, he does not analyze, does not moralize, and does not reflect upon himself or the culture that seeks to control him; consequently, he neither asks the questions nor draws the conclusions that would cause him to reject the given world. Responding with the same sensitivity as the others to the same exhibitions of human depravity, he concludes that *he* is not fit for the community, rather than it for him. His very lack of egocentrism is the factor that saves him from despair; he does not feel that the community must be reformed because it does not conform to his expectations. Rather, he discovers a spiritual otherworld within the confines of the given one. Like the periods of respite experienced by the other narrators, Huck's experience of harmony with nature is fragile and intermittent, but while he is surrounded by the river, away from the world of men, he is happy. Instead of accepting his society's evaluations of the necessary and the good, he finds a landscape of spiritual repose and substitutes the plenitude of nature for the inadequacy of human relationships.

In a letter to his fiancée, Olivia Langdon, in 1868, Twain referred to "home" as "that type and symbol of heaven" from which he felt he was in exile, and he described his response as a "great blank," and "awful vacancy."[9] When he claimed that in visiting home he saw his family "taking delight in things that are new to me and which I do not comprehend," he was describing an emotional and temporal chasm that, to him, was as wide as the one Hank Morgan was later to perceive between himself and the nineteenth-century world to which he so reluctantly returned. It has often been noted that temporal and cultural distance represents emotional loss in Twain's work.[10] The narratives he sets in the Middle Ages seem more like science fiction than historical novels because the sense of alienation that rules their narrators' consciousness shows how distant they feel themselves to be from the historical contexts of their stories. These novels do not reconstruct the Middle Ages; rather, the narrators are so disaffected that they become the critics instead of the interpreters of their societies. As characters, they (like Clarence and his boys) find themselves with no nation to which they can return when they have completed their education. Spiritually afloat, as Twain phrased it in his letter to Livy, they drift between the centuries, searching for "that pillow of weariness, that refuge from care, and trouble, and pain ... Home."[11] Yet each of these novels indicates that a spiritual refuge does exist, if only it can be located. In *Joan of Arc* it is evoked through a myth of innocence; in "No. 44, The Mysterious Stranger" through a brief vision of freedom from corporeality, in *A Connecticut Yankee* through association with a woman and child.

In *Huckleberry Finn,* the earliest written of these novels, the sense of drift that signals loneliness in the historical novels is transformed into Twain's most famous, and perhaps his own favorite, image of repose. Here the vacancy that exile from the community engenders is filled by the plenitude of nature: out on Jackson's Island, before he meets Jim, when Huck is lonely he goes and sits by the river because "there ain't no better way to put in the time when you are lonesome; you can't stay so, you soon get over it" (*HF,* p. 34). On the river the violence, selfishness, and death that Huck associates with the community are annulled by the continual transformation of one form of life into another, and Huck is joyous because he perceives life on the river as a process of continual becoming. Removed from the specter of human disasters, he feels that he is freed from imprisonment; far from feeling isolated, he feels that when he and Jim are alone on the river they have substituted the cycle of natural rebirth for the sequence of human decay. Out on the river Huck in effect abandons human time.

Thus if the sensitive Twain narrator feels estranged from his society, he also discovers a means of escape from his loneliness. Images of childhood, of nature (especially associated with water), or of women predominate in these interludes, both for the narrators we have seen and for many of Twain's other characters.

These images play similar roles in many of Twain's travel narratives, essays, speeches, and private papers. By studying the contexts in which they appear we will be able to better understand their function as centers of consciousness, as symbols that provide Twain, as well as his characters, with an alternative to his increasingly pessimistic vision of the human condition.

NOTES

[1] *Adventures of Huckleberry Finn,* edited by Henry Nash Smith (Boston: Houghton Mifflin, Riverside Editions, 1958), p. 18, Twain's emphasis. Hereafter abbreviated as *HF* and cited in the text.

[2] The critical controversy about Huck's attitude toward his society is far less vehement than that about Hank Morgan's; however, while everyone agrees that Huck is uneasy around "Shore People," to use Henry Nash Smith's term, they are not agreed over the degree to which Huck "rejects" the values of his society. A sampling of recent views illustrates typical similarities and differences. Thomas Blues, for instance, feels that Twain thwarted Huck's incipient anarchism when he brought him back into the fold during the Phelps episode (*Mark Twain and the Community* [Lexington: University Press of Kentucky, 1970, pp. 19–21], but Maxwell Geismar feels that Huck Finn "*defied* all the proprieties, including . . . wealth, success, social position, and conventional religion" (*Mark Twain: An American Prophet* [Lexington: The University Press of Kentucky, 1970], p. 87). Analyzing Twain's style, in *Mark Twain: The Development of a Writer* (New York: Atheneum, 1974), Henry Nash Smith claims that Huck's and Jim's flight "obviously translates into action the theme of vernacular protest" (p. 115), and Robert Regan, in *Unpromising Heroes: Mark Twain and His Characters* (Berkeley: University of California Press, 1966), sees Mark Twain as "at pains to emphasize the false, the dishonest, and the hypocritical side of St. Petersburg life" (p. 135). In *The Art of Mark Twain* (New York: Oxford University Press, 1976), William Gibson, too, sees the "continual drama of foolish and ferocious citizens . . . 'the damned human race'" as "a second major motif" in the novel (p. 113); and James M. Cox, in "Toward Vernacular Humor," *The Virginia Quarterly Review* 46 (Spring 1970): 311–30, sees Huck's "rejection of civilization" at the end of the book as "the radically negative vision which his doubly negative grammar embodies." Moreover Alan Trachtenberg, in "The Form of Freedom in *Huckleberry Finn,*" *The Southern Review* 6 (October 1970): 954–71, sees Huck's conflict with his society as one of "conformity versus autonomy." The crucial point, for all readers, rests on Huck's assumption that he, rather than the society, is wrong, and the argument concerns to what degree this constitutes "rejection." With those critics who view Huck's stance through an analysis of his style—Henry Nash Smith, Gladys Bellamy, James M. Cox, Alan Trachtenberg, and Richard Poirier, for instance—I feel that Huck's alienation from "Shore People" is implicit in his vernacular stance (that is, in his position as a character who is not conventionally "respectable") and in the metaphors through which he portrays what he sees.

[3] The portrayal of human nature through the delimitation of the types of people Huck and Jim meet during their journey is the major reason most readers see *Adventures of Huckleberry Finn* as, in part, Mark Twain's criticism of pre–Civil War society and as a precursor of Twain's later invectives against "the damned human race." Again, a brief sampling of recent criticism should provide an overview of the whole. Believing that "Huck's socially anxious voice never carries fully the implications of social contempt and rejection that govern the metaphorical pattern of the book," Richard Poirier nevertheless believes that "we are seeing in these repeated metaphors Mark Twain's own alienation from that society" (*A World Elsewhere: The Place of Style in American Literature* [New York: Oxford University Press, 1966], pp. 152–53, 179–80). Smith, in *Mark Twain: The Development of a Writer,* claims that "the satire of the towns . . . insists . . . that the dominant culture is decadent and perverted" but that Huck's inability to respond openly detracts from his full development as a character (pp. 117–18). Geismar sees the "real form" of *Huckleberry Finn* as "a series of long, over-done, brutal . . . forays of 'civilization' . . . onto the raft" alternating with "the return into . . . a natural existence on the blessed raft" (*An American Prophet,* p. 96). Perhaps one of the most thorough of recent treatments of these episodes is in Gibson's *The Art of Mark Twain,* where he analyzes each episode as he shows that "in the second half of the novel Mark Twain plans primarily to illustrate life in small towns along the Mississippi" (p. 106) and that Huck's comment that "human beings *can* be awful cruel to one another" is a response to the great number of characters who "deserve damnation for their actions" (pp. 113–14).

[4] The narrative irony of *Huckleberry Finn* is, for this reader, its most interesting stylistic aspect: critics who concentrate on Mark Twain's style have contributed to our understanding of it. Henry Nash Smith set the stage for this kind of analysis in the "Sound Heart and Deformed Conscience" chapter of *Development of a Writer.* James M. Cox may state the problem most clearly in *Mark Twain: The Fate of Humor* (Princeton: Princeton University Press, 1966): "The vernacular ... created the means of control within the reader's mind ... first ... Huck's incorrect language implied standard, correct, literary English. Second, Huck's status as a child invited an indulgence from the reader. Finally, Huck's action in time and place ... ensured moral approval from the reader" (pp. 168–69). Trachtenberg, in "The Form of Freedom," also addresses this question, often in opposition to Smith; interested in the problem Mark Twain encountered in transforming oral into written art, Trachtenberg sees Huck's major mode of speaking as "deadpan," that is, as saying less than he means. Trachtenberg finds that this technical device thwarts Huck's full realization as a character, first, because he cannot be allowed to "know" what he means (which would destroy his naiveté), and second, because the deadpan voice precludes complete innocence. Both Cox and Trachtenberg throw the full realization of the moral intentions of the book back onto the reader; with this, if not with minor points, I am in full agreement.

[5] James M. Cox, *Mark Twain: The Fate of Humor,* p. 168.

[6] Poirier, *A World Elsewhere,* pp. 150–51.

[7] For a seminal account of Mark Twain's innovations in constructing Huck's landscape descriptions see Leo Marx, "The Plot and the Passenger: Landscape Conventions and the Style of *Huckleberry Finn,*" *American Literature* 28 (May 1956): 129–46. In "The Form of Freedom," Trachtenberg approaches my view of Huck's narrative function when he claims that our assessment of Huck's double role—as both actor and storyteller—"precedes assessment of the meaning of freedom" (p. 960).

[8] Maurice Merleau-Ponty, "What Is Phenomenology?," in *European Literary Theory and Practice: From Existential Phenomenology to Structuralism,* edited by Vernon W. Gras (New York: Dell Publishing Co., 1973), p. 69.

[9] *Mark Twain's Collected Letters,* vol. 1, 1853–1869, edited by Lin Salamo (Berkeley: University of California Press, forthcoming), #251.

[10] One of the broadest and most interesting discussions of this theme is Roger B. Salomon's "Realism as Disinheritance: Twain, Howells, and James," *American Quarterly* 16 (Winter 1964): 532–44.

[11] *Mark Twain's Collected Letters,* vol. 1, 1853–1869, edited by Lin Salamo, #251.

R. J. Fertel

SPONTANEITY AND THE QUEST FOR MATURITY IN *HUCKLEBERRY FINN*[1]

Health is to be won by "free living," then. . . .
But now, who has given you such a false im-
pression of analysis?[2]

At the heart of Mark Twain's *Adventures of Huckleberry Finn* contradictory assessments of spontaneity's nature and value vie for supremacy. On the one hand, as if to prove Emerson's observation that "Every surmise and vatication of the mind is entitled to a certain respect,"[3] the novel attacks those who cannot achieve spontaneity in their lives and art; on the other, it attacks the debased Romantic notion of spontaneity, the view that unmediated behavior alone suffices us as social and moral beings. However "full of Emersonian inclinations,"[4] the novel is also, but more subtly, akin to Mill's nearly contemporaneous rationalist attack on "the vein of sentiment so common in the modern world . . . which exalts instinct at the expense of reason. . . ."[5] Paradoxically, *Huckleberry Finn,* whose hero tells us he goes "a good deal on instinct,"[6] both affirms this consecration and, like Mill, negates it. This paradox creates the novel's central expressive tension, the resolution of which is a necessary qualification of spontaneity as moral and aesthetic ideal.

What has in part blinded readers to this tension concerning the nature and value of spontaneity is the prevailing assumption that *Huckleberry Finn* is an improvised creation, like many Romantic documents before it a "spontaneous overflow of powerful feelings." Twain himself fosters this assumption.[7] But while he presents the novel, in Huck's voice and in the famous first notice, as improvised, he makes a counter generic claim that also shapes our experience of the book.[8] He introduces the novel with not one notice, but two, and together they present fundamentally opposite aesthetic and moral premises. The first *seems* to claim (we shall see that more is claimed in a moment) that what follows will be a carefree, improvised tale:

NOTICE

Persons attempting to find a motive in this narrative will be prosecuted; persons attempting to find a moral in it will be banished; persons attempting to find a plot in it will be shot. (p. 2)

From *Modern Language Quarterly* 44, No. 2 (June 1983): 157–77.

Romantic writers like Keats distrusted art that "has a palpable design upon us"[9] because such art betrayed the meddling of moralistic rationality; Twain, on the basis of this notice, seems to enlist in the romantic camp. To be without motive or moral or plot is to be free of rhetoric and artifice: it is to speak from the unimpeachable heart. The basic moral and aesthetic premises most often extracted from this first notice are these: natural, spontaneous, unconniving man and his works are good; artificial, conventional, designing man and his society are corrupt. But as we shall see, other, quite different premises are in fact discernible in this notice.

The second notice conveys more obviously the contrasting message of careful craftsmanship:

EXPLANATORY

In this book a number of dialects are used, to wit: the Missouri negro dialect; the extremest form of the backwoods South-Western dialect; the ordinary "Pike-County" dialect; and four modified varieties of this last. The shadings have not been done in a hap-hazard fashion, or by guess-work; but pains-takingly, and with the trustworthy guidance and support of personal familiarity with these several forms of speech.

I make this explanation for the reason that without it many readers would suppose that all these characters were trying to talk alike and not succeeding. (p. 2)

Now it is not the heart or the imagination, but experience and intellect that guide us. We are asked to trust this not as a sport, but rather as a well-considered and well-honed document. The language of law ("to wit"), the parallel clauses, the masterful manipulation of tone and phrasing in the concluding "snapper," all convey the value of intellect, reason, and care. We are invited to experience and to appreciate this narrative in terms of its thought, its thoughtfulness, and its craft. These moral and aesthetic terms call in question the premises of the first notice.

In fact, these premises are questioned even within the first notice. The second notice is patently in Twain's voice; although some readers have heard Huck's in the first, surely we at least hear Twain's snickering behind it. For one thing, in contrast to the "naturalness" of Huck's speech patterns that follow in the novel proper, Twain here creates a sentence of well-formed Ciceronian balance. Huck's normal grammatical mode of stringing clauses together by conjunctions (polysyndeton) here gives way to polished, elliptical asyndeton: clauses balanced upon semicolons. Where Huck achieves a spontaneous flow of speech that generates natural climaxes of image and theme, we have here an example of classical *gradatio*, underscored by anaphora ("persons ... motive ... prosecuted; persons ... moral ... banished; persons ... plot ... shot") and climactically reinforced by internal masculine rhyme ("plot ... shot"). While it is no doubt possible to find equally sophisticated rhetorical constructions in Huck's oft-praised "natural" style, Twain pointedly and masterfully obscures the debt of Huck's speech to rhetorical artifice. The first notice, by contrast, the novel's initial claim for naturalness and spontaneity, draws our attention, however subconsciously, to the artifice of the claim. The implicit humor in the claim—for no one, however he reads, expects to be prosecuted, banished, or shot—further undermines the claim. The tension between tenor and vehicle calls in question the assumptions and premises of the tenor, the affirmation of spontaneity and naturalness. The second notice reinforces our doubts about these assumptions, enlisting the novel in the camp of intelligent craftsmanship. From the very beginning of *Huckleberry Finn* the premises upon which critics either praise or blame the novel—its celebration of primitive naturalness and unmediated spontaneity—are called in question by Twain himself.

For, since the 1950s, critical treatment of *Huckleberry Finn* has in large part centered upon themes associated historically with the Romantic movement: spontaneity, primitivism, unmediated experience and vision, and the attack upon artifice and conventionality. While critics differ over the interpretation of symbolic patterns or over the assessment of the ending, they divide in their evaluation of the Romantic tendency of the whole, praising or condemning Twain for celebrating these Romantic themes in his characterization of Huck. William Van O'Connor well exemplifies those who condemn.[10] Describing Huck as one "who reject[s] the evils of civilization" out of hand, O'Connor argues that the novel is insidious because it "appeals to our desire for a condition of innocence" (p. 10). Henry Nash Smith, voicing the majority opinion, praises; after comparing the language of the novel to that of the *Lyrical Ballads*, he commends Twain's stylistic achievement, symptomatically echoing Coleridge's *Biographia Literaria:*

> the systematic elimination of conventional associations removes the cake of custom from the visible universe and fosters a completely fresh treatment of landscape. A vision not distorted by inherited modes of perception, once fresh themselves but long since grown lifeless through over-use, can report sensory experience with supreme vividness.[11]

For Smith, Twain's satiric target is the fact that Shore society does not "react to situations spontaneously but according to stereotyped patterns of feeling and behavior" (p. xiv). Huck's style and character dramatize a different model, a "voice of freedom, spontaneity, autonomy of the individual" (p. xvi).[12] Between these two poles of blame and praise stand those critics who examine the attack on Romanticism implicit in the book; but these critics essentially oppose such themes as Tom and Emmeline's artificial and romantic "nonsense" to Huck's greater naturalness and spontaneity, thus substituting a "better" set of Romantic premises for a "worse," a true Romanticism (Huck's) for a false (Tom's).[13]

Much of the satire in *Huckleberry Finn* is, of course, based upon a Rousseauvian opposition between the artificiality and conventionality of the Shore society and the more fluid, natural spontaneity of Huck. Huck shows up Tom's artificial romancing, the evangelicals' rigid conventionalism in the camp-meeting episode, the Grangerfords' sophisticated feuding, even Emmeline's pseudo-spontaneity in her one-note versifying. With a writing-voice "blood-warm" Huck travels down the Mississippi like an embodiment of Emerson's "Man Thinking," helping us to see the "sluggish and perverted mind of the multitude."[14] In a sense Twain does substitute his truer, purer Romanticism for the received, debased notion of that movement. He shows in effect that the riverboat *Walter Scott* is well sunk, the boiler of the *Lally Rook* well blown, and he floats Huck's innocent raft in their stead. So much is clear. What needs further clarification, however, is the way Twain also concerns himself with some of the negative aspects of Huck's noble innocence. Huck, the naïve unmasker of society's corrupt sophistications, is also to some degree unmasked. Twain questions Romantic premises in a more thorough fashion than has been perceived. I wish to offer a reading of *Huckleberry Finn* which does not condemn Twain either for reneging on his celebration of a primitivist Huck in a "flawed" ending (it is flawed but not for that reason), or for the immaturity of carrying his celebration through (he does not). I will examine Twain's fundamentally ambivalent treatment of primitivism and related ideas. I will, finally, argue for recognition of the ultimate moral maturity—for Twain at least—of Twain's ambivalent posture.[15]

The novel's opening chapters reinforce the opposition between innocent spontaneity and untutored naturalness, and the value of care, craft, and thought. In contrast to the ending, these chapters have not attracted much critical attention. Bernard DeVoto called them "just 'Tom Sawyer' and pretty poor 'Tom Sawyer,'" and argued that they have "no dynamic purpose."[16] T. S. Eliot defended the ending by arguing that "it is right that the mood of the end of the book should bring us back to that of the beginning,"[17] and left it at that. Leo Marx argues that the ending does not live up to its serious beginning: the opening portrays "Miss Watson ... the Enemy" who "exhibits all the outstanding traits of the valley society" which "Huck and Jim ... symbolically repudiated when they set forth downstream" (p. 427), implying that the repudiation was to Twain's mind fully justified.[18] In sum, the received reading of the opening is that it portrays the "sivilization" from which the innocent, asocial Huck will rightly flee. But the opening is far richer than *Tom Sawyer*. Beneath its light tone lies the weight of moral concerns. Beside its ironic portrayal of "the Enemy" is set the far more positive portrayal of the Widow Douglas, the embodiment of all the good in society.

The first paragraph still pursues the issue of authenticity we met in the notices. Like most art which claims to be improvised, this work begins with an attack upon the falseness of other literary endeavors. *The Adventures of Tom Sawyer*, we hear,

> was made by Mr. Mark Twain, and he told the truth, mainly. There was things which he stretched, but mainly he told the truth. That is nothing. I never seen anybody but lied, one time or another, without it was Aunt Polly, or the widow, or maybe Mary. Aunt Polly—Tom's Aunt Polly, she is—and Mary, and the Widow Douglas, is all told about in that book—which is mostly a true book; with some stretchers, as I said before. (p. 7)

"Made" books, Huck is saying, are mere fabrications. On the other hand, this spontaneous, designless, and lived account is true. With all its bad grammar—even because of its bad grammar—this is the real thing. Even so, the reader knows better than to take this opposition between Twain and Huck at face value: behind the claim of greater naturalness and truth Twain stands grinning. As in the notices, the humor questions the idealization of unschooled, careless spontaneity.

Imbedded in Huck's attack and counterclaim is our introduction to the Widow Douglas. Mary will have no role in this adventure, and Aunt Polly only a walk-on at the conclusion. Most critics would agree, however, that the widow symbolizes to Huck and to us civilization, conscience, and religion. But in granting her this symbolic importance, most critics conflate her with Miss Watson. As Kenneth Lynn has written, most speak "of Miss Watson and the Widow Douglas in the same breath, as a double-headed symbol of familial suffocation" (p. 345).[19] In fact, as I hope to show, the two women are strictly and consistently distinguished. We should note that at her first entrance the Widow Douglas is set in opposition to confirmed liars; despite Huck's subsequent reactions to her, the novel never really contradicts this positive and sympathetic portrayal.

For Huck's negative assessments of the widow are always susceptible to a double reading: we first applaud his boyish rejection of her; then, catching ourselves up, we realize that like Huck we are overreacting, responding like a naïve child. Indeed, the humorous texture of his portrait insists that we read again and repeal our initial response.[20] Huck's next statement about the widow evokes this ambivalent dynamic:

> The Widow Douglas, she took me for her son, and allowed she would sivilize me; but it was rough living in the house all the time, considering how dismal regular and decent the widow was in all her ways; and so when I couldn't stand it no longer, I lit out. (p. 7)

While the child in us agrees with Huck that it is "rough living in the house all the time," the adult remembers the civilized truth that houses are handy in bad weather. Twain calls up in us this impulse to qualify Huck's statement by making Huck speak in excessive and categorical terms: "all the time." The same dynamic of appeal and repeal is evoked by the third phrase of Huck's portrait, "how dismal regular and decent the widow was in all her ways." Here opposite connotations evoke the child-adult swing of responses. Huck, perhaps despite himself, plays upon the etymology of "regular": according to rule. "Decent" from Huck's point of view connotes its opposite: hypocritical. Having to be "regular and decent," being acculturated, in short, is what Huck and the child within us resist. But our adult voice should interrupt with the words' opposite connotations, their more colloquial meanings: "what more could you ask for, Huck, than a foster parent who is regular (*consistent*) and decent (*fair*)," indeed, as Huck says, "in all her ways." Read this way, Huck's adverbial adjective "dismal" hints at something amiss in the speaker—if only an excess of childishness. The power of Twain's language to evoke the two voices in the reader is masterly.

The humor of Huck's responses to the widow's crying over him as a "poor lost lamb" ("she never meant no harm") and to her grumbled mealtime prayers ("there warn't really anything the matter" with the food) depends upon the same kind of double, ironic readings. Huck's next stroke in the widow portrait is an especially evocative one, again despite his own understanding of it:

> After supper she got out her book and learned me about Moses and the Bulrushers; and I was in a sweat to find out all about him; but by-and-by she let it out that Moses had been dead a considerable long time; so then I didn't care no more about him; because I don't take no stock in dead people. (pp. 7–8)

This passage is no doubt usually read as but another Twainian satire of Sunday School didacticism and the "goody-goody" tradition, satires which, as Sydney J. Krause rightly argues, were "part of the critical impetus that launched him on his first significant novels, *Tom Sawyer* and *Huckleberry Finn.*"[21] But the widow's Sunday School lesson differs significantly from those satires: in form it lacks the pat apothegm which for Twain was the hallmark of the morally false; in substance it expresses love and acceptance, not hate and cooptation. Twain may have had his goody-goody satires in mind and yet he goes beyond them.

For in the passage Twain subtly turns the satire from the widow toward Huck. What Huck misses—and critics seem to have missed it too—is that in a most important way Moses still lives. According to Protestant custom, the widow has chosen her text for its application to present affairs. Like the "poor lost lamb" or prodigal son, who when found is of greater worth than all who remain in the fold, so the Moses found in the "Bulrushers" is analogous for the widow to Huck. She is telling Huck how much she prizes and loves him. Huck misunderstands because of the civilization he lacks and scorns—notice the misheard "Bulrushers." To miss this message of love and acceptance, so much the goal of Huck's quest, is, it can be argued, to become inevitably lost. Huck will float down the river like Moses: the image looks forward to his journey. But by means of the image the widow hopes to say that his journey is over.

In the next paragraph Huck adds a stroke to the widow's portrait which sticks in many minds: her hypocrisy. Huck wishes to smoke and she won't let him. "And," he adds sarcastically, "she took snuff too; of course that was all right, because she done it herself." But before agreeing with Huck's assessment of the widow as hypocrite, we must note the context of his sarcastic attack:

> She said it was a mean practice and wasn't clean, and I must try to not do it any more. That is just the way with some people. They get down on a thing when they don't know nothing about it. Here she was a bothering about Moses, which was no kin to her, and no use to anybody, being gone, you see, yet finding a power of fault with me for doing a thing that had some good in

it. And, she took snuff too; of course that was all right, because she done it
herself. (p. 8)

The context, along with the humor, qualifies Huck's charge of hypocrisy and all but
demolishes it. Compared to Huck's blindness to the meaning and good intention
behind the Moses story here reinvoked, the widow's fault shrinks to a mere foible.
Huck's general assessment of hypocrites turns back on him in particular: "They get
down on a thing when they don't know nothing about it." If Huck cannot see the
purpose of her "bothering about Moses," that by analogy Moses and Huck are both
"kin to her," then who is he to judge the widow's intentions? The upside-down
world of ironic satire, where the fool instructs the righteous, here turns right-side
up: the ironic mask slips as his instructions betray both the error of his ways and the
essential rightness of the Widow Douglas.

Let us not lose sight of the spareness of Twain's portrayal of the widow. But
her portrait, finished not by Huck but by Twain's subtle ironies, is sharply drawn.
And the succeeding contrasts with her spinsterish sister, Miss Watson, bring the
widow's sympathetic character, and Huck's wrongheadedness, into still sharper
focus. The contrasts between the two women further consolidate our sympathy
for the widow and for the positive version of civilization she represents.

Huck introduces Miss Watson in the next paragraph. She is "a tolerable slim
old maid, with goggles on," and, coming to live with her sister, she takes "a set at
me now, with a spelling-book" until "the widow made her ease up" (p. 8). Here the
language is too strong for us to do anything but lend Huck all our sympathy.
Appealing to the sexism of his audience with a stroke right out of fairy tale, Twain
undermines her in terms of her marital status: "old maid." And to be "set at" with
a "spelling-book" is different from studying spelling, though we may doubt that
Huck could distinguish between the two. The spinster is "sivilization" at its very
worst—repressed and repressive, vindictive and lacking in sympathy, and very
much in contrast with her sister: "the widow made her ease up."

But the point is not merely that the widow protects Huck from her sister. The
opposition between the two women raises more important questions. Why does
Twain introduce Miss Watson into this narrative at all? What is her narrative
agency? Could not the Widow Douglas have carried her part?

There is in fact nothing in *Tom Sawyer* which would have prevented the
widow from being Jim's owner, and from being as cruel as need be to set him, and
Huck, on the road to freedom. Since Tom's Aunt Sally takes over the widow's role
as Huck's adopter and civilizer at the end of the tale, there is no reason why Twain
could not have killed the widow off and made *her* recant and set Jim free. In short
the Widow Douglas could have been "the Enemy" of whom Marx speaks. Twain
could have embodied the civilization that Jim and Huck flee in one religious,
slave-holding woman.[22]

He did not. Instead, two characters exist to represent and embody two
distinct versions of civilization. Presented through the eyes of Huck, neither is

immediately attractive—and under Huck's influence the reader conflates them. But, trusting the tale and not the teller, we see beyond Huck's vision of things to the fact that one is far more acceptable than the other. The Widow Douglas is even attractive—if not to Huck, at least to us. As is often the case with first-person narrations, the narrator tells us more than he knows, especially about himself. One of the first things we learn from Huck, who will do his all to evade civilization, is that civilization is not all bad. The contrast between the two women comes to a head when, after a night out with Tom's Gang, Huck gets what he deserves from both:

> Well, I got a good going-over in the morning, from old Miss Watson, on account of my clothes; but the widow she didn't scold, but only cleaned off the grease and clay and looked so sorry that I thought I would behave a while if I could. (p. 14)

The widow's gentler response, pained not paining, always works better on the ever-responsive Huck, as we see later by the effect of Jim's "trash" speech. Her response is set in sharp contrast to the spinster's self-righteous castigation. The latter makes us feel for Huck; the former makes us feel for Huck's victim.

The contrast between the widow and the spinster continues as they respond in turn to his questions about the nature of prayer. Miss Watson calls him "a fool" (p. 14) for trying to pray for fishhooks; she is blind to the fact that her own definitions of prayer are largely responsible for Huck's self-seeking misconception. The widow's response, on the other hand, is warm, gentle, and pious correction:

> she said the thing a body could get by praying for it was "spiritual gifts." This was too many for me, but she told me what she meant—I must help other people, and do everything I could for other people, and look out for them all the time, and never think about myself. This was including Miss Watson, as I took it. I went out in the woods and turned it over in my mind a long time, but I couldn't see no advantage about it—except for the other people—so at last I reckoned I wouldn't worry about it any more, but just let it go. Sometimes the widow would take me one side and talk about Providence in a way to make a boy's mouth water; but maybe next day Miss Watson would take hold and knock it all down again. I judged I could see that there was two Providences, and a poor chap would stand considerable show with the widow's Providence, but if Miss Watson's got him there warn't no help for him any more. (p. 15)

A reader who insists upon Twain's atheism and upon his horror of the hypocrisy of the "damned human race" might prefer Huck's skepticism to the widow's homespun piety. But the contrast between the two women is an important element in the texture of the passage and the key to our local response. Like the two Providences, there are two versions of religion in the novel. Compared to her sister, the widow is unexceptionable. In seeing no advantage about Christian charity and prayer "except for the other people," Huck, as so often, exaggerates her meaning and misses the point.

This more positive reading of the theme of religion in the novel has a bearing on our reading of the celebrated moral crisis Huck later undergoes. His basis here for deciding between "the two Providences"—on the way they feel—is shown there to be misleading. Miss Watson, not the Widow Douglas, will be the controlling presence, a presence he finally overcomes. But he does not substitute for his "yaller dog" (p. 183) conscience one that enables him to stop Tom's Evasion schemes. And throughout the crisis he does not take responsibility for Jim's plight.

The first chapters also present Huck's alternative to these two forms of civilized religion: superstition. Huck's indirect response to Miss Watson's oppressions is a passage often celebrated as an example of Huck's unmediated, precivilized imagination. Like the primitive, he projects his feelings into the landscape:

> Miss Watson she kept pecking at me, and it got tiresome and lonesome.... I felt so lonesome I most wished I was dead. The stars was shining, and the leaves rustled in the woods ever so mournful; and I heard an owl, away off, who-whooing about somebody that was dead, and a whippowill and a dog crying about somebody that was going to die.... (pp. 8–9)

Stylistically the passage is justly celebrated: Huck achieves immediacy and naturalness in his projection of a mental landscape and wins our heart. But by emphasizing the cause and source of Huck's mythopoeic rumination, Twain calls attention to a moral problem. Huck may deal "directly" with nature here, but like many a child he deals not with the source of his malaise, Miss Watson, but merely with the symptoms. Avoiding the source of conflict remains ever characteristic of Huck. In the next chapters he associates superstition by turns with Jim's dream of the devil and his hairball, with Tom's romancing, and with Pap. Later in the narrative Huck blames Jim's rattlesnake bite and all their mutual troubles not on his own behavior, but on his having touched a molted snakeskin on Jackson's Island. In his moral crisis Huck's "yaller dog" conscience makes him feel guilty for everything but his role in getting Jim sold back into slavery. Huck's recurrent failure to assume responsibility begins here. Superstition is Huck's way of adapting to evil in the world.[23] But according to the terms of the novel, superstition fails as an alternative to religion because it betrays elements of childish irresponsibility and passivity.

I do not wish to overstate the ironic undermining of Huck in the opening chapters. To ignore his attractions is to miss an important aspect of the dynamics of the book. But it is equally wrong not to acknowledge that Twain draws the reader's attention to the negative underside of his best characteristics. To say this is in part only to remark that the opening chapters delineate the problems the protagonist will have to face in the balance of the book: he will have to grow up by becoming responsible for his actions; he will have to cast off the influence of Tom's romantic adventurism, of Pap's and Jim's superstition, and of Miss Watson's version of civilization and religion. In sum he will have to see through the worst of society and religion to its better aspects. In short, the problem the opening chapters forcibly present is this: he must see his way into society or become like Pap.

By chapter 4 Huck is getting so he can stand "sivilization": "the longer I went to school the easier it got to be" (p. 18). By chapter 6 Huck has adapted to the horrors of cabin life:

> It was kind of lazy and jolly, laying off comfortable all day, smoking and fishing, and no books nor study. Two months or more run along, and my clothes got to be all rags and dirt, and I didn't see how I'd ever got to like it so well at the widow's, where you had to wash, and eat on a plate, and comb up, and go to bed and get up regular, and be forever bothering over a book and have old Miss Watson pecking at you all the time. I didn't want to go back no more. (p. 24)

Typically, only the pain of Pap's "hick'ry" induces Huck to leave this questionable comfort: "I was all over welts" (p. 24). Huck's powers of adaptation and loyalty, so often praised by critics, are called in question by such passages as the above, where the horror lies so close beneath the surface of the "lazy and jolly" life. Huck's floating loyalty will attach itself to anything that passes before his ever-responsive consciousness.

Huck's passivity culminates of course in his tacit participation in the belittlement of Jim in the Evasion sequence. No apology has yet succeeded in palliating the horror of his behavior there. This horror is foreshadowed in many respects: in Huck's unquestioning responsiveness to the King and Duke; in his celebration of the "free and easy" raft; indeed, in the journey south itself. I shall focus on these three aspects of the journey and on how they keep us uncomfortable about Huck's ability fully to mature.

While Marx and others read the moment Huck and Jim pass Cairo as the moment Twain loses control of his novel (Marx, p. 432), Twain in fact keeps firmly in view the significance of passing the Ohio. Huck is continually enthralled by whatever passes before his responsive consciousness: the sunken *Walter Scott,* the Grangerford feud, the escapades of the King and Duke, a circus, or the river itself. Huck has a good time and expects the reader to enjoy his tale. But while part of the reader does enjoy it, another part knows better and is disturbed. The many episodes in which Huck's concern for Jim is at a low ebb are symptomatic not of Twain's loss of control over the theme of slavery, but of Huck's over his moral responsibility to Jim. There is no room for anxiety when all drifts along so "free and easy." We see everything through Huck's eyes, yet Twain makes it clear that continuing south is wrong and that Huck's passive responsiveness is a major cause of the error. Twain enforces our judgment of Huck's "carefree" journey south by subtle manipulation of diction, narrative context, and the dramatic irony implicit in the southward journey itself.

A significant example of dramatic irony occurs just after Huck meets the King and Duke. Noting that Jim and Huck cover the raft by day, they ask if Jim is "a runaway nigger" (p. 102). Huck's reply is ironically resonant: "Goodness sakes, would a runaway nigger run *south?*" (p. 103). The reader, after enjoying Huck's quick-wittedness, asks in kind, "Indeed, would he?" This dramatic irony turns the humor, as so often, back at Huck. Huck's quick-witted reply gets them out of the frying pan and into the fire: the Duke responds by printing the slave bills that enable their rafting by day and that lead ultimately to Jim's being sold back into slavery. Huck's ready improvisations often have this effect: they are good for putting off trouble, not getting rid of it. The trouble comes back with a vengeance.

Twain forces us to judge the southward journey by insisting, through Huck's own narration of events, upon the lengthy passage of time spent on the journey. The famous dawn scene begins, "Two or three days and nights went by . . ." (p. 96). Huck's obliviousness to clock-time is attractive—surely it contributes to the pastoral idyll which follows—but such uncertainty is misplaced when getting back to Cairo is the pressing concern. We wonder about Huck's good faith when he elaborates, "I reckon I might say they swum by, they slid along so quiet and smooth and lovely" (p. 96). He has merged with the landscape but at the expense of his union with Jim and Jim's problem. The opening of chapter 31 again emphasizes the lapse of time as well as distance traveled. For "days and days" they "kept right along down the river." Huck's description of the locale is worth close scrutiny:

> We was down south in the warm weather, now, and a mighty long ways from home. We begun to come to trees with Spanish moss on them, hanging down from the limbs like long gray beards. It was the first I ever see it growing, and it made the woods look solemn and dismal. So now the frauds reckoned they was out of danger, and they begun to work the villages again. (p. 165).

The frauds are out of danger but Huck and Jim are evidently in pretty deep. The warm weather, the distance from home, and the Spanish moss ("the first I ever see it growing") underscore just how far they have come. The imagery further suggests that Huck himself half-recognizes their error. According to his habitual mode of emotional transference, he evokes the specter of a judgmental authority figure: "moss . . . like long gray beards . . . solemn and dismal." Daunted but taking no action, Huck and Jim passively drift ever southward.

Huck's love for the "free and easy and comfortable" raft, though it is the mainstay of many critics' celebration of Huck, also invites our recognition of this passive trait in him. The context in which Huck first enunciates this creed calls the creed in question. He has just evaded the Grangerford feud. His response to the feud is often praised for its understated horror. Yet the understatement is in part symptomatic of his failure to judge fully the nature and implications of the action. His escape to the raft enables him simply to drop the subject:

> I never felt easy till the raft was two mile below there and out in the middle of the Mississippi. Then we hung up our signal lantern, and judged that we was

free and safe once more. I hadn't had a bite to eat since yesterday; so Jim he got out some corn-dodgers and buttermilk, and pork and cabbage, and greens—there ain't nothing in the world so good, when it's cooked right—and whilst I eat my supper we talked, and had a good time. I was powerful glad to get away from the feuds, and so was Jim to get away from the swamp. We said there warn't no home like a raft, after all. Other places do seem so cramped up and smothery, but a raft don't. You feel mighty free and easy and comfortable on a raft. (pp. 95–96)

The famous dawn scene follows. As I have argued, the reference to time ("Two or three days and nights . . . swum by") hints that Huck is not fully in control. Huck's *aubade* and pastoral idyll are justly celebrated, but his lingering over details again forces us to ask if this relaxation is appropriate to the narrative. What about Cairo and freedom? The juxtaposition of the Grangerford feud with Huck's pastoral enjoyment suggests that Huck's rechristening in the river is in part mere evasion. At its worst his warm pastoral represents an improvident responsiveness to the drift of experience; like Keats's "cold pastoral," it is cut off from the pressing realities of life.

At the end of the idyll passage, Huck finds the canoe that could take them to freedom but instead gets them involved with the King and Duke when Huck goes to "get some berries" (p. 98)—even though their coffers are brimming with "corn-dodgers and buttermilk, and pork and cabbage, and greens." Huck's submissive behavior toward these con men raises a disturbing question: why does he not evade them? In chapter 31 we will be struck by how easily Huck skips out on the pair; but by that time it is too late: they have already sold Jim back into slavery. As early as chapter 19 Twain focuses the question sharply. Happy that the King and Duke had made friends, "for what you want, above all things, on a raft, is for everybody to be satisfied," Huck explains:

> It didn't take me long to make up my mind that these liars warn't no kings nor dukes, at all, but just low-down humbugs and frauds. But I never said nothing, never let on; kept it to myself; it's the best way; then you don't have no quarrels, and don't get into no trouble. If they wanted us to call them kings and dukes, I hadn't no objections, 'long as it would keep peace in the family; and it warn't no use to tell Jim, so I didn't tell him. If I never learnt nothing else out of pap, I learnt that the best way to get along with his kind of people is to let them have their own way. (p. 102)

This is the passage, this is the "human credo," that Marx argues "constitutes the paramount affirmation" (p. 431) of the novel. By extension, this is the family which Lionel Trilling calls "a community of saints."[24] But however immediately appealing Huck's code is, the context of Jim's quest for freedom puts all this in question. Why does he not tell Jim that the King and Duke are charlatans and capable of anything? Considering their potential for violence, Huck's desire to avoid conflict and confrontation is wise. But telling Jim about them need not result in "a quarrel," but only in evasion, where for once evasion is the wisest course. Even the notion of avoiding conflict is undermined in the passage by association with Pap Finn, the worst of all role models in the novel. The final blow to this code of adapt-at-all-costs is delivered when we realize that it echoes the King, who has already said, "Make the best o' things the way you find 'em, says I—that's my motto" (p. 102). These are indeed Pap Finn's "kind of people." Huck adapts to the King and Duke at the price of the trip northward and at the moral cost of participating in their criminal schemes. Huck's behavior to the King and Duke, and toward Jim, betrays the ugly side of his ready responsiveness: misplaced sympathy, undue loyalty, and failure to judge and to act.

But beyond Huck's improvident responsiveness we finally see that he is attracted to the King and the Duke because their characters are similar to his own. Like him, the King and Duke are improvisers, always ready with a tall tale or scheme or counter scheme with which to manipulate others. Huck's improvising is by contrast harmless, brought to bear on others only to avoid trouble. But the King and Duke make trouble with their lies, and one wonders if this is just what Huck will do, grown up. Situated at the center of the novel, their confidence games are the dark side of Huck's spontaneous improvising and further call spontaneity and its premises into question. Through the King and Duke, improvising is associated with lying, the human behavior first deprecated in the novel. What is wrong with lying, in the world of the novel, is that it creates a habit of mind that leads ultimately to self-deception. The King and Duke are such invidious role models because they have attained that unfortunate state of mind. As the Duke says when Huck complains that Jim was "mine": "We never thought of that. Fact is, I reckon we'd come to consider him *our* nigger; yes, we did consider him so—goodness knows we had trouble enough for him" (p. 171). The Duke's repetition makes the statement ring true; this is not just another lie meant to placate Huck. The final self-delusion is the Duke's believing that Jim caused them trouble, not they him. Self-delusion is the common state of the Shore, implicit in the Shore's hypocrisy and conventionality, and in slavery itself. Huck at his worst, like the King and Duke whose schemes he admires, is no better. Responding to the Duke, Huck complains that Jim was his "only property" (p. 171). We are left wondering how long until Huck, too, begins to believe his lies. Improvisation, free living, passivity, and misplaced sympathy together make a pretty sorry pathway to maturity. The novel makes it clear how strait is the gate through which Huck must pass.

Marx was surely right to say that "Huck [grows] in stature throughout the journey" (p. 428), but Huck's promising growth never comes to fruition. He comes to appreciate more and more the "whiteness" of Jim and he commits—and recommits—himself to Jim's escape from slavery; he learns that "you can't pray a lie," and that, given the general, "spurious Christian morality" of the Shore (p. 431), it would be better to forsake such godliness and go to hell. But what is finally in question in the world of the novel is not moral awareness but moral action. As Huck himself says earlier, "So the question was, what to do?" (p. 72). What he is asked to do by the terms of the book is to learn to take responsibility for his actions. Huck's deflations, which we saw in the opening chapters, are sustained and elaborated through the course of the book. Huck's moral backsliding in the Evasion sequence comes with a sad inevitability.

The novel's conclusion makes us uncomfortable, as the many attacks on the ending attest. But we must recognize that these evasions, though overdone and overlong, are thoroughly prepared for from the beginning of the novel, and that their purpose is to culminate our uneasy responses to Huck's character. Whatever negative strokes in his portrait we perceive, we do come more and more to value, even to love, Huck. And, perceiving his failings, we do not disapprove but sympathize, for the child-adult swing of responses has shown us that Huck's failings are our own. Like most "children's stories," *Huckleberry Finn* flatters children (and adults) in their childishness, but at the same time elicits their maturation. The novel is about an attractive boy's failure to grow, and it makes perfectly clear what prevented his growth.

The final stroke in Twain's portrait of failure is the most resonant, and it has been among the most debated. Marx long ago argued that the decision to "light out for the territory" is Huck's final "confession of defeat" (pp. 438–39). But despite Marx's inferences, Twain is fully in control of the confession. This is Huck's final admission that he can adapt to all the evil in the world, as we have seen, but also that he cannot see through to, and adapt to, the *good* in "sivilization." Miss Watson and Pap are gone: the worst of society and of anarchy have died a ritual death. Society is ready for Huck but Huck is not, and perhaps never will be, ready for society. The Widow Douglas and her delicious Providence drop from Huck's view.

In *Huckleberry Finn,* Mark Twain does not simply oppose a corrupt society and "depraved conscience" to the innocence of Nature and the spontaneous human heart. His moral vision embraces the difficulty of entering society, which can be corrupt, but which after all is the fruit of our fall and the condition of our prospering. To see this implicit vision in the novel is to see the Twain of *Huckleberry Finn* as less thoroughly atheistic and less cynical in his view of man and society. Through the opposition of River and Shore, the novel shows that Huck's finer qualities—spontaneity, immediacy, responsiveness—are important moral equipment if ever we are to break free of outworn conventions and artifice. But the novel makes it equally clear that they are not sufficient provisions in the journey to maturity. Twain's narrative demonstrates how especially difficult our entrance into adult society is when we approach it with "soul-butter and hogwash" (p. 132) notions of an innocent, spontaneous heart. In fact he implies, like many Christians before him, that not only the "yaller dog" conscience but the heart itself is essentially fallen and depraved. In effect Twain gives the lie to Emerson's optative trust that "if the single man plant himself indomitably on his instincts, and there abide, the huge world will come round to him" (*The American Scholar,* p. 69). Trust in our instincts,

Twain suggests, will not only fail to convert the world, but will prevent our seeing and converting to the best in it. Huck cannot intuitively distinguish the Widow Douglas from Miss Watson, or sense to whom he should attach his free-floating loyalty. Instinct teaches Huck that Jim, among many bad choices, is his truest father, but it cannot show him how to abide by and act upon the perception. By portraying the limitations of Huck's innocence, the novel dramatizes the necessity of adding to the heart's spontaneous workings whatever care and insight the mind can provide. Through Huck's attractions Twain tempts us to see Huck's journey as a happy fall; but he makes it clear to the adult ever nascent within us that maturity and redemption are never so easily won.

NOTES

[1] For reading and responding to various drafts, I wish to thank Fred W. Anderson, Gordon Boudreau, Eugenia Delamotte, Lilian Furst, James Hoopes, Patrick Keane, Will Lee, Cynthia Lewis, and Roger Lund; for funds used in completing the essay, I thank Le Moyne College.

[2] Sigmund Freud, A General Introduction to Psychoanalysis, trans. Joan Riviere (Garden City, N.Y.: Garden City Publishing, 1943), p. 375.

[3] Nature, The Collected Works of Ralph Waldo Emerson, ed. Robert E. Spiller and Alfred R. Ferguson, I (Cambridge: Belknap Press of Harvard University Press, 1971), 41.

[4] Richard Poirier, A World Elsewhere: The Place of Style in American Literature (New York: Oxford University Press, 1966), p. 153.

[5] John Stuart Mill, "Nature," Essays on Ethics, Religion and Society, ed. J. M. Robson, F. E. L. Priestley, and D. P. Dryer (London: Routledge & Kegan Paul, 1969), p. 392. "Nature" was first published in Three Essays on Religion in 1874.

[6] Samuel Langhorne Clemens, Adventures of Huckleberry Finn, ed. Sculley Bradley et al., 2nd ed. (New York: W. W. Norton, 1977), p. 174. All quotations from the novel are from this edition.

[7] Bernard DeVoto, Mark Twain at Work (1942; rpt. Boston: Houghton Mifflin, 1967), e.g., pp. 52, 91–92, was perhaps the first to treat Twain as an improviser. For more recent treatments on this order see Sydney J. Krause, "Twain's Method and Theory of Composition," Modern Philology, 56 (1959), 167–77; and Chadwick Hansen, "There Warn't No Home . . . Like a Balloon Ballooning across the Sahara: Mark Twain as Improviser," in Directions in Literary Criticism: Contemporary Approaches to Literature, ed. Stanley Weintraub and Philip Young (University Park: Pennsylvania State University Press, 1973), pp. 160–67.

[8] Alan Trachtenberg anticipates the present essay when he writes that the novel "is born for us . . . under the aegis of a dual tradition, a dual vision of art" and that the two "are not always in accord with each other" ("The Form of Freedom in Adventures of Huckleberry Finn," Southern Review, n.s., 6 [1970], 957). Unlike Trachtenberg, I argue that this discord leads not to the novel's failure but to its success.

[9] To J. H. Reynolds, 3 February 1818, The Letters of John Keats: 1818–1821, ed. Hyder Edward Rollins, 2 vols. (Cambridge: Harvard University Press, 1958), I, 224.

[10] "Why Huckleberry Finn Is Not the Great American Novel," College English, 17 (1955), 6–10. Leo Marx's attack on the conclusion is in many ways an attack on Twain's Romantic, primitivist premises; see his "Mr. Eliot, Mr. Trilling, and Huckleberry Finn," American Scholar, 22 (1953), 423–40. See, however, his qualifying note in The Machine in the Garden: Technology and the Pastoral Ideal in America (New York: Oxford University Press, 1964), p. 326. See also V. S. Pritchett, "Books in General," New Statesman and Nation (London), August 2, 1941, p. 113. In a manner typical of this strand of criticism, Pritchett concludes, "It is not a book which grows spiritually . . . and it is lacking in that civilised quality—the quality of pity."

[11] Introduction to Adventures of Huckleberry Finn (Boston: Houghton Mifflin, 1958), p. xxv. Cf. Coleridge's description of the inception of Lyrical Ballads: "Mr. Wordsworth . . . was to propose to himself as his object, to give the charm of novelty to things of every day, and to excite a feeling analogous to the supernatural, by awakening the mind's attention from the lethargy of custom, and directing it to

the loveliness and the wonders of the world before us; an inexhaustible treasure, but for which, in consequence of the film of familiarity and selfish solicitude we have eyes, yet see not, ears that hear not, and hearts that neither feel nor understand" (*Biographia Literaria*, ed. J. Shawcross, 2 vols. [Oxford: Oxford University Press, 1907], II, 6).

[12] The strands of praise and blame are not perfectly separate. Smith takes up the attack in part, bemoaning "the tendency toward primitivism that is implicit in *Huckleberry Finn*" (p. xxviii). But Smith's own general tendency is to praise the novel in terms of its achieved Romantic premises. For other examples of this laudatory treatment of Twain's primitivism, see Daniel Hoffman, "Black Magic—and White—in *Huckleberry Finn*," in *Form and Fable in American Fiction* (New York: Oxford University Press, 1961), pp. 317–42; Chadwick Hansen, "The Character of Jim and the Ending of *Huckleberry Finn*," *Massachusetts Review*, 5 (1963), 45–66; Maxwell Geismar, *Mark Twain: An American Prophet* (Boston: Houghton Mifflin, 1970); and Edward J. Piacentino, "The Ubiquitous Tom Sawyer: Another View of the Conclusion of *Huckleberry Finn*," *Cimarron Review*, 37 (1976), 34–43. Kenneth S. Lynn seems to have this strand of criticism in mind when he tries to rescue the novel from what he calls "the Dropoutsville interpretation"; see his "Welcome Back from the Raft, Huck Honey!" *American Scholar*, 46 (1977), 338–47. My differences with Lynn's interpretation will be explained below, note 19.

[13] See, e.g., Richard P. Adams, "The Unity and Coherence of *Huckleberry Finn*," *Tulane Studies in English*, 6 (1956), 87–103; Thomas Arthur Gullason, "The 'Fatal' Ending of *Huckleberry Finn*," *American Literature*, 29 (1957), 86–91; Gilbert M. Rubenstein, "The Moral Structure of *Huckleberry Finn*," *College English*, 18 (1956), 72–76; and Robert Penn Warren, "Mark Twain," *Southern Review*, n.s., 8 (1972), 470–72.

[14] Emerson, *The American Scholar, Collected Works*, I, 68, 53, 56.

[15] Albert J. von Frank, "Huck Finn and the Flight from Maturity," *Studies in American Fiction*, 7 (1979), 1–15, anticipates my own reading in his treatment of a tension in the novel concerning the "roseate vision of romantic primitivism" (p. 13). I differ in seeing Twain in control of this tension and guiding the reader's response to it in the ways that I set forth below. There are also some points of contact between the present study and George C. Carrington, Jr., *The Dramatic Unity of* Huckleberry Finn (Columbus: Ohio State University Press, 1976), e.g., his rejection of "interpretations of the novel as a hymn to nature" (p. 6); his willingness to look unflinchingly at Huck's faults and failings; and his view that "the novel is full of premonitions of disaster; the ending is that disaster" (p. 155). But contrary to Carrington's view that a "moral reading" is inadequate, I here attempt to show that it is necessary and, indeed, demanded by the terms of the book. Although Carrington argues that *Huckleberry Finn* looks forward to the radically skeptical, nihilistic vision of *What Is Man?* and the *Mysterious Stranger* MSS, it is important to consider the extent to which *Huckleberry Finn* proceeds from a far more conservative, humanistic perspective.

[16] *Mark Twain's America* (Boston: Little, Brown, 1932), p. 311; *Mark Twain at Work*, p. 54.

[17] Introduction to *The Adventures of Huckleberry Finn* (London: Cresset Press, 1950), p. xv.

[18] Poirier writes that "Huck's socially anxious voice never carries fully the implications of social contempt and rejection that govern the metaphorical pattern of the book" (pp. 152–53), thus implying that the desire to fit in is categorically wrong and, with Marx, that the repudiation of society is fully justified.

[19] For an example of the way the widow and the spinster are conflated under the single, opprobrious term "Christianity," see James D. Wilson, "*Adventures of Huckleberry Finn*: From Abstraction to Humanity," *Southern Review*, n.s., 10 (1974), 80–82. In attacking such conflations, Lynn successfully distinguishes the two women; but I do not think he has fully explained the narrative function and symbolic role of the widow. Lynn, furthermore, attacks Twain for dropping the widow from view in the conclusion; but, as we shall see, it is Huck who drops her from sight in a way fully appropriate to his character. See below.

[20] Cf. Carrington's "alienating process," p. 122.

[21] *Mark Twain as Critic* (Baltimore: Johns Hopkins Press, 1967), p. 90. See Krause's fine discussion of Twain's treatment of the "goody-goody" tradition, pp. 82–96.

[22] This seems to have been Twain's plan as late as 1883. Interpolating the "Raft Passage" from the manuscript of *Huckleberry Finn* into *Life on the Mississippi*, Twain sets the scene with these significant words: Huck "has run away from his persecuting father, and from a persecuting good widow who wishes to make a nice, truth-telling, respectable boy of him; and with him a slave of the widow's has also escaped" (ed. Edward Wagenknecht [New York: Heritage Press, 1944], p. 16). Here the "persecuting" widow is linked with "persecuting" Pap Finn; it is she who owns Jim. In the finished novel she will remain "good" in just the ambiguous way that "good widow" suggests. That is, she will retain her wish to "sivilize" Huck, but Twain will force us to see the action from two points of view: Huck's and the "adult" reader's. The spinster Watson was added to help us see this positive side of the widow's goodness. Many thanks to Fred W. Anderson for bringing this passage to my attention.

[23] Daniel Hoffman's more positive treatment of the theme of superstition in the novel must be mentioned here (see note 12). Hoffman rightly notes that Twain makes superstition an appealing counterreligion; but I am saying that he *also* forces us to judge the premises and ends of such a religion. Typifying those who find Romantic premises in the novel, Hoffman writes that Huck needs to have no truck with the widow's form of religion, because "this 'spiritual gift' the Widow urges Huck to seek is something he already has; it comes to him and to Jim without the machinery of prayer.... The spiritual gift is natural goodness" (pp. 324–25). Cf. also Carrington, who argues that "magic is the religion of the novel" (pp. 8, 92, 126).

[24] *"Huckleberry Finn," The Liberal Imagination: Essays on Literature and Society* (1948; rpt. New York: Viking Press, 1950), p. 108.

Roger Asselineau

A TRANSCENDENTALIST POET NAMED HUCKLEBERRY FINN

Mark Twain has often been regarded as an uncouth barbarian for daring to make fun of Ralph Waldo Emerson, Henry Wadsworth Longfellow, and Oliver Wendell Holmes in the after-dinner speech he delivered in Boston in 1877 for the seventieth birthday of John Greenleaf Whittier. William Dean Howells, who introduced him that night, was horrified and the listeners petrified. "There fell," he said, "a silence weighing many tons to the square inch, which deepened from moment to moment, and was broken only by the hysterical and blood-curdling laughter of a single guest."[1] Poor Twain felt completely disgraced and, thirty years later, could still remember "Mr. Emerson supernaturally grave, unsmiling."[2] Actually the reason why Emerson did not smile was that he was stone-deaf and could not hear one word of what was being said, as his daughter wrote to Mark Twain in answer to the letter of abject apology he sent a few days later.[3]

Twain felt all the more dejected as he had meant well and even had probably written his speech for the purpose of showing that he was familiar with the works of the New England poets.[4] He quoted in particular a line from "Brahma," "I am the doubter and the doubt," and a passage from "Mithridates":

> Give me agates for my meat;
> Give me cantharides to eat;
> From air and ocean bring me foods,
> From all zones and latitudes.

True, he did not only quote, he also irreverently parodied and did not even respect "Brahma," a passage from which became:

> They reckon ill who leave me out;
> They know not well the subtle ways
> I keep.———I pass, & deal again!

From *Studies in American Fiction* 13, No. 2 (Autumn 1985): 219–26.

He similarly mistreated "Song of Nature": "I tire of globes and aces, Too long the game is played" replaced "I tire of globes and races, Too long the game is played." He wanted to prove that he was not an unlettered Westerner, a mere clown, that the intrepid rider on the Jumping Frog of Calaveras County[5] had changed into a well-read New England gentleman.

These were not unfounded claims. He had apparently read not only Emerson's[6] and Longfellow's and Holmes' poems, but also Henry David Thoreau's books, which was not so common in those days. He referred in a letter to Howells to Thoreau's "happy narrative talent."[7] He appreciated him because there was a kinship between them. They had the same mastery of concrete details and the same keen sense of observation. It is surprising and almost shocking that Ernest Hemingway did not put them side by side in his literary Pantheon when he talked literature in the green hills of Africa. One cannot help suspecting him of lying when he said that he had not read Thoreau yet. If he had not, he would not have devoted so much space to him.[8] When he was interviewed for the *Paris Review* later, he was franker and fairer. This time he placed Thoreau in the list of his "literary forbears" together with Mark Twain.[9] There is indeed the same idyllic quality in *Walden* as in *Adventures of Huckleberry Finn,* and the way in which Huck lazily drifts down the Mississippi on his raft is not dissimilar from the way Thoreau and his brother spent a week on the Concord and Merrimack rivers. Twain, besides, was as much aware as any Transcendentalist of the presence of imponderable elements at the heart of things in nature. In his pilot days, he had frequent occasions of worshipping "nature's God" while sailing down the Mississippi: "The primeval wildness and awful loneliness of the sublime creations of nature, nature's God, excite feelings of unbounded admiration," he once wrote.[10] In art, he could discern with keen insight "the subtle something," "the nameless something which differentiates real narrative from artificial narrative."[11] He knew as well as Emerson that "the value of genius to us is in the veracity of its report. Talent may frolic and juggle; genius realizes and adds."[12] In short, unknown to himself, he was in some ways a crypto-Transcendentalist.

No wonder he created Huckleberry Finn, that Gavroche of the Middle-West, with his dead-pan face and dreamy eyes, so different from that smart-aleck of a Tom Sawyer and all the other boys of Hannibal, a lonesome orphan even in the company of others, a waif lost in the great vacuum of the American continent. Had Huck Finn been more literate, he would have written his own version of "Waldeinsamkeit." He was indeed Emerson's and Whitman's child asking "what is the grass?" and "fetching it ... with full hands." In Twain's interior universe, he was Joan of Arc's dirty-faced junior brother (with the same transvestite tendencies), a pure-hearted idealist in a world of crooks and criminals.

Tom Sawyer, that very shallow boy with nothing in his head except the cops and robbers stories he had read, with no interior life of his own, was a bad influence on him. Huck could be himself only when Tom was not near him. The two boys are perfect illustrations of the distinction Samuel Taylor Coleridge made in his

Biographia Literaria between fancy and imagination. Tom has "no other counters to play with but fixities and definites"[13] borrowed from "pirate books and robber books," as he acknowledged himself.[14] He can "throw style" into everything, transform the discovery of a wreck in the Mississippi into "Christopher Columbus discovering Kingdom-Come" (p. 57). Huck, on the contrary, sees things as they are but with the sense of wonder of a true child of Nature (rather than of Old Man Finn). The wreck of the steamboat "laying there so mournful and lonesome" is to him essentially a mystery (p. 56). Everything to him is a mystery. He has a sense of beauty and of infinity. When Huck and Tom go together at night, from the hill-top Huck "looked down into the village and could see three or four lights twinkling, where there was sick folks, maybe; and down by the village was the river, a whole mile broad, and awful still and grand" (p. 11). There is no way of knowing what Tom thought at the time since the narration never gets inside him, but the chances are he was only thinking of founding "Tom Sawyer's Gang."

Huck is never so happy as when he is all by himself, floating on water or dreaming in the grass in the middle of nature, realizing the infinity of the universe:

> [I] laid down in the bottom of the canoe and let her float. I laid there and had a good rest and a smoke out of my pipe, looking away into the sky, not a cloud in it. The sky looks ever so deep when you lay down on your back in the moonshine; I never knowed it before. And how far a body can hear on the water such nights (pp. 32–33).

Whenever he feels lonesome, as on the island on which he has taken refuge after escaping from his father's shack, he only has to look at the stars and listen to the current of the river to find comfort: "By and by it got sort of lonesome, and so I went and set on the bank and listened to the currents washing along, and counted the stars and drift-logs and rafts that come down, and then went to bed" (pp. 35–36). Jim's presence by his side did not change anything. At night, on the raft, "it was kind of solemn drifting down the big still river, laying on our backs, looking at the stars, and we didn't even feel like talking loud ..." (p. 55). The days and nights they thus spent together on the river were just perfect. They were cut off from the rest of the world and formed an ideal society of two. They did not have to take part in "dialogues of business, love or strife,"[15] but were free to let their eyes wander over the scenery, spontaneously realizing that what was needed was "not to look at all, but a true sauntering of the eye,"[16] as Thoreau put it. No film of custom had covered Huck's eyes yet, and he could see the sun in all its glory, whereas most people fail to see it at all, as Emerson noted. He watched the sun rise on the Mississippi with the eye of a landscape painter and all the excitement of a Romantic poet:

> The first thing to see, looking away over the water, was a kind of dull line—that was the woods on t'other side—you couldn't make nothing else out; then a pale place in the sky; then more paleness, spreading around; then

the river softened up, away off, and warn't black any more, but grey ... and you see the mist curl up off the water, and the east reddens up, and the river, and you make out a log cabin on t'other side of the river ... and next you've got the full day, and everything smiling in the sun, and all the song-birds going to it.[17]

In the central part of the *Adventures of Huckleberry Finn,* the narrative is thus constantly interspersed with lyric interludes celebrating the sights and sounds of Nature in prose-poetry worthy of Thoreau. Huck can sing the awful grandeur of a storm as skillfully as the beauty of a serene summer night:

It would get so dark that it looked all blue-black outside, and lovely; and the rain would thrash along by so thick that the trees off a little ways looked dim and spider-webby; and here would come a blast of wind that would bend the trees down and turn up the pale underside of the leaves; and then a perfect ripper of a gust would follow along and set the branches to tossing their arms as if they was just wild; and next, when it was just about the bluest and blackest—*fst!* It was as bright as glory ... and now you'd hear the thunder let go with an awful crash and go rumbling, grumbling, tumbling, down the sky towards the underside of the world ... (p. 43).[18]

Brander Matthews called this "an instantaneous photograph of a summer storm" (p. 278) because the cinema had not yet been invented, but it was neither a snapshot nor a film sequence but a poem.

A poet could appropriate some of these passages and print them as "found poetry," the beginning of Chapter 8, for instance:

I could see the sun at one or two holes,
but mostly it was big trees all about,
and gloomy in there amongst them.
There was freckled places on the ground
where the light sifted down through the leaves,
and the freckled places swapped about a little,
showing there was a little breeze up there.
A couple of squirrels set on a limb
and jabbered at me very friendly (p. 34).[19]

Like Whitman, Huck dutifully obeyed Emerson's recommendation to integrate industry into poetry. The intrusion of steamboats on the Mississippi did not shock him at all. On the contrary, he represented them as things of beauty: "Once or twice of a night we would see a steamboat slipping along in the dark, and now and then she would belch a whole world of sparks out her chimbleys, and they would rain down in the river and look awfully pretty ... (p. 97).[20]

So Huck was, in a way, a Transcendentalist poet capable of singing the immensity of the universe and of looking at the ground as much as at the sky, as if he had heard Thoreau's warning: "Heaven is under our feet as well as over our heads."[21] He faithfully expressed in demotic language feelings and thoughts his creator expressed elsewhere more directly as the omniscient narrator of other stories and even in his own name in his *Autobiography*. At the beginning of *The Gilded Age,* all the younger members of the Hawkins family and the Negro slaves he portrayed sitting on a log after supper and contemplating "the marvellous river":

> The moon rose and sailed aloft through a maze of shredded cloud wreaths; the sombre river just perceptibly brightened under the veiled light; a deep silence pervaded the air, and was emphasized at intervals, rather than broken, by the hooting of an owl, the baying of a dog, or the muffled crash of a caving bank in the distance.

It was "a world of enchantment," Mark Twain concluded.[22] He had lived in it as a child, when he spent summer vacations on his uncle John Quarles' farm, near Florida, Missouri, and, many years later, while dictating his *Autobiography,* he could still remember "the solemn twilight and mystery of the deep woods and the earthy smells, the faint odors of the wild flowers.... I can call it all back," he added, "and make it as real as it ever was, and as blessed."[23] It was then, no doubt, that he acquired that sense of mysterious presences in Nature which Huck shared with him and experienced in Arkansas when he arrived at the Phelps' farm:

> When I got there it was still and Sunday-like and hot and sunshiny.... There was them kind of faint droning of bugs and flies in the air that makes it seem so lonesome and like everybody's dead and gone; and if a breeze fans along and quivers the leaves, it makes you feel mournful, because you feel like it's spirits whispering—spirits that's been dead ever so many years ... (p. 171).

He could have exclaimed like the boy Wordsworth after a nutting expedition, "there's a spirit in the woods!"[24] In his old age, he rationalized these childish intimations and wrote in his *Notebook:*

> The Being who to me is the real God is the one Who created the majestic universe and rules it. He is the only originator of thoughts; thoughts suggested from within not from without; the originator of colors and of all their possible combinations; of forces and the laws that govern them; of forms and shapes of *all* forms.[25]

In short, his God was a pantheistic deity, an oversoul, not the Creator transcending and distinct from His Creation but a confluence of forces, a force responsible for all the wonders and miracles he sometimes listed in catalogues worthy of Whitman:

> The materials of the leaf, the flower, the fruit; of the insect, the elephant, the man; of the earth, the crag and the ocean; of the snow, the hoar-frost and the ice—may be reduced to infinitesimal particles and they are still delicate, still faultless; whether he makes a gnat, a bird, a horse, a plain, a forest, a mountain

range, a planet, a constellation of diatom whose form the keenest eye in the world cannot perceive, it is all one.[26]

His God was an immanent, omnipresent Divinity, forever going forward, mindless of consequences, a Whole as splendidly indifferent to the fate of its parts as Emerson's Brahma: "God cares not a rap for us—nor for any living creature,"[27] he affirmed.

Huck, however, was far too young to embark on such lofty speculations. He was closer to Thoreau and Whitman than to Emerson. His enjoyment of Nature was more sensuous than spiritual, but, unlike Whitman's, not in the least sensual. He was no "caresser of life." Nevertheless, like Thoreau, who occasionally indulged the luxury of "walking up and down a river in torrid weather with only a hat to shade the head," or like Whitman, sun-bathing at Timber Creek, he loved lying stark naked on the raft, presumably to feel the warmth of the sun and the coolness of the breeze. This was the only sensual excess he was guilty of, for, like New England Transcendentalists, he lived in a sexless world, whatever he may have claimed later in the *True Adventures of Huckleberry Finn,* which he told to John Seelye.[28] His innocence is easy to understand. He was practically an orphan (since his mother had long been dead and his absentee father hardly counted). So he suffered from no Oedipus complex, unlike all normal persons, and was as pure as if his birth had been the fruit of some immaculate conception.

Eros played no part in his life, but Thanatos, on the contrary, looms as large in his book as in *Leaves of Grass.* Of course, it was not the sea that "whispered" to him "the low and delicious word death,"[29] but the woods and the night-birds and the river:

> The stars was shining, and the leaves rustled in the woods ever so mournful, and I heard an owl, away off, who-whooing about somebody that was dead, and a whippowill and a dog crying about somebody that was going to die . . . and I couldn't make out what it was, and so it made the cold shivers run over me. . . . I felt so lonesome I most wished I was dead (pp. 8–9).

He heard this call repeatedly and was strangely fascinated by it, as if he were drawn by the other world and were not quite of this one. Later, when he arrived at the Phelps', he "heard the dim hum of a spinning-wheel wailing along up and sinking down again; and then I knowed for certain I wished I was dead for that *is* the lonesomest sound in the the whole world" (p. 171).

However, unlike Young Goodman Brown, Huck did not expect to meet the Devil in the woods. He even made fun of Jim, who believed he had once been taken all over the world by witches and given a five-cent piece by the Devil himself in exchange for three candles, whereas he had actually been the victim of one of Tom Sawyer's pranks (p. 9). Like a good little Transcendentalist, Huck did not believe in the reality of evil, even when he saw proof of it. And he did see quite an abundance of proof in the course of his adventures, with his own father trying to murder him in a fit of delirium tremens, the sanguinary feud in Kentucky, Colonel Sherburn killing a harmless old drunk in cold blood, and finally, the Duke and the King, whose behavior was "enough to make a body ashamed of the human race" (p. 130). But it was not yet "the damned human race" of Mark Twain's bitter old age. All that Huck found to say was that "human beings can be awful cruel to one another" (p. 180). He deplored such events, but did not believe in their essential existence or necessity. For all his experiences, he kept singing songs of innocence. Though morally and physically as invulnerable as Candide, he never shared his illusions, never regarded the world as the best of all worlds possible. Like Margaret Fuller, on the whole, he accepted the world with resignation rather than enthusiasm. Though misfortunes and disappointments rained upon him, he remained as dry as a duck in a storm, immune to evil.

He was apparently born free of original sin and, although he lived in a guilty society, he never shared its guilt. True, at first, since everyone around him took slavery for granted, he found it perfectly natural. He considered Jim a mere superstitious Negro, "a runaway slave," "Miss Watson's nigger," somebody's property he was guilty of stealing, but, whereas to Tom Sawyer other persons were objects one could play with as with toys, to Huck they were subjects with feelings of their own. If originally he regarded Jim as object, he soon discovered he was a subject experiencing love and pride, terribly hurt when he was lied to for fun (p. 71), and heart-broken whenever he thought of the wife and children he had left behind, for "he cared just as much for his people as white folks does for their'n" (p. 124). So, after a cruel internal debate, Huck reached the conclusion that he had rather go to hell than betray Jim. He gave priority to the dictates of his conscience over the law Church and State wanted to impose on him. In short, he instinctively rediscovered all by himself the basic principles of *Civil Disobedience*. Like the Transcendentalists, he virtually became an abolitionist. To him, Jim was "white inside" (p. 215). This phrase has sometimes been mistaken for an unconscious affirmation of racial superiority. Actually it was Huck's way of proclaiming the fundamental equality of the black and white races in the only terms at his disposal. In this moral crisis, he felt painfully different from all those who surrounded him, but, if he had thought of it then, he would have drawn comfort from the only valid thing the King ever said: "The fools ... ain't that a big enough majority in any town?" (p. 141). Emerson was of the same opinion, since he confided to his *Journal:* "Majorities, the argument of fools!"[30]

No wonder Huck was always "in a sweat" when on land among his fellow-men, and life in society gave him "the fantods." There was only one way out for him, "to light out for the Territory ahead of the rest," in search of something beyond a reality he was too pure to endure. His adventures end on the final apotheosis of an incorrigible idealist. He almost disappears like Whitman at the end of *Song of Myself* in the form of a comet.

Mark Twain said of *The Adventures of Tom Sawyer* that it was "simply a hymn, put into prose to give it a worldly air" (p. 318). This is much truer of the

Adventures of Huckleberry Finn, for Huck corresponds to something deeper in Twain, who was both Tom Sawyer the prankster and Huckleberry Finn the Transcendentalist poet. He kept their portraits, the portraits of his two selves, not in his garret like Dorian Gray, but in the books he had devoted to them, and, thanks to this trick, he never aged himself. T. S. Eliot noted that "Huckleberry Finn is the boy Mark Twain still was at the time of writing his adventures."[31] Unlike Dorian Gray's portrait, though, the portraits of the two boys never aged either and Mark Twain never had to stab them.[32]

It may seem surprising that the same book should be both extremely humorous and highly poetical almost in the same breath, but humor and poetry are opposite poles of the same reality. Peter Viereck's poem "Which of Us Two?"[33] thus treats lyrically a theme Mark Twain developed humorously in the famous story in which he told how he and his twin brother were once put in the same bath and one of them got drowned and no one afterwards could ever tell which one. In the same way, the raftman's extravagant boasts in the chapters of the *Adventures of Huckleberry Finn* which Mark Twain transferred to *Life on the Mississippi* sometimes sound very much like some of Whitman's lyrical outbursts in *Song of Myself* or "Salut au Monde": "When I am playful I use the meridians of longitude and parallels of latitude for a seine" (p. 231) is not much different from "Within me latitude widens, longitude lengthens. . . ."[34] Strange as it may seem, both the humorist and the poet were, each in his own way, the spiritual heirs of Emerson and followers of Transcendentalism as a result of elective affinities, or, in the case of Twain, some pre-established harmony.[35]

NOTES

[1] Quoted by Albert Bigelow Paine, *Mark Twain: A Biography* (New York: Harper & Brothers, 1912), II, 605. Actually, as Henry Nash Smith has proved in a brilliant essay, "That Hideous Mistake of Poor Clemens'," *Huntington Library Bulletin,* 9 (1955), 145–80, the reaction of the audience on that night seems to have been on the whole quite favorable, but Twain and Howells were disconcerted by the coldness and reticence of some of the listeners, who resented the disrespect they perceived in Twain's speech for New England values and culture in general, not only for the writers mentioned.

[2] Paine, p. 604.

[3] Paine, p. 608.

[4] The whole speech has been reprinted by A. B. Paine in Appendix O of his *Mark Twain: A Biography,* III, 1643–48, and by H. N. Smith in his essay on the reception of the speech.

[5] This is how he was represented on a poster announcing his lectures in California in 1867.

[6] Thanks to the patient research of Alan Gribben, who has drawn up an inventory of Twain's library and annotated it with admirable precision, we know for certain that Twain had in his library both Emerson's *Essays* (New York, 1886) and *Selections from the Writings of R. W. Emerson, Arranged under the Days of the Year* (Boston: Houghton, Mifflin, 1889). Both books, it is true, were subsequent to the *Adventures of Huckleberry Finn,* but their presence in Twain's library (especially the presence of the second book) shows the persistence of his interest in Emerson, to whom he had tried to pay a visit in the company of W. D. Howells in 1882, a few days before his death. See Alan Gribben, *Mark Twain's Library: A Reconstruction* (Boston: G. K. Hall, 1980), I, 220–22.

[7] Henry Nash Smith and William M. Gibson, ed., *Mark Twain–Howells Letters* (Cambridge: Harvard Univ. Press, 1960), I, 138.

[8] See Ernest Hemingway, *Green Hills of Africa* (Harmondsworth: Penguin, 1966), pp, 24–25.

[9] See Van Wyck Brooks, ed., *Writers at Work: The* Paris Review *Interviews* (London: Secker, 1963), p. 191.

[10] *Life on the Mississippi* (New York: Harper & Brothers, 1923), p. 258.

[11] See Mark Twain's letter to Howells dated Jan. 10, 1904, in *Mark Twain–Howells Letters*, II, 778.

[12] "The Poet," in *Selected Writings of R. W. Emerson*, ed. Brooks Atkinson (New York: Modern Library, 1970), p. 324.

[13] Samuel Taylor Coleridge, *Biographia Literaria* (London: Everyman's Library, 1930), p. 160.

[14] Samuel Langhorne Clemens, *Adventures of Huckleberry Finn* (New York: W. W. Norton, 1962), p. 12.

[15] William Wordsworth, "Ode on Intimations of Immortality," in *Poetical Works*, ed. Thomas Hutchinson (London: Oxford Univ. Press, 1913), p. 589.

[16] Henry David Thoreau, *Complete Works* (Boston: Houghton, Mifflin, 1906), X, 351.

[17] See also the description of Mark Twain's trip down the Neckar in *A Tramp Abroad* (Hartford: American, 1880), particularly the last three paragraphs of Chapter 14, pp. 126–27.

[18] Another storm occurs in Chapter 20, p. 103.

[19] Walt Whitman's "To the Man-of-War Bird" was probably the earliest example of "found poetry" in American literature. He "found" it in Michelet's *The Bird*. The Scottish poet Hugh MacDiarmid was a great practitioner of this art. His habit of incorporating material quarried from the mass of reading stored in his head or in his notebooks was discussed in "Letters to the Editor," in *Times Literary Supplement*, Jan. 28 and Feb. 4, 1965.

[20] In *The Gilded Age*, the Negro slaves even mistake a steamboat at night with her "deep coughing sound," "huge duplicated horns" spitting smoke and sparks, for "de Almighty." See *The Gilded Age* (London: Chatto & Windus, 1928), p. 19.

[21] H. D. Thoreau, *Complete Works* II, 313.

[22] *The Gilded Age*, pp. 17–18.

[23] *Mark Twain's Autobiography* (New York: Harper & Brothers, 1924), I, 109–10.

[24] William Wordsworth, "Nutting," in *Poetical Works*, p. 186.

[25] *Mark Twain's Notebook*, ed. Albert Bigelow Paine (New York: Harper & Brothers, 1935), pp. 360–61.

[26] *Mark Twain's Notebook*, p. 361.

[27] *Mark Twain's Notebook*, p. 362.

[28] John Seelye, *The True Adventures of Huckleberry Finn* (Evansville: Northwestern Univ. Press, 1970).

[29] Walt Whitman, "Out of the Cradle Endlessly Rocking," in *Leaves of Grass: Comprehensive Reader's Edition*, ed. Harold W. Blodgett and Sculley Bradley (New York: New York Univ. Press, 1965), p. 252.

[30] Ralph L. Rusk, ed., *The Journals of Ralph Waldo Emerson* (Boston: Houghton, Mifflin, 1909–1914), VII, 148.

[31] T. S. Eliot, "Introduction," *Adventures of Huckleberry Finn* (New York: Chanticleer, 1950), p. viii.

[32] Actually, though Mark Twain never wrote any book showing Tom Sawyer and Huck Finn in their old age, he once imagined them returning to Hannibal when sixty years old (see *Mark Twain's Notebook*, p. 212). He sees them both as "desolate" because their "life has been a failure." Huck is even "crazy." Mark Twain does not say why, but probably because Huck has been unable to adapt himself to the civilization which eventually caught up with him in the territory where he had sought refuge.

[33] Quoted in *The Penguin Book of Modern American Verse*, ed. Geoffrey Moore (Melbourne: Penguin, 1954), p. 284.

[34] Walt Whitman, "Salut au Monde," in *Leaves of Grass*, p. 137.

[35] James Johnson, in *Mark Twain and the Limits of Power: Emerson's God in Ruins* (Knoxville: Univ. of Tennessee Press, 1982), has also underlined a number of correspondences between Twain and Emerson, but he places himself exclusively on the ethical plane and completely ignores the aesthetic aspect of the problem. He sees in Huckleberry Finn a potential saint rather than a Transcendentalist poet.

Millicent Bell

HUCKLEBERRY FINN AND THE SLEIGHTS OF THE IMAGINATION

Like the second half of *Don Quixote*, *Huckleberry Finn* begins with a reference by the hero to his previous existence as a literary character: "You don't know about me, without you have read a book by the name of *The Adventures of Tom Sawyer*, but that ain't no matter. That book was made by Mr. Mark Twain, and he told the truth, mainly. There was things which he stretched, but mainly he told the truth" (p. [17]). It is sometimes thought that this opening is a remnant, merely, of Twain's intention to write a sequel to his earlier success made up out of discarded portions of it, parts he might have eliminated as the book grew into an independent and very different act of the imagination.[1] But the literary self-consciousness introduced by Huck's awareness of his status as fiction is perhaps quite significant. Borges remarks that it disquiets us to know that Don Quixote is a reader of the *Quixote* because "if the characters in a story can be readers or spectators, then we, their readers or spectators, can be fictitious."[2] Making allowance for Borges's particular readiness to see fictionality in existence, we still can take note of the way in which fiction and "life" are mixed as the result of the promotion of character to reader. And as the author, the maker of fictions, becomes the author of what is also "real," we are also reminded of reality's fictionality.

Huckleberry Finn seems to eliminate the author by the superior authority of its hero's first-person narrative. Yet it admits, indeed incorporates into that pretended reality, a profounder awareness than its predecessor of the role of the imagination in all human gestures. The three opening chapters are, in fact, highly relevant to this awareness, as are the last ten chapters, so often considered a regrettable superfluity that Twain would have done better to eliminate.[3] John C. Gerber has properly identified *Huckleberry Finn* as a "modified frame story" because Tom Sawyer, instead of Huck, is the major character in these opening and concluding sections.[4] Technically, of course, the narration is still Huck's, but Tom's mind is omnipresent in these parts since the action is primarily dictated not only by what Tom does but also by his way of thinking, his version of life. And this version is now felt—as it is not so deeply felt

From *One Hundred Years of* Huckleberry Finn: *The Boy, His Book, and American Culture*, edited by Robert Sattelmeyer and J. Donald Crowley (Columbia: University of Missouri Press, 1985), pp. 128-45.

in *Tom Sawyer*—decidedly to be a fiction, a viewpoint that consciously constructs reality into certain formal arrangements. The Tom Sawyer frame serves to prepare the reader to regard what it encloses as also structured by imaginative invention.

We say at once that Tom's imagination is "literary." He represents that side of Twain's own mind that was capable of absorbing a multitude of literary models. Twain recognized in himself, indeed, a tendency to "unconscious plagiarism" and approved the statement of Dumas, "The man of genius does not steal; he conquers; and what he conquers, he annexes to his empire."[5] *The Adventures of Tom Sawyer* has been shown to utilize suggestions and details from literature at every level—from the work of native Southwest or Yankee humorists, from dime novels and melodramas, and from the tradition of belles lettres. Among literary re-spectables from whom it borrows are Dickens, Charles Reade, Wilkie Collins, and Poe—the grave-robbing scene in the book can be related to an episode in *A Tale of Two Cities,* for example, and the digging for buried treasure to "The Gold Bug." The absorption of literary models and suggestions continues in *Huckleberry Finn,* which uses some of these same sources.[6]

Both works, in being openly imitative of known literary and popular models, tend toward parody, making comment not only on life directly but on other versions of life. In its earliest form as "The Boy's Manuscript," *Tom Sawyer* began, probably, as a literary burlesque, suggested by David Copperfield's courtship of Dora.[7] The suggestion of parody reminds us that what we are reading is itself only another text, another fiction without absolute standing as a version of experience. But *Huckleberry Finn* goes further than *Tom Sawyer* in this direction, as I have said, partly because it also replicates and comments upon its own predecessor by the same author. It reproduces certain situations from the earlier novel—such as Huck's discussion with Tom about the lives of pirates and robbers or the behavior of prisoners—that particularly reflect the conventions of literature. In the con-text of Huck's narration these discussions become self-conscious references to the art of fiction as practiced by Tom himself as well as by his creator. More covertly than by the direct reference of the opening sentence but still significantly to the recognizing reader who knows the earlier book, the text of *Huckleberry Finn* informs one that it is a text and suggests the textuality of experience.

When we say that Tom Sawyer's imagination is "literary" we also remind ourselves that he is one of the great examples, like Quixote, of the mind saturated with literature almost to the point of delirium. This is true not only because Tom wants to make reality conform to literary models and consciously invokes these models as "authorities" but also because his concept of "style" is the governing principle that directs his actions. *Style,* after all, is a term only restrictedly applied to art; in a more general sense it is a way of describing human behavior as it approximates some ideal pattern. Tom's preoccupation with form, evident throughout *Tom Sawyer* and still more conspicuous in the portions of *Huckleberry Finn* in which he is present, persists in the "interior" parts of the book where Sawyerism is felt as a continuing presence even though Tom is gone, an element internalized sometimes in Huck himself.

Yet Huck's mind is fundamentally opposed to Tom's, as Sancho's is to Quixote's. Huck has only recently become literate, and his speech is still free of the elegancy or obfuscation induced by written models. Huck's moral imagination is also free, despite the "deformed conscience"[8] that seems to overwhelm it from time to time. His "primitive" responses to experience have no available justification or even name; they remain outside the patterns of approved social value and of language as well. Yet his personal speech, the governing voice of the book, is as near a literary equivalence of his existential ethic as it is possible to imagine, a miracle of the emergence of validity out of the unlearned powers of mind and the least refutable aspects of perception.

Huckleberry Finn's colloquial autobiographical mode effected, of course, an alteration in the relation between language and literature in our culture. It converted an oral-comic tradition, previously employable only in sub-literature or journalism, to the highest literary ends. After Twain, in fact, there is no longer any reason to distinguish between low and high styles at all. But the immediate impact of this novel derived from the fact that the distinction, at the time of its writing, was still a powerful one. Colloquial speech, the speech of a half-educated country person, was adapted in this unclassifiable prose to ends that proved serious, even "poetic" in an unprecedented way. Yet, because of its thrust against the traditional mode for such expression, it was felt to be subversive. This historic subversiveness had obvious objects: literary genteelism, to begin with—but literary genteelism was linked in Twain's mind with the social pretensions of aristocracies in general and with the self-justifications of a defunct Southern aristocracy in particular. Twain, connecting styles of life and language he judged equally dishonest, related the false dignity and claims of refinement of the slaveowners to their defensive rhetoric. He thought there were particular sources for both in literature itself, specifically in the novels of Sir Walter Scott, which he accused of poisoning literature with "wordy, windy, flowery 'eloquence,' romanticism, sentimentality" and with bringing on the Civil War.[9]

We only faintly sense this political motive in *Huckleberry Finn*'s stylistic innovation. But, a hundred years later, we can still perceive how the book opposes all aspects of *any* dominant culture with what Henry Nash Smith has called the "vernacular attitude."[10] Twain's skepticism seems wholesale and modernist. His suspicions that all social forms—not merely American Southern aristocratic ones—might be impositions had already begun to surface in this, his greatest work. Eventually they would reach that nihilism visible in the writings of his last years which belong so clearly to our own century. It is this total distrust of received values and meanings that earlier had energized his propensity to satire and burlesque of any and every propriety. Nor do Twain's biographers stress irrelevantly the fiasco of the *Atlantic Monthly* Whittier dinner in 1876,[11] when Twain was working on the early chapters of the novel. On this occasion, to his own chagrin, some inner demon caused him to hold up to ridicule those distinguished fellow guests and cultural idols, Longfellow, Holmes, and Emerson. Twain's mockery knew its own ultimate objects despite his "deformed" inner censor.

Huckleberry Finn expresses this same irreverence filtered through Huck's innocent humorlessness. To every cultural or social pretension, the novel's mode of narration opposes an anti-stylistic style. Scrupulously pruned of rhetoric, reduced in syntax and vocabulary to simple elements of plain statement, Huck's first-person retrospection appears, in the best passages of the book, to be artless. It is nothing of the sort, of course, but it was *designed* to seem so, to convey the effect of spontaneity because the spontaneous, the untutored, was a value to be set against that which surrounded it, the behavior patterns and language dominant in the culture and expressing its bad faiths. Devoid of literary and social preconceptions, this pseudo-oral style was made to seem the direct record of honest sensation and feeling.

This subversion of "style" as such is part of a general antiformal impulse in the work. We should, I think, take with utmost seriousness Twain's notice to the reader: "persons attempting to find a moral in it will be banished; persons attempting to find a plot in it will be shot" (p. [5]). Twain discarded quite deliberately the apocalyptic fictional form long dominant in the novel and drew instead on an early, looser model, the picaresque, with its license to disjunctive, open-ended narrative and to a hero who does not develop as his history progresses. The correspondences of Huckleberry Finn with Don Quixote are less fundamental than one might suppose, despite the obvious parallels.[12] Cervantes's view of Quixote is more complex than Twain's view of Tom; Huck is very different from the pragmatic Sancho. But the "open form" resulting from what Robert M. Adams calls an "unresolved tension" between Cervantes's pair[13] may have provided a suggestive design along with adapted details. Twain himself, we know, greatly approved the Spanish classic and contrasted it, in the passage in Life on the Mississippi already referred to, with Scott's Ivanhoe, because it "swept the world's admiration for medieval chivalry-silliness out of existence,"[14] while Ivanhoe restored it. In his own attack on the same delusions, he may even have identified himself with Cervantes but been influenced more than he was aware by the subtle rejection of resolution that makes the Spanish masterpiece so different from such a work as Scott's.

The title of Twain's book expresses the fact that Huck has "adventures," has, that is, engagements with chance, and that the incidents he relates are not caused by him and do not change him. Of course, we are tempted to think that something else is going on, despite the picaresque form, for Huckleberry Finn does more with its hero than conduct him, in the picaresque way, through the layers of his society, so revealing them to us. The work does not seem to be a comic journey without goal, for Huck appears to "grow," like the hero of tragedy, as he passes along the stages of his downriver voyage with Jim. We are even likely to see in his experience one of the standard patterns of the novel of character, the penetration of illusion, the coming to maturity through trial, of the youthful protagonist. But reading the book in this way brings us up (with a cry of critical anguish, generally) against the ending. For if Huck *has* changed and grown, if we have really gone somewhere with him, what is the meaning of that return, in the Phelps Farm chapters, to the exact conditions of the opening when he is enrolled in Tom Sawyer's band of make-believe robbers and Jim is merely the object of a boyish practical joke?

It is my contention that we must understand *Huckleberry Finn* in some other way than as a novel of development—and that still the book is "serious." It expresses not only Twain's view of his own society but also his understanding of human life in general as a condition of precarious continuity in which identity is maintained only by our willingness to accept definition of ourselves from the norms of society and the expectations of others. Huck's experiments with freedom, the sloughing off of old habits of thought and action, are the experiments of utopia, the utopia of the raft. That utopia cannot survive on the shore, which finally even invades and destroys the raft itself. Huck's adventures involve him in the greatest risk because of their continued invitation not so much to the discovery of a new self as to the loss of membership altogether in human society, the source of all role and all selfhood. It is no accident that the narrative is permeated by references to death and by the narrator's own death thoughts, lyric moments in which he seems ready to surrender selfhood altogether, to merge with the flow of natural forces that bear him onward, not to any landing where he and Jim can continue as they are, but toward a sea of silence.[15]

If indeed the plot of *Huckleberry Finn* can thus be described as an antiplot, a frustration of our expectations of development and consequence, it may suggest that life in general may not possess inherent design. Plot, character, formal closure, even "theme" are, after all, ways of saying that life has inherent form. If these can be seen as the inventions of the human imagination, we are reminded that life is not, after all, a coherent story and that we can only pretend that we know who we are. This, of course, is itself a statement, a theme, and perhaps *Huckleberry Finn,* while undermining more obvious themes, leaves this one on our hands.

The mark of such an intention is the obsessive stress in the book on the games literature plays in imposing its designs upon life and the interpretation of social forms as games perfectly analogous to the games of literature. The Phelps Farm coda is distinguished from what has gone before only because the emphasis on language and literature—present earlier too—takes over completely from the social and psychological interests that are finally revealed in all their desolating vacuity as make-believe. It is indeed a pessimistic reduction from the previous richness of Huck's moral effort and hope. His story-telling is over now, subdued to Tom's art-for-art's-sake view of life as an aesthetic opportunity. Huck escapes at the very end with a vow of silence, "If I'd a knowed what a trouble it was to make a book I wouldn't a tackled it and ain't agoing to no more" (p. 366): Tom's art prevails and survives, however; his is the unresting imagination forever generating roles for himself and others out of the conventions of society and the formulas of literature.

As I shall try to show, the literary imagination, chiefly identified with Tom at the start as at the end, comes to stand for all lies imposed by social life. But what forms of social life are not lies? The literary imagination is the enemy of Huck's existential freedom and yet, paradoxically, it is the only means of his survival. His adventures, even when he is separated from Tom—as he is for most of the story—involve him in the play-acting, the charades and deceits of others, an assortment of characters who represent both the respectable and the disreputable in society. Only the private life established between Huck and Jim on the raft is free from such deceits, though Huck can play games that make "trash" out of Jim's feelings in the early stages of their relationship and though he subscribes to society's cruel fiction that a human being can be regarded as a piece of property. But even more benignly Huck is compelled in his contacts with a lying society to resort to life-saving fictions; Huck's own fertility of self-invention produces a succession of impersonations that both express, in a symbolic mode, his orphanhood and peril and combat the destructive designs of society. Thus, the descent in tone, the tedious burlesque of the ending with its emphasis on game-playing pure and simple, is anticipated in the whole of the work more than critics have been willing to admit. The Phelps chapters are not so much an anticlimax as consistent with much that has gone before.

The ending also implies a cyclicity rather than a linearity in experience, for though Huck initially resists the seductions and sleights of Tom's imagination, he submits to the forms of respectability, agrees to go to live with the Widow Douglas, as the price of that same membership in the gang, joining the make-believe of society and of the gang at the same time. It is clear that respectability, membership in societies, is the same in both the larger world of adults and the imaginative world of the boys. The final paragraph tells us that he will be joining Tom for new adventures over in the Territory but will somehow manage to evade Aunt Sally's intention to adopt and "sivilize" him. Yet we cannot help seeing here only the temporary rebellion and self-exile that had preceded his original submission in the first chapter. Tom's price will be the same as before. The whole narrative, indeed, exhibits a continuation of such resistances and returns, and anticipates the end. One may mention, for example, Huck's decision not to oppose the pretenses of the Duke and the Dauphin "'long as it would keep peace in the family" (p. 166), recognizing as he does that lies are somehow the very essence of social cohesion.

There is no real difference, it is plain at the start, between the making-up of reality by the gang and the Bible stories Huck is told by the widow. He loses interest in the latter when he learns that "Moses had been dead a considerable long time . . . because I don't take no stock in dead people" (p. 18). He finds that religion asks him to interest himself in either an imagined past or an imagined future, and Miss Watson's theology leaves him cold: "All I wanted was to go somewheres; all I wanted was a change, I warn't particular" (p. 19). Tom's preference for art over nature exhibits itself just as promptly and just as bewilderingly to Huck. On the night of their first escapade he wants to tie the sleeping Jim to a tree "for fun" until Huck points out that this would wake him, but still "nothing would do Tom but he must crawl to where Jim was, on his hands and knees, and play something on him" (p. 23). This "play" is the first of the three practical jokes inflicted on Jim during the course of the story, the first of the three impositions of fancy that become increasingly dangerous until Huck rejects all such games as a way of dealing with his friend. A staple of American humor that Twain himself found detestable, the practical joke is essentially a fiction, a made-up explanation of appearances intended to deceive and when the deception is disclosed to embarrass the victim. Jim's own self-seduction by fantasy collaborates here when he finds his hat hung on a tree to make him think that he has been acted upon by witches and is then tempted himself into extravagances of story-telling as he develops an account of what happened in more and more fanciful versions. Story-telling thus begets more story-telling.

The inspiration for Tom's robber-band is openly literary. Tom's "beautiful oath" to which all must swear comes, he admits, only in part "out of his own head," the rest "out of pirate books, and robber books" (p. 26). Tom—or Twain—draws, in fact, on sources as diverse as Carlyle's *History of the French Revolution,* Dickens's *A Tale of Two Cities,* and Robert Montgomery Bird's *Nick of the Woods* for details here.[16] The fidelity to formula is, indeed, compulsive: Huck is almost excluded because he hasn't a family to be killed if he tells the gang's secrets. The business of the gang is routine, *"only* robbery and murder" (emphasis mine), but it is no mere unimaginative burglary: "We ain't burglars. That ain't no sort of style," says Tom. "We are highwaymen. We stop stages and carriages on the road, with masks on, and kill the people and take their watches and money" (pp. 26–27). "Killing people" is part of the prescription for proper style, except perhaps when the robbers hold their captives for ransom, a variation permitted by some "authorities," which is to say, by some texts. Tom doesn't really know what the word *ransom* means, and when Ben Rogers says, "Why can't a body take a club and ransom them as soon as they get here," he answers, "Because it ain't in the books so—that's why" (p. 67).

After a month of playing robber, Huck and the other boys resign from the gang. Realists, they tire of fancy: "We hadn't robbed nobody, we hadn't killed any people, but only just pretended" (p. 30). Tom alone retains the taste for calling things what they are not—only for him are hogs "ingots," turnips "julery." The attack upon a camp of Spanish merchants and A-rabs "warn't anything but a Sunday-school picnic, and only a primer-class at that" (pp. 31–32). When challenged about wonders the others fail to see, Tom refers Huck to *Don Quixote* and explains that "enchantment" had converted the A-rabs and elephants into picnickers. Tom is thus explicitly identified with Cervantes's hero, and the twist of logic that makes him argue that *appearances* are what is unreal suggests that the consequence of believing in the reality of fantasy is, as Borges (in the remark quoted earlier) observes, that one must suspect the fantasy of reality. So, Huck tries to work the enchantment himself by rubbing an old tin lamp, "calculating to build a palace and sell it," but he gets nowhere: "all that stuff was only just one of Tom Sawyer's lies" (p. 33). It is a famous deflation of the literary imagination at its game of reversing the relation between fancy and fact, a game more serious than it seems at this early point, for though we can laugh easily at the harmless nature of Tom's play-acting, more serious fictions upon which society's very existence bases itself—such as racial inequality—will soon be posing as reality.

Huck himself is getting used to the artifices of society, though various signs tell him that Pap—the demon presence behind the fine appearance of the social world—is around. Then Pap appears, the destroyer, it would seem at first, of all civilized lies, with a particular hatred for literature; Huck is reading about George Washington when the old man whacks the book out of his hand and shouts, "First you know you'll get religion, too" (p. 40), correctly—from Twain's point of view—connecting the fictions of history and religious belief. But, of course, Pap is no real enemy of these things—he is the Master of Lies, expert in his own right in all pretenses and fabrications sanctified by social usage. Gaining the sympathy of the judge by enacting the convention of father-love, he takes him in further by his parody of "reform." Pap is really a subscriber to society's formulas, for all his seeming unregeneracy—as his drunken reproaches to Huck that he has been cheated of the due rewards of fatherhood and his denunciations of the state of Ohio for letting a "nigger" vote both illustrate. He is, in fact, the wicked soul of conventionality, his hypocrisy simply more blatant still than that of respectable society.

Huck makes his escape from both respectable and disreputable versions of constraint, from the Widow and Pap, by a device of make-believe, his own faked murder. On the one hand this is symbolically veracious and life-saving; Huck must "die to" an old life in order to reach for freedom, and this reaching must threaten to extinguish the sense of self by which one survives in society. It can be contrasted with the theatrics of Pap that precipitate it—Pap's drunken delusion that Huck is the "Angel of Death." But Huck is right to recognize, on the other hand, that he is engaging himself, out of necessity, in the very mode he is bidding farewell to, the mode of fiction-making. He acknowledges that his is an inferior achievement to what Tom might have devised: "I did wish Tom Sawyer was there, I knowed he would take an interest in this kind of business, and throw in the fancy touches" (p. 57). Yet henceforth such story-telling as Huck engages in will, for the most part, be enforced by the necessity, paradoxically, of keeping himself free from the world of social lies or of protecting Jim from its designs.

Only occasionally is he afterward tempted to regress to idle, mischievous make-believe. The second practical joke on Jim, the snakeskin laid at the foot of his bed, brings the dead snake's mate to bite Jim on the heel. Jim thinks that bad luck has been invoked, but Huck knows that the misfortune has been brought on not by handling the snakeskin as such but by his own undisciplined impulse toward "fun." Then directly, Huck must himself, again, needfully make-believe to find out the state of things in St. Petersburg, and he goes onshore as a girl, with a tale of a sick mother needing help. Detected as a boy, he is quick with another tale—this one of a runaway orphan bound to a mean, old farmer—and is believed, his story-telling thus having served the function of keeping him safe from discovery while truly, in this second case, representing his condition of orphanhood and flight.

He is tempted again by the lure of motiveless "adventure," the distractions so often offered him by Tom, who is, in this sense, still present within him when he goes aboard the wrecked steamboat despite Jim's misgivings. He is thinking of Tom, indeed, as he says to himself, "wouldn't [Tom] throw style into it?" (p. 97). His reproof is the harrowing sight of the murderers aboard the wreck and the loss, temporarily, of the raft—admonishment, as after the snakeskin trick, of the consequence of idle fancy. To do what he can for the murderers, now trapped on the sinking vessel, he resorts to another invented story to the ferryboat watchman, trying to rescue them by his tale as he had tried to safeguard himself and Jim by his tales to Mrs. Loftus, for, as he says, "there ain't no telling but I might come to be a murderer myself" (p. 103). But imagination cannot work its life-saving magic this time, and the vessel sinks before help can come.

She is called, of course, the *Walter Scott,* and with her, taking this opportunity to mock once more the novel's antimodel, Twain sinks Huck's appetite for romance. As for Jim, he "didn't want no more adventures," the word now signifying Tom Sawyer–style escapades, and Huck concludes, "he was right; he was most always right; he had an uncommon level head, for a nigger" (p. 109). Part of the "truck" they have carried off from the *Walter Scott* is, not surprisingly, "a lot of books," from which the recently literate Huck reads to Jim—"about kings, and dukes, and earls, and such" (p. 109)—and they discuss the ways of such fabulous beings. They also discuss the ways of the greatest of Old Testament kings, Solomon, who wanted to cut a baby in half, and Jim thinks him plagued by the "dad-fetchedes' ways" (p. 111) he has ever seen. Jim scores, too, over Huck's book-learning by "proving," with irrefutable logic, that although cats and dogs "talk" differently, Frenchmen and Americans must talk alike. All this conversation may seem simply a comic interval between significant action unless we realize its import—Jim, the illiterate and even more alienated refugee from society, must teach Huck the futility of the "truck" of notions he has rescued from the sinking vessel of his social membership.

It is at this point, however, when the raft and the canoe are separated in the fog, that Huck loses Jim, his instructor in pragmatic wisdom. When he finds him again, he has forgotten what he learned about idle story-telling and plays the third of his practical jokes on Jim, pretending never to have been gone at all, even though Jim has worried solely about him. Jim's reproach, his reduction of cruel fantasy to truth, is telling: "Dat truck dah is *trash;* en trash is what people is dat puts dirt on de head er dey fren's en makes 'em ashamed" (p. 121). Again the word *truck* stands for the useless—and sometimes dangerous—freight of lies that even the raft is carrying, as the *Walter Scott* had, something that is no better than "trash." Huck's apology, as every reader notes, is a giant step in his moral progress. It also represents his resolution to dispense with Tom-Sawyer-foolery. He will tell no more false tales, unless he has to, to save life. So, he immediately lies again, but only for this reason, with a lie that is better than the truth he intended to tell the men with guns who are on the lookout for runaway slaves. Not even Tom could have improved upon his suggestion, by implication, that his family is afflicted with smallpox. That he does not actually say this—but leaves the specification to the imagination of the bounty-hunters, is probably significant; Huck's restraint is more than strategic, for it may represent his disinclination, now, for elaborating even necessary fictions.

Again separated from Jim when the steamboat collides with the raft, Huck must once more reinvent himself as "George Jackson," just fallen off the steamboat, a fiction of orphaning symbolically justifiable. But it is not Huck who is the source of the engulfing and ultimately murderous fiction of the Grangerfords, whose adopted son this orphan becomes. At first he is delighted to find himself in such a fine family, one so completely equipped with all the standard appurtenances and practiced in the appropriate rituals of gentility. Huck has never before seen a house that has "so much style" (p. 136), so many objects too elegant to function, like the mantel clock, with the picture of a town painted on it and a beautiful tick, which would "start in and strike a hundred and fifty before she got tuckered out" (p. 137) after a traveling peddler repaired it, or the crockery basket filled with painted plaster fruit. Indeed, the house is *all* style without substance, filled with what might be called stage-props rather than realities.

Of course, the Grangerfords possess books. There is *Pilgrim's Progress,* which Huck summarizes, in his ignorance, as "about a man that left his family it didn't say why" (p. 137), a Bible, a gift-book annual full of poetry, a home medical manual, Henry Clay's speeches, and a hymn book. The collection is ironically significant, as Walter Blair has pointed out, enforcing "the evidence of fraudulent pretense"[17] in the Grangerford way of life. Though they subscribe to "Friendship's Offering," though they possess the religious texts that instruct one to love one's neighbor, though they can learn from the medical volume how to treat the injured and save life, the Grangerfords inhabit a house of hatred and death where the most powerful feeling is enmity for one's neighbor and a desire to injure and destroy him. And in this family of fictionizers there has even been one literary creator, the lamented Emmeline, whose grotesquely sentimental verses and drawings not only parody a tradition of false art but also demonstrate the falsifying artifice of Grangerford being.

For in this House of Fiction, the greatest fiction of all is the Grangerford family itself. At the Grangerfords', social behavior is as ritualized as the ceremonies of Tom Sawyer's band, got up from the best authorities. The fine manners and high principles, like the accumulations of artifacts in their house, are as much a fiction as are the practices of the make-believe boy-robbers, as much a structure of the imagination unrelated to reality. But, unlike the boys' games, the Grangerfords' pretenses are not for fun; the feud will become murderous and cost the lives of all the male members of the clan, even down to young Buck. Buck, save for a letter of his name, is Huck himself, who is nearly dead with horror as he witnesses the slaughter of his twin. But Buck, because of his implication in the gang-war of the adults, is also that other brother to Huck, his friend Tom, the young knight of pretenses and the willing collaborator in the social game.

Huck escapes this death of self and the imagination by the narrowest squeak and reaches the eden, once more, of the raft. But it is soon invaded by those final virtuosi of story-telling, the Duke and the Dauphin. They are, even more obviously than the Grangerfords, literary fabricators, conscious tellers of tales, inventors of false identity. These scoundrels perpetrate frauds that are parodies of social roles, dramatic impersonations behind which no definable selfhood or meaningful history exists. When first encountered each has got into trouble for a false tale—one for vending a dentifrice that really melts the enamel off teeth, the other for running a temperance revival while swigging the jug on the sly. The first soon tells his story of his descent from the Duke of Bridgewater, only to have it immediately topped by the other's claim to be Louis the Seventeenth, the lost Dauphin. It doesn't take Huck long to discern that the liars "warn't no kings nor dukes at all, but just low-down humbugs and frauds," but he raises no fuss, understanding by this time that society is sustained, peace is kept in the family, by lying tales. "If I never learnt nothing else out of Pap," Huck observes, "I learnt that the best way to get along with his kind of people is to let them have their own way" (p. 166). The Duke and the Dauphin, then, are replications of his own terrible father, representatives of the deceitful, pretending, and enslaving parent-culture to which, for the sake of family peace, Huck has learned to accommodate himself.

To protect Jim, whom the scoundrels immediately suspect of being a runaway slave, Huck must still another time subdue himself to the mode of pretense and tell his false identity tale (in which he is again, so *truly*, the orphan with no one but Jim to cling to). But the Duke soon devises new identities for Jim, supposedly also meant for protection but really bringing him into closer correspondence with the endangering condition of criminal and racial outcast, printing his picture on a "Reward" poster to be used when they want to claim him as their captive or making him up to represent a "sick Arab." None of the Duke and the Dauphin's lies can have any effect, in the end, but destruction—it is they who soon enough will collect a forty-dollar reward for turning Jim in.

The inventions of the Duke and the Dauphin elaborate Twain's ridicule of the formulas of society. Religion, the object of satiric contempt in almost everything Twain wrote from *Innocents Abroad* to *The Mysterious Stranger*, is immediately represented not only by the campmeeting sermon but also by the King's pose as repentant pirate, itself reminiscent of Pap's earlier posturing as repentant sinner. At the Wilks funeral, again, the false piety of society at large is only echoed by the hypocrisy of the King posing as the preacher uncle from Sheffield. The funeral sermon of the Reverend Hobson is less significant to his audience than the racket of the dog who has caught a rat in the cellar of the house, and at the auction of the Wilks property the King is on hand, "looking his level piousest . . . chipping in a little Scripture, now and then, or a little goody-goody saying" (p. 249) to the general edification.

But the most significant pretenses of the Duke and the Dauphin are parodic of language itself. The garbled Shakespeare speeches may seem tedious unless we realize that Twain has undercut the dignity of the most profound passages by mixing lines that almost coalesce; all coherence is mocked when one's ear is lulled into accepting the false connectedness of "To be or not to be; that is the bare bodkin/That makes calamity of so long life," (p. 179) and so on. Similarly, the coherence of history is a little later made ridiculous by Huck when he undertakes to explain to Jim that "kings is mostly rapscallions" (p. 199), mixing the Domesday Book and the Arabian Nights, the lives of Henry VIII and the Duke of Wellington, and conflating the mistresses of Henry II, Edward IV, and Charles II.

The question of language as the source of deceits and fictions is crucial, and Twain seems willing to turn even upon the colloquial style he has reserved for Huck's monologue and to show that it, too, can be the container of corruption and conventionality. At Bricksville, that devastating second look at St. Petersburg, the common men who exchange their banalities as they lounge along the filthy main street are quite deserving of the contempt of Colonel Sherburn who, like another Grangerford, has shot down the drunken lout Boggs out of offended dignity. The lecture he delivers to the crowd that thinks it wants to lynch him is couched in a style as formally correct as it is coldly superior in logic and truth to that of his hearers. But the Duke and the Dauphin are capable of parodying all styles, high and low. Their final caper, the attempt to fleece the Wilks family, exhibits them as polite gentlemen from the birthplace of the idea of the gentleman, old England, while constantly revealing, as though through the rents in their shoddy costumes, their true coarseness. The speeches of the King—"tears and flapdoodle" (p. 212), as Huck says—are never more deliciously comic versions of the rhetoric of high occasions than when they focus on a malapropism, his use of the word *orgies*. When he even offers a pseudo-etymology to justify it, Huck declares, "He was the *worst* I ever struck" (p. 217). Yet their imperfect command of their roles proves their undoing, for it is their speech that distinguishes them from the genuine English relatives and gives the cue to Doctor Robinson.

To foil the plotters Huck must rouse himself from his customary passivity and, devising a plot himself, make a confidante of Mary Jane so that she may witness to the truth after he has escaped. He knows that his plot is in the Tom Sawyer mode, but beneath Tom's purity of impracticality and superfluous style. "I judged I had done it pretty neat—I reckoned Tom Sawyer couldn't a done it no neater himself," says Huck, though he admits, "Of course he would a throwed more style into it, but I can't do that very handy, not being brung up to it" (pp. 248–49). His stratagem has rested on truth rather than falsity, an unorthodox procedure indeed. As he reflects after his revelation to Mary Jane:

> I reckon a body that ups and tells the truth when he is in a tight place, is taking considerable many risks, though I ain't had no experience, and can't say for certain; but it looks so to me, anyway; and yet here's a case where I'm blest if it don't look to me like the truth is better, and actuly *safer* than a lie. I must lay it by in my mind, and think it over some time or other, it's so kind of strange and unregular. I never see nothing like it. Well, I says to myself at last,

I'm agoing to chance it; I'll up and tell the truth this time, though it does seem most like setting down on a kag of powder and touching it off just to see where you'll go to. (P. 240)

To tell the truth—not to "make up a story"—is, of course, to deny the superiority of fiction to fact, to deny the validity of pretense, to deny Tom Sawyer. Huck's resolution to dispense with falsehood this time fills him with misgiving, goes against his sense of what he *ought* to do, and is a crisis in which his heart triumphs over his conscience, anticipating the more famous crisis that immediately follows. Before this happens he turns, ineptly, to lying again, trying to describe life in the pretended English home of the fake Wilks uncles and himself, and Levi Bell, the lawyer, observes, "I reckon you ain't used to lying, it don't seem to come handy; what you want is practice. You do it pretty awkward" (p. 254).

He makes his most famous repudiation of lying when he discovers that he cannot pretend to himself that he wants to turn Jim in: "You can't pray a lie" (p. 270), he observes, and, though he proceeds to write the letter to Miss Watson, he decides to damn himself and "steal Jim out of slavery again" (p. 272), and so tears up the letter. Paradoxically, he is full of inventive ingenuity on behalf of the truth to which he has committed himself and successfully talks his way out of obstruction by the two knaves as he makes his way to the Phelps Farm—he must still resort to life-saving fiction to combat a world of lies.

When he arrives at the Phelps Farm in Chapter 32, he is once again in one of those moods of melancholy transcendence to which I have referred and even wishes himself dead as the breeze whispering of dead spirits quivers the leaves. And he is ready for his last relapse into the character of Tom Sawyer, ready to accept Tom's name and serve Tom's imagination. His own existential truthfulness, his independence of the lies and the fictions of the social world, must be surrendered. But if what I have been maintaining is true, we should not be surprised. The last ten chapters are no reversal, after all. If Huck is to survive he must reattach himself to his world and to its lies, fabricate the self out of them. At this moment, indeed, Huck is, for once, without a prepared selfhood. He is a ghost without a name, listening to the words of others for a cue to his identity: "I wanted to get them [the children] out to one side, and pump them a little, and find out who I was" (p. 281). When he is at last "recognized" as Tom, he is overjoyed: "if they was joyful, it warn't nothing to what I was; for it was like being born again. I was so glad to find out who I was. . . . Being Tom Sawyer was easy and comfortable" (pp. 282–83). The exhausting struggle for free formlessness of being is over, and he is easy and comfortable in the role of the inventor of fictional selves and stories, Tom Sawyer.

Tom himself greets Huck as an impersonating ghost and warns him, "Don't you play nothing on me, because I wouldn't on you" (p. [284]), which is a joke, we will realize, for Tom *is* about to "play" a joke on Huck—one of those practical jokes that hurt—to pretend to be a "nigger-stealer," willing to help him free Jim. It is Tom's deception underlying all the deceptions the boys will now practice together upon others. Meanwhile, he welcomes Huck back, in effect, to the robber-band. He is full of praise when he hears how Huck made his escape from Pap by the faked murder: "I warn't ever murdered at all—I played it on them," says Huck with some pride, suggesting by "them" some vaguely general social audience. Tom calls Huck's story, "a grand adventure, and mysterious" (p. 285). As Huck says, "it hit him where he lived" (p. 285).

So, under the rule of Tom's imagination, made-up history, appearance as costume, and theatrical improvisation all flourish. Tom pretends to be someone else before he assumes the "true" (but really still false) identity of Sid. When the Phelpses see him at their door, says Huck, he has "his store clothes on, and an audience—and that was always nuts for Tom Sawyer. In them circumstances it warn't no trouble to him to throw in an amount of style that was suitable" (p. 286). So, first he claims to be William Thompson, a young traveler from Hicksville, Ohio—which then appears to be one of those practical jokes so relished by the Sawyer imagination when he "reveals" himself to Aunt Sally as Sid. She declares, "I'd be willing to stand a thousand such jokes to have you here. Well, to think of that performance" (p. 289), not realizing that "Sid's" disclosure is but another layer of performance. Unlike Huck's disguises, Tom's are prompted not by need but by his insatiable appetite for histrionics.

Sleights and disguises are all, indeed, that we will ever get from Tom, who is not, when finally revealed as himself, ever reduced to a final essence, an unalterable core, since he is always precisely no more than what he appears. Huck is awed as Tom begins to develop schemes for the liberation of Jim, and he yearns to complete his own submergence in the mode of the protean imagination, already signaled by the adoption of Tom's name: "if I had Tom Sawyer's head, I wouldn't trade it off to be a duke, nor mate of a steamboat, nor clown in a circus, nor nothing I can think of" (p. 294). No particular role can offer more delight than the artist's, for his is the capacity to impersonate all roles. For the artist there is, really, no "authenticity."

Huck realizes that his own capacity for creating plot is rudimentary compared to Tom's. His plan for freeing Jim has the defect of mere functionality (as Tom says, "it's *too* blame' simple; there ain't nothing *to* it"), whereas Tom's own, Huck says, "was worth fifteen of mine, for style, and would make Jim just as free a man as mine would, and maybe get us all killed besides" (p. 294). The fantasy that entails *real* danger, even the threat of death, is the best of all, as Tom had long before pointed out to his boy-robber companions when he insisted that they were highwaymen who "killed people" and could get killed themselves, and not mere burglars. The Grangerford fantasy proved its excellence by its murderous—and suicidal—consequences. And this elegant plan of Tom's will nearly get Jim and themselves killed, as it turns out.

When Huck suggests with plain practicality that Jim escape through the cabin window, Tom reproaches him, "I should *hope* we can find a way that's a little more complicated than *that,* Huck Finn," and proposes that they dig the prisoner out. At the house, the back-door fastened by a latch-string "warn't romantical enough for

Tom Sawyer: no way would do him but he must climb up the lightning-rod" (p. 297). Tom is actually distressed by the altogether too "easy and awkward" conditions they confront—"It makes it so rotten difficult to get up a difficult plan. There ain't no watchman to be drugged—now there *ought* to be a watchman. There ain't even a dog to give a sleeping-mixture to. And there's Jim chained by one leg, with a ten-foot chain, to the leg of his bed: why, all you got to do is lift up the bedstead and slip off the chain" (p. [300]).

The absence of the conventional plot ingredients enforces artistic creation: "You got to invent *all* the difficulties." But the more to be invented the more honor to the artistic imagination: "there's more honor in getting him out through a lot of difficulties and dangers, where there warn't one of them furnished you by the people who it was their duty to furnish them, and you had to contrive them all out of your own head" (p. 301). Of course, getting them out of one's own literary head means getting them from the "best authorities" and examples—among whom Tom names Baron Trenck, Casanova, Cellini, King Henry IV of France, and Dumas's *The Man in the Iron Mask* and *The Count of Monte Cristo,* getting the idea for titling his escapade on "evasion" from Dumas's *L'Évasion du Duc de Beaufort.* Tom is proud to claim an authority for everything—the rope ladder that Jim has to hide in his bed, the "journal" that Jim must write on his shirt, though he can't write, and so on.

When Tom finally agrees to use pick and shovel instead of case knives to dig Jim out, he admits it isn't moral, reversing the sense of *morality* to make it mean aesthetic impracticality, inefficacy. Huck's stubborn anti-aesthetic *im*morality (as Tom would judge it) makes him insist, "Picks is the thing, moral or no moral; and as for me, I don't care shucks for the morality of it, nohow. When I start in to steal a nigger, or a watermelon, or a Sunday-school book, I ain't no ways particular how it's done so it's done. What I want is my nigger; or what I want is my watermelon; or what I want is my Sunday-school book; and if a pick's the handiest thing, that's the thing I'm agoing to dig that nigger or that watermelon or that Sunday-school book out with; and I don't give a dead rat what the authorities thinks about it nuther" (p. 310). *Morality* here is absolutely synonymous with *conscience* as Huck has used the latter word, the "deformed" conscience of social modes that reproves the instinctive promptings of his heart.

Even Tom must yield, somewhat, to the practical, though in that case the pretense of impracticality must be maintained. Picks must be thought of as case knives and stairs as the lightning rod it is really too difficult to climb. But wherever possible the complications of imagination are to be preferred to the merely efficacious, especially if the former are *less* efficacious. Jim, who could be freed by the quick application of a cold chisel to his shackles, must be subjected to the tedious, the distressing, even the dangerous devices of Sawyerism. "Tom was in high spirits. He said it was the best fun he ever had in his life, and the most intellectural; and said if he only could see his way to it we would keep it up all the rest of our lives and leave Jim to our children to get out" (p. 313). Jim must be a proper literary prisoner, with tools or rope ladders smuggled to him in a pie, must scratch inscriptions and a coat of arms on the wall, and must adopt a pet rat and plant a garden, however incomprehensible these things are to him. And the Phelps household must be thrown into confusion by the disappearance of sheets and shirts and spoons and the escape of the rats and snakes the boys have collected. It is all almost as tiresome to the reader as it is to Jim himself, and even to Huck.

The warnings and anonymous letters that Tom now insists upon prove, however, the source not merely of "style" but of near disaster, though perhaps one should say that high style requires a flouting of the utilitarian to the point of a deadly indifference. Jim and his two liberators make it to the raft despite the real pursuit they have generated, and even Jim must admit, "It 'uz planned beautiful, en it'uz *done* beautiful; en dey ain't *nobody* kin git up a plan dat's mo' mixed-up en splendid den what dat one wuz." Tom himself is positively delighted that make-believe has almost had fatal consequences: "Tom was the gladdest of all, because he had a bullet in the calf of his leg" (p. 344). "Boys," he says, "we done it elegant!" (p. 344). Tom is consistent enough to instruct that the doctor now needed must be kidnapped and brought blindfolded, but Huck is practical enough to employ his own lower kind of make-believe in a story about a brother hurt in a hunting accident. This tale, though not very convincing, is a correct and consistent summary of what actually happened: "He had a dream," Huck tells the doctor, "and it shot him." And the doctor comments, "Singular dream" (p. [347]). Indeed, dreams or fictions play real and sometimes dire roles in our lives, as the dreams of the Grangerfords and Shepherdsons have already done in the novel, or, as Twain probably thought, the dreams of North and South had done in the country's recent history.

Yet, now that the Evasion is ending, Huck is ready to be reconciled to the dreams by which life sustains itself. Aunt Sally, it seems, is much nicer than the widow, though the cyclicity of the plot tells us that she is really a duplication of that matriarchal authority from which he has been in flight. Huck cannot stand any longer the deception he has practiced on her and swears to himself that he "wouldn't never do nothing to grieve her any more" (p. 354). Society now offers him its most self-flattering versions of itself. Though Jim is put back into chains, he is acknowledged, after the doctor's report, to be "a nigger ... worth a thousand dollars—and kind treatment, too," and the Phelpses take one or two of his chains off and let him have meat and greens with his bread and water. Huck no longer thinks of Jim's freedom—or of his own.

So it is time for Tom's revelation that Jim has been free all along because of Miss Watson's will. It does not matter that her death-bed repentance for her resolution to sell him downriver is blatantly improbable, a formula of cheap romance. As for Tom's commitment, even temporarily, to the project of setting a free nigger free, it is clear, now, that this has been only another of his make-believe adventures, a fiction. If it had succeeded it would only have been the start of further adventures; the three would have continued downriver on the raft and had "adventures plumb to the mouth of the river," and only then, perhaps, would Tom and

Huck tell Jim that he was a free man and take him "back up home on a steamboat, in style, and pay him [forty dollars] for his lost time" (p. [364]). Tom does give Jim forty dollars for being a patient prisoner. Is it only an accident that this is the same sum for which the Duke and the Dauphin had sold him back into slavery? Huck, at any rate, is ready for "more howling adventures," and he will even be member enough of respectable society to be able to purchase the necessary outfit, his six thousand dollars having been kept safe for him all this while by Judge Thatcher.

With deliberate irony the last chapters overturn any expectations we have cherished, despite Twain's numerous hints and warnings, that the search for a meaningful design in experience is anything but a game. That Jim was free all along makes Tom's Evasion properly titled. His plan had been, as he would claim, "beautifully" purposeless, an evasion of the whole issue of personal freedom. And all Huck's efforts, earlier, to help Jim gain freedom, those struggles, even against conscience, to stand by his friend, to protect him from those who would keep him a slave—these too, in retrospect, become plot without motive, pure art or adventure in the Tom Sawyer sense. Huck has risked social selfhood, the only identity society allows, in his passage down the river, but now he accepts once more his role as Tom Sawyer's lieutenant, becomes the willing accomplice in the sleights of the imagination.

NOTES

All citations to *Adventures of Huckleberry Finn* are taken here from the reproduction of the first American edition of 1885 included in *The Art of* Huckleberry Finn: *Text, Sources, Criticism,* edited by Walter Blair and Hamlin Hill (San Francisco: Chandler Publishing Co., 1962).

[1] Compare *Adventures of Huckleberry Finn,* ed. Sculley Bradley et al. (New York: W. W. Norton & Co., 1977), n. 1, p. 7.

[2] *Other Inquisitions: 1937–1952* (New York: Simon & Schuster, 1968), p. 46.

[3] A considerable literature has accumulated on this point, but the most famous expression of dissatisfaction with Twain's ending of the novel may be the comment of Ernest Hemingway (in *Green Hills of Africa* [New York: Charles Scribner's Sons, 1935], p. 22): "If you read it you must stop where the Nigger Jim is stolen from the boys. That is the real end. The rest is cheating." Bernard DeVoto wrote of the ending, "Mark was once more betrayed. He intended a further chapter in his tireless attack on romanticism, especially Southern romanticism, and nothing in his mind or training enabled him to understand that this extemporized burlesque was a defacement of his pure work" (*Mark Twain's America* [1932], excerpted in *Huckleberry Finn,* ed. Bradley et al., pp. 302–3). Twain's denouement was defended, though only casually, by Lionel Trilling, who remarked in 1948 that it permitted Huck to "return to his anonymity, to give up his role of hero which he prefers, for he is modest in all things," and by T. S. Eliot in 1950: "Huck Finn must come from nowhere and be bound for nowhere . . . he is in a state of nature as detached as the state of the saint." In 1953 Leo Marx responded to both in an essay maintaining that Twain had "jeopardized the significance of the entire novel" by an ending in which Huck's search for freedom is surrendered and his growth of character denied (all three essays reproduced in *Huckleberry Finn,* ed. Bradley et al., pp. 318–49). To Marx there have been a number of important replies, among them those of Frank Baldanza ("The Structure of *Huckleberry Finn,*" *American Literature* 27 [1955]: 347–55) and Richard P. Adams ("The Unity and Coherence of *Huckleberry Finn,*" *Tulane Studies in English* 6 [1956]: 87–103), who argue for the coherence of the whole book including the ending as a result of rhythms of repetition and variation and patterns of

imagery. My own argument for the meaningfulness of Twain's ending finds a start in the statement of James M. Cox that "after Huck reached his unknown destination, the Phelps farm, the only terms on which he could exist were Tom's terms." Cox sees the ending as a "sad initiation" into respectable society ("Remarks on the Sad Initiation of Huckleberry Finn," *Southern Review* 62 [1954]: 389–405).
[4] "The Relation between Point of View and Style in the Works of Mark Twain," *Style in Prose Fiction,* English Institute Essays: 1958 (New York: Columbia University Press, 1959), p. 165.
[5] Compare Walter Blair, *Mark Twain and Huck Finn* (Berkeley: University of California Press, 1960), p. 60.
[6] Blair, ibid., has demonstrated the relation of both novels to "the literary flux." Compare pp. 58–67, 111–30.
[7] Henry Nash Smith, *Mark Twain: The Development of a Writer* (New York: Atheneum, 1967), p. 81.
[8] In 1895 Twain wrote concerning Huck's decision in Chapter 16 not to betray Jim, "I should exploit the proposition that in a crucial moral emergency, a sound heart is a safer guide than an ill-trained conscience. I sh'd support this doctrine with a chapter from a book of mine where a sound heart and a deformed conscience come into collision and conscience suffers defeat" (Blair, *Mark Twain and Huck Finn,* p. 143).
[9] *Life on the Mississippi* (New York: Signet, 1961), p. 267.
[10] Smith, *Mark Twain.*
[11] See ibid., chap. 5.
[12] The parallels with *Don Quixote* were pointed out by Olin H. Moore, "Mark Twain and *Don Quixote,*" *PMLA* 37 (1922): 337–38.
[13] *Strains of Discord: Studies in Literary Openness* (Ithaca: Cornell University Press, 1958), p. 73.
[14] *Life on the Mississippi,* p. 267.
[15] I have elaborated this interpretation in *"Huckleberry Finn:* Journey without End," *Virginia Quarterly Review* 58, no. 3 (1982): 253–67.
[16] Blair, *Mark Twain and Huck Finn,* p. 117.
[17] Ibid., p. 229.

Lee Clark Mitchell

THE AUTHORITY OF LANGUAGE IN *HUCKLEBERRY FINN*

Tom Sawyer notoriously usurps the plot in *Adventures of Huckleberry Finn* and impairs the novel's moral structure by setting a "free nigger free." Or so many readers have claimed. The reenslavement for sheer *adventure* of a man Tom knows is legally free seems on the face of it merely grotesque; and Huck's bewildered assistance only diminishes his earlier triumphant decision to "go to hell" on behalf of Jim. Moreover, as Laurence B. Holland cogently argues, the timing of Miss Watson's manumitting will a full month before Huck's bout with conscience grants a merely "ritual" status to the scene and a tone of "futility" to the conclusion.[1]

Our discomfort, however, results less from a betrayal of Huck's decision, or even from its suppressed irrelevance, than from the lurking suspicion that his decision and the ending do not differ all that much. While we cringe at Tom's "Evasion" scheme for its deliberate and gratuitous cruelty, we cringe even more as we realize how starkly it enacts questionable terms in Huck's famous gesture. After all, Tom does no more than exploit to the fullest the principle behind Huck's reliance on "right" feeling—a principle that justifies behavior as well for nearly everyone else in the novel. Far from forming an "Evasion" of the ethical model that Huck supposedly represents, the concluding "raft of trouble" drifts to the limits of the novel's problematic implications for conduct. Even more radically, the ending confirms how dependent upon language are feelings themselves, and suggests in the process that the authority of words dictates far more than the shape of particular events. Discursive conventions actively structure the terms of personal identity in the novel—a novel that, as much as anything, is about the authoring of a self. Through the course of his narrative, Huck will create himself no less willfully than anyone else, and will do so in ways that come to seem no more self-justifiable.

The sequence of the following essay, from morality to identity to language, charts a progression among Huck's most cherished certainties about what it is possible to assume. Each one of these categories seems to him somehow more

From *New Essays on* Adventures of Huckleberry Finn, edited by Louis J. Budd (Cambridge: Cambridge University Press, 1985), pp. 83–106.

"natural" than the one preceding, and he confidently believes each stands more or less independent of the other two. Yet his narrative itself reveals language and identity (no less than morality) as social conventions, whose arbitrary and interdependent status is fully exposed only at the Phelps farm. Contrary to what most readers have suspected, then, Tom's "Evasion" appropriately concludes the novel, in terms of both formal coherence and moral obscurity. This clear thematic appropriateness notwithstanding, Tom invariably has seemed less scrupulous than Huck. And it is that falsely invidious distinction we must address first, since it results from a narrative strategy that disguises the novel's troubling resistance to fixed categories, whether moral, psychological, or linguistic.

I

That strategy begins in the boyish innocence that allows a river-rat to describe manners and mores with comic incomprehension. When Huck remarks on Miss Watson's prayerful "grumble" over food, or wonders at an undertaker's "softy soothering ways," or admires Emmeline Grangerford's lugubrious "style," the social construction of reality tumbles into view. Sometimes ridiculous, otherwise cruel conventions of behavior emerge *as* mere conventions, the more compellingly as Huck remains steadfastly oblivious to the very possibility that they are arbitrary, not natural. Yet everyone else is likewise oblivious. Miss Watson, for example, never doubts a biblical exegesis that leads her to pray in the closet, while with firmly clenched guns the Grangerfords and Shepherdsons admire a sermon on brotherly love. In obedience to the dictates of a "gentleman's" code, Colonel Sherburn will shoot a drunken Boggs. From Huck's perspective, social convention is nearly always unpredictable, violating life and sense with equal ease. Everywhere and at every level of seriousness, people justify behavior by assuming its naturalness; and because things turn out as expected, they assume their categories must be right. Only Huck's solemnly wondering gaze exposes the choplogic of such categorical imperatives.

Of course, Huck cannot question even circular reasoning, since he has yet to learn the power of intellectual abstraction. But as a child, he can impulsively reject the more brutal dictates of social convention, and he does define with Jim an apparent alternative to the self-centered, self-authorizing pattern of southern society. Their idyllically drifting hours together teach Huck a goal that should justify action—one best expressed after the squabbling King and Duke first rock the raft, only to make up: "Jim and me was pretty glad to see it. It took away all the uncomfortableness, and we felt mighty good over it, because it would a been a miserable business to have any unfriendliness on the raft; for what you want, above all things, on a raft, is for everybody to be satisfied, and feel right and kind towards the others." Huck accommodates the two men to preserve the peace, not naively or out of misplaced respect. He sees through their fraudulent claims, unlike Jim, but nonetheless defers for the general welfare.

However attractive at first glance, this conjunction of Christian charity with Rousseauistic natural virtue is deeply troubling—far more so, in fact, than its quietism suggests. The problem is a logical one, and results from an inherent conflict between concepts Huck unwittingly elides in his concern to "feel right." The phrase collapses together antithetical categories by implying that emotion can legislate a standard of reason, that ethical issues can be measured affectively. Yet no external vantage point is left when morality depends so exclusively upon the authority of the self, and ethics therefore is reduced to a series of circular considerations. Huck's justification of riverside thefts, for example—"We warn't feeling just right, before that, but it was all comfortable now"—wryly masks a logic as self-confirming as that expressed by the Duke and the King, by Pap, indeed by the shore world in general. From the beginning, Huck's good "feelings" translate into considerations that can too easily be self-serving, whether of the physical comfort in smoking, eating, and wearing old clothes, or the "thrift" in refusing to spend money for the circus— "there ain't no use in *wasting* it on them." A gentle humor appears to redeem his excuses, but he transgresses convention and breaks the law out of criteria as self-reflexive as everyone else's.

That Huck at times acts self-servingly or immorally is hardly consequential, however. For the crucial point is that feeling itself—any feeling whatever—cannot serve to justify. Ethics and emotion should not be confused, since the terms by which we make sense of the one differ radically from the criteria for the other. And yet Huck consistently confuses them. Take, for example, the defrauding of the Wilks girls: His emotional barometer registers first "ornery and low down and mean," then "ruther blue," and finally "dreadful glad," once he has recovered the money. While these sympathetic responses prompt him to actions that we interpret favorably, we do so despite the fact that ethical considerations are masked by the emotional drama itself. Huck laudably helps the Wilks girls because they are kind, although their kindness to him has no logical bearing on their claim to the money. The feelings that lead him to assist, in other words, are irrelevant to the girls' legal rights.

Irrelevant as emotion is to ethics, Huck nonetheless repeatedly confuses the two. Earlier, for instance, in a playful mood, he convinces Jim that a real fog was merely a dream, only then to learn that trust and good faith give greater pleasure than teasing lies. The premise again disguised by the scene, however, is that affective standards, not logical ones, have become the measure of moral conduct.[2] Huck, of course, cannot be expected to know this, since the narrative requires a childish sensibility ever ignorant of moral abstractions. Yet that strategy itself has a disturbing effect. For by celebrating an inability to distinguish the personal from the social—his own desire from collective right—the novel reduces Huck's behavior to the same self-confirming logic as everyone else's. Morally commendable as he may seem, the novel provides no terms by which that status can be confirmed. And in the end, the "right feelings" of a "sound heart" seem as arbitrary and capricious as the cruel conventions of town.

Most severely testing the category of "feeling right" are Huck's three encounters with a troubled conscience. The first, dismissively brief scene reveals only his fear of ignominy: Even though "people would call me a low-down Ablitionist and despise me," he promises to keep Jim's escape a secret. In Chapter 16, when friendship conflicts with the bad "conscience" that had prompted him to inform on Jim, Huck predictably opts for "whichever come handiest." And given an emotional economy in which "the wages is just the same," he vows to go on doing so. Here as elsewhere, the narrative strategy precludes the questions implicit in that vow: How will he determine his desire? What constitutes a "sound heart"? Why prefer one action over another given contradictory feelings of equal weight?

Huck's third bout with conscience only compounds these questions and further exacerbates the issue. Having considered writing North to save Jim, he rejects the idea for three reasons: Miss Watson might resent her slave's ingratitude; Jim would be universally despised; and, most importantly (in a reversion to the first scene's rationale), "it would get all around, that Huck Finn helped a nigger to get his freedom." He therefore attempts to escape his "wicked and low-down and ornery" feeling by trying to "pray a lie." The impulse might seem an improbable one, given his professed theological skepticism, but here most dramatically the novel shows that feelings are not logical. Nor are they appropriate, as he finds when his effort all too predictably fails, a failure that in turn prompts him to prepare for prayer by the ploy of drafting an experimental letter. The letter's curious effect is to leave Huck feeling "light as a feather"—curious, because the letter itself is responsible for eliciting a condition of grace, instead of forming merely the preliminary to a prayerful state: "I felt good and all washed clean of sin for the first time I had ever felt so in my life." The narrative has again conflated categories, masking the fact that Huck never intended to mail the letter that has left him "all washed clean of sin." He gains absolution, as it were, despite a contrition that is only partial. Still, the result is that Huck recalls Jim's loving-kindness, and in the "close place" dividing conscience from heart, decides to rip up the letter and "go to hell."

This crucial scene dramatizes as nowhere else the problematic aspects of Huck's behavior, by exposing the novel's radical equation of emotion, morality, and language. Quite simply, Huck's "decision" rests on nothing more than feeling. The "conscience" of a slave-holding South, however evil, represents at least a coherent social system, just as the Grangerford-Shepherdson feud illustrates a system of prescriptive rules, however vicious. Not so Huck's seemingly humane alternative, which lacks either system or logic that might link "feeling" to something outside the self. Social conventions alone allow behavior to be both anticipated and justified, and only by organizing raw feeling into a set of predictive categories can conduct then be measured. Lacking any terms other than the narrowly personal, Huck can judge action by nothing but his own pulse. That pulse may indicate a "sound heart" on the one hand, and beat calmly to what we sense as "right feelings" on the other, but the metaphor itself reveals a morality far more circular than the conventional ethos of "conscience." Even more troubling from a larger perspective is the lack of constraints on the self. For when feeling dictates value rather than the other way around, an unmoored self risks being battered by its own inconsistent energies. This may explain why the "awful" words of Huck's supposed moral triumph seem to emerge independently, as if unintended: ". . . but they was said. And I let them stay said." Conversely, when southern values earlier impelled him to identify Jim, "the words wouldn't come"—an experience repeated when he tries to "pray a lie." Unable to structure emotion through language, Huck finds that language at times opposes "conscience," at other times expresses it.

II

But Huck's inability to tie morality to language does not result simply from his dependence on feeling. Language in the novel more generally seems free-floating, especially as a form of self-definition. People everywhere adapt selves and adopt identities all by mere assertion: A con man becomes the late Dauphin, then in turn a pirate, Edmund Kean the Elder, the Reverend Elexander Blodgett, and Harvey Wilks; Jim becomes a "sick Arab" just as Tom becomes Sid; and Huck becomes Sarah Williams, George Peters, and George Jaxon, then Adolphus the valet, and finally Tom. Aunt Polly alone relies on ocular proof, sternly claiming to know Tom "when I *see* him"; yet her metonymic appearance as a mere pair of spectacles suggests that her logic persuades less than her tone. She knows Tom only by sight in a novel where trust in one's senses is unreliable at best and at worst quite dangerous. As the con men realize all too well, desire invariably mediates vision. An expectant Aunt Sally, for instance, actively creates the prospect of Tom out of Huck, who in the event can only perplexedly affirm her opening query: "It's *you* at last!—*ain't* it?" Later, she embraces the real Tom after his casual assurance that he is Sid, and continues the process of social creation—as the Wilks sisters had earlier kissed the two frauds, and likewise granted them a social authority.

Indeed, selves proliferate wherever desire emerges. Blithely inventing a series of identities, the Duke and the King gain beds, two servants, hundreds of dollars, and at least one bottle of whiskey.[3] The King talks the Duke "blind" at first, and then "warbling and warbling right along . . . he was actuly beginning to believe what he was saying, *himself.*" Yet although both only temporarily convince a town to take "empty names and facts . . . for *proofs,*" their exposure hardly gives comfort to those hoping for an assurance of "actuly" true identities. The novel provides after all not a shred of evidence proving that the real Wilks brothers "are who we say we are." Despite a full chapter of narrative suspense, they are vindicated by neither writing sample nor alleged tattoo. If "you couldn't tell them from the real kind," as Huck had earlier observed of the two frauds, the converse holds with at least equal force in a novel rarely given to evidential "proofs." " 'Here's your two sets o' heirs to old Peter Wilks,' " yells the crowd; " 'you pays your money and you takes your choice!' "

Huck, however, seems oblivious to the possibility, unaware of how readily language creates selves. Ever the naive realist, he continues to assume that words stand transparently for things, and believes in a literalism so severe that even prayer continues to mystify him—"I couldn't see no advantage about it."[4] The irony, of course, is that Huck himself appears as no more than a voice in the text. Constitutionally unable to accept the broader implications of figurative discourse, he cannot appreciate the terms of his own novel in which language everywhere shapes experience. His very lies assume that words mirror reality rather than constitute the way things are; and with a scrupulous sensitivity to context, he fabricates tales only for self-survival (as when he quick-wittedly misleads Pap), or to protect others (as with Mrs. Judith Loftus, the slave-hunters, and Joanna Wilks), or to find Jim. True, he too seems at times "to believe what he was saying, *himself.*" But he is unable to recognize the ways in which "false" identities do alter his "true" self—an inability that both results from and contributes to his confidence in that self.

Even his dramatically experienced rebirths encourage no self-conscious sense of change. His resurrection on Jackson's Island, for example, follows the cabin death he stages for Pap, just as later he is reborn to Jim after returning to the raft. At the Phelps farm, the process recurs most explicitly when Aunt Sally suddenly names him Tom: "If they was joyful, it warn't nothing to what I was; for it was like being born again, I was so glad to find out who I was." Huck's three rebirths form a telling progression, from the physical through the social to the linguistic; and mired in words at last, he cleverly abets Sally in creating himself as Tom. Yet comically as he exposes here the set categories of language, the scene's humor depends on the exposure being unwitting, on Huck's being a mere victim of linguistic convention. His relief, in fact, results from discovering not who he is but whom others take him to be, since again he assumes that an unaltered self persists under an infinitely flexible mask. That romantic faith in a unique being somehow independent of behavior—of an inner self untouched by its expression—remains steadfast right through to the closing "Yours Truly."

Such confidence in an empirical self seems in part a bold front, however, masking a more general uncertainty in the novel between Huck's dual identities as character and author. Deny the latter role as he will, he finds it increasingly difficult to hide his authorship. Of course, an unhesitating narrative voice bespeaks an unquestionably unified self—one that must know its feelings precisely because the self at that moment *is* those feelings. And Huck seems no more able to deviate from his voice than language can veer from the illusion of referentiality. But the point (and the problem) is that his wonderfully immediate voice is indeed an illusion, fostered in the novel by his radical conflation of dual roles. Huck disguises the gap between past and present, between himself as actor and as recollective writer, by emphasizing a single identity as the coherent, fully self-consistent "I" of the text. As we shall see later, however, the narrative inadvertently belies his efforts, and reveals despite itself the evolution of an authorial voice.[5]

Despite the book's spoken modulations, in other words—so clearly heard we could almost assume it was recited—the most salient feature of the prose is that it is written. We think of Henry James's late novels, by contrast, as too plainly written and rewritten, although as it happens they were each dictated. The reason for this is that James's characters so often confess an inability to get things "right," doing so nonetheless with such verbal adroitness that we are ever aware of the shaping powers of language. Huck, on the other hand, deftly masks his discursive skills by never doubting that things are as he says. And again, the reason he does so is because he must seem somehow innocent of literary conventions—the very conventions of which he has been "sivilized" by writing the book. This admittedly characterizes a structure common to first-person narratives of the past; bridging the disjunction between events and their recounting, they recapture antecedent ignorance from a perspective of recollective knowledge. Pip in *Great Expectations,* say, or Ishmael in *Moby Dick,* or Miles Coverdale in *The Blithedale Romance:* Each suppresses and alters information in the necessary process of establishing a narrative line. Yet none of these suppressions approaches that of *Huckleberry Finn,* in part because none of those novels so forthrightly represents the conflict of innocence and convention. Nor do the narrators themselves enter the recollected past so transparently as to make their authorial roles seem to disappear.

Huck's very narrative strategy, in fact, directly controverts his alleged faith in an integrated self that might stand somehow outside of society. The novel, that is, divides an acting self committed to the truth and ready to lie only for humane reasons, from an authoring self that willfully compounds those lies in order, as Tom says, merely to "make . . . talk." Of course, this only expresses in less charitable terms the conventional observation that Huck's limited comprehension contributes to the novel's dramatic irony: He sees bifocally, doing right by judging wrong. Yet that formulation disguises Huck's fundamental desire to disguise his narrative authority—his wish to tell his story at the same time that he denies any responsibility for doing so. He cannot express the desire forthrightly, for the expression itself would belie the claim; but the impulse sometimes betrays itself, as when he falls asleep during his own narrative. Unlike the retrospective view taken in the "go to hell" scene and sustained in his concluding "I slept the night through," these scenes effectively mask Huck's role as author standing outside the text. They allow him as passive character instead to shape temporal gaps into narrative suspense. Chapter 6 closes with him guarding his drunken Pap, for example, and then Chapter 7 begins: " 'Git up! what you 'bout!' I opened my eyes and looked around, trying to make out where I was."[6]

Yet Huck's authorial status disappears more dramatically when as character he suddenly loses his breath—a speechlessness, indeed voicelessness, that occurs in the novel with surprising regularity. Sophia Grangerford, for instance, suddenly embraces him for having acted as a go-between: "I was a good deal astonished, but when I got my breath I asked her. . . ." And a few pages later, he escapes from the feuding families only to discover that "the raft was gone! My souls, but I was scared! I couldn't get my breath for most a minute."[7] The first-person immediacy of Huck's experience is intensified in these breathless moments of narrative stasis. Perhaps especially in a novel that exists to "make ... talk," scenes that subvert speech paradoxically heighten the character's sensibility, and do so again at the expense of the author's controlling presence.

When Huck does at last catch his breath, he attempts further to confirm an authorial transparency by asserting the primacy of physical experience. Unlike Tom, who engages language as a play of signifiers, Huck at every point looks for verification to "reality." His relief that he swears on a dictionary, not a Bible, only seems to imply disrespect for the former; far from acknowledging the empty authority of words, his superstitious glance instead registers how fully he believes in their scriptural status. For him, they speak to an actual order beyond any conventional syntax or particular grammar. Fixed definitions tie words to a world that ever precedes them, and seems therefore more immediate.[8] Indeed, Huck at times authenticates the "reality" of experience by claiming that words too readily evoke painful experiences—as in the recollected horror of the Grangerford-Shepherdson feud. Elsewhere, he suggests the transparency of language by asserting that his adventures exceed descriptive powers, his own or anyone's.[9] Events always precede discourse for Huck, and language can do no more than turn us back to that prior order. By blinding us to the gap between life and history—by dissolving the distinction between an event and its recounting—he fosters an allusion that experience is everywhere fully present and unmediated.[10]

⟨. . .⟩ Although the novel depends nominally on an older Huck's memory, the fact that he has apparently matured not at all calls the very terms of memory into question. To put the matter simply, has a narrating Huck actually remembered what happened, or inadvertently "painted it up considerable"? When Aunt Sally claims to " 'disremember,' " or admits to being " 'most putrified with astonishment,' " or when Tom suggests Jim send a " 'message to let the world know where he's captivated,' " are the malapropisms theirs or Huck's? The point is that, given the narrative strategy, we are not meant to measure the distance a recollective Huck has come from his earlier naive expectations. The narrative's comic effectiveness depends precisely on his ignorance of solecisms, his complete lack of amusement at the play of language that everywhere serves private interests.

All these efforts notwithstanding, a retrospective Huck cannot help stumbling into view. Slips of expression reveal a narrative self, and even his authorial presence is confirmed by the notoriously misspelled "sivilized"—an obviously written, not spoken error.[11] At other times, he makes larger narrative missteps, as when a few chapters after using the word confidently, he seems altogether innocent of the meaning of "sivilized": "so cramped up and sivilized, as they call it." But when later knowledge slips into a narrative recounted months after the events, Huck's dual perspective breaks apart—precisely because the self assumed by "Huck" can no longer appear unified. His self-consciously retrospective tone in fact emerges clearly at least twice: first when, like Hank Morgan, he cannot scratch an itch—"Well, I've noticed that thing plenty of times since"—and second, following Mary Jane Wilks's departure—"I hain't ever seen her since, but I reckon I've thought of her a many and a many a million times."

More confusing is Huck's revelation upon first seeing Jim on Jackson's Island, when he admits to not being "afraid of *him* telling the people where I was." For Huck does not know yet that the slave is a runaway, as his subsequent surprise makes all too clear, and therefore can have no assurance that an exuberant Jim would not bear the glad tidings back to town. Likewise, late in the narrative he describes with knowing impatience Uncle Silas's "pretty long blessing"; but earlier, he had wondered why the widow should "grumble a little over the victuals, though there warn't really anything the matter with them." This progression certainly represents a gain in knowledge from Huck's point of view as a character (he now is familiar with the social ritual of grace before meals); but from his larger authorial perspective, the inconsistency suggests more narrative manipulation. And although manipulation of events for narrative suspense forms a basic convention of first-person accounts, manipulation of language does not.

The verbal slips that bring an authoring Huck to life reveal as well the novel's narrative law—the same expensive premise that structures Jim's story of bewitchery: "... every time he told it he spread it more and more." From the opening reminder ("without you have read a book") on through to Tom's concluding escapades, the novel assumes the constant expandability of stories. Huck breathes life into each of them, linking each into the circular narrative line of the novel—from the widow's account of Moses, to Jim's bewitched flight and his hairball prediction, to Tom's renditions of Scott and Cervantes, to Huck's school-prize account of George Washington, and many others. Once again, the expansive nature of these stories highlights Huck's authorial role, directing us from the narrative subject back to the narrating shaper. ⟨ . . . ⟩

III

⟨. . .⟩ The play of language has a dizzying effect upon no one so much as Huck, largely because he more than others is motivated by the oxymoronic desire to "feel right." On the way to the Phelps farm, for example, he agreeably trusts to the very "Providence" that a chapter earlier was "slapping me in the face and letting me know my wickedness." But now he reflects that "Providence always did put the right words in my mouth, if I left it alone." The contrary assertions reflect Huck's continuing uncertainty about the status of his words and therefore of his self. Not only does he confuse Providence with instinct ("I go a good deal on instinct"), but this time he will be left "up a stump," without the "right words" he needs.[12] On the other hand, when "Providence" does put words in his mouth, he feels alarmed—as when he tells Mary Jane that her slaves will be reunited: "Laws it was out before I could think! ... I see I had spoke too sudden, and said too much."

Despite what Huck has learned from Jim on the raft, the formidable "resks" posed by sincerity and honesty continue to trouble him:

> I reckon a body that ups and tells the truth when he is in a tight place, is taking considerable many resks ... and yet here's a case where I'm blest if it don't

look to me like the truth is better, and actuly *safer,* than a lie. I must lay it by in my mind, and think it over some time or other, it's so kind of strange and unregular. I never see nothing like it. Well, I says to myself at last, I'm agoing to chance it; I'll up and tell the truth this time, though it does seem most like setting down on a kag of powder and touching it off, just to see where you'll go to. (Chapter 28)

Like the notion of a transparent language, uncontingent truth seems explosively unreliable to someone who has so often seen others shape words to ends they happen to define as true. In the ensuing conversation with Mary Jane, for example, Huck continues to speak honestly (if not quite straightforwardly). And yet language still seems self-dictating: "Saying them words put a good idea in my head." With much the same effect as it had earlier in the novel, when he races back from Mrs. Judith Loftus, language seems to be speaking through Huck. Yelling unreflectively— "Git up and hump yourself, Jim! . . . They're after us!"—he never considers that the slave-hunters are not in fact actually looking for him. After all, he is safely "dead" and no longer an object of pursuit.

Although this impulsive identification with Jim defines a praiseworthy change in Huck's character, it also points to the troublingly unstable intersection of language and the self in the novel. Huck at some times relies on an independent "truth" that as here seems to speak through him, and at other times on a verbal talent that self-protectively disguises the truth. Yet in either case, truth is less at issue than the fact that words seem beyond conscious control. Incapable of using language to separate public ethics from private impulse, unable to distinguish the abstract from the immediate, Huck can only be startled by, and sometimes even balk at, his own behavior.

The simple way to maintain composure in the sort of world that Huck describes is to acknowledge how fully language creates the self. Of course, selves created wholly in this fashion invariably reshape the structure of language—by which paradoxical standard, Tom Sawyer becomes the novel's hero. Appearing in the opening sentence as a character in another novel, his intertextual identity extends to his verbal defense: "Because it ain't in the books so, that's why." He too compels words to mean what he wants, equating ransom with murder and pickaxes with case knives, then recreating garter snakes as rattlers, huts as prisons, and stairs as lightning rods. Tom will "let on" that the proposed escape took all of thirty-seven years, and will arbitrarily deny both Ned's and Aunt Sally's assumptions that things are what they manifestly seem. In this, he differs little from Aunt Sally herself, who delights in fooling her long-suffering husband about Huck's arrival: " 'I'll play a joke on him.' " For them, as for the Duke, the King, and Huck, conventional expectation offers just the toehold imaginative play requires. And it is important to recognize that although Tom's antics may pall long before Jim complains—" 'Yes . . . but what kine er time is *Jim* havin?' "—his efforts "to set a free nigger free" serve the sole end of sheer exuberant adventure.[13] Unlike the two frauds, unlike Huck himself, Tom has in mind no practical motive.[14] Huck's naive admiration of his imaginative spirit, of Tom's willingness to treat everything as an adventure of language, contributes to the novel's ironic power; but that admiration also reflects how much Huck's narrative celebrates the kind of inventive style Tom embodies.

Although Tom's "Evasion" exceeds in cruelty anything Huck does, then, their moral (and linguistic) categories nonetheless seem in the end to differ little. Huck, no less than Tom, relies on the self-justification of "feeling right," and although his feelings are largely benign, even beneficent, they are no more legitimate than anyone else's. Indeed, his major scenes of conscience vindicate a "sound heart" only by dramatizing his inability to ground right action in anything other than feeling. Just as the ending's narrative structure resembles that of the rest of the novel, its causal and moral progressions play out the pattern everywhere implicit. The very unsavoriness of Tom's plan highlights the logical inconsistency of the terms by which Huck has been acting all along. Tom flagrantly ignores consequences, it is true, but Huck pays them little more attention, and dismisses them altogether in his major bouts with conscience. With none of the families he meets, moreover, does he need the elaborate schemes he devises. The escape plan he develops at the Wilkses', like the lies he tells the Grangerfords and the Phelpses ("they froze to me for two hours; and at last when my chin was so tired it couldn't hardly go, any more") differs in degree but not kind from Tom's plot. When Jim protests that boarding the wrecked *Walter Scott* involves too much " 'resk,' " Huck retorts: " 'Do you reckon Tom Sawyer would ever go by this thing? Not for pie, he wouldn't. He'd call it an adventure.' "

Indeed, the novel links language and adventure by tacitly broaching this question of "resk"—a question best defined, as it happens, in Jim's response to Solomon's supposed wisdom. He rejects the biblical judgment, failing to realize that Solomon only pretended a threat and never intended to harm the infant. Yet as Jim wisely notes, " 'de *real* pint is down furder,' " for had its mother not spoken, the child might well have been destroyed.[15] No risk had existed prior to his threat, but through the action of language Solomon introduced danger, and whatever his intention, the effect is the same. Fake threats, in other words, become real by virtue of contexts (particularly royal ones) that require them to be interpreted as such. Similarly, Tom's escape plan, like Huck's narration, creates for others a series of increasing hazards. Or as Huck incisively explains in response to the doctor's query about Tom's wound: " 'He had a dream, and it shot him.' " To follow Jim's advice and " 'run no resk' " is not merely to defuse adventures, but as well in the process to void language of its power.

The problem in *Huckleberry Finn* is that it disguises the dangers it seems to reveal by leading us to believe that Tom's cruelty and Huck's kindness are motivated differently. The two boys in fact differ far less than appearances would suggest. With seeming innocence, Huck repeatedly claims to want not to act, and yet nonetheless does so as contrivedly as Tom. Listen to the way he deplores his efforts at the Wilkses:

Now how do *I* know whether to write to Mary Jane or not? Spose she dug him up and didn't find nothing—what would she think of me? Blame it, I says, I might get hunted up and jailed; I'd better lay low and keep dark, and not write at all; the thing's awful mixed, now; trying to better it, I've worsened it a hundred times, and I wish to goodness I'd just let it alone, dad fetch the whole business! (Chapter 27)

Yet in the end, Huck controls all "pretty neat—I reckoned Tom Sawyer couldn't a done it no neater himself." He may earlier have dismissed "Tom Sawyer's lies," but on the raft, he readily plays a "sivilizing" guide to Jim's guileless incomprehension. Too much should not be read into the role that Huck accepts with belated relief—"Being Tom Sawyer was easy and comfortable"—but the identification is hardly gratuitous. For the fundamental similarities between the two boys structure a novel that maintains a consistent set of assumptions, one more troubling in its consistency than most readers have allowed.

Tom's "raft of trouble" at the Phelps farms, in other words, resembles the raft that has drifted through the rest of the novel. The ending does no more than extend and elaborate the early questioning of straightforward claims for morality and identity, and more generally, for language. Not slavery alone, but all codes and structures, are exposed as arbitrary human conventions, denying therefore the inherent validity of any institution. Early and late, the novel dismisses the notion that language represents rather than creates, just as it undermines belief in the possibility of fixed, unchanging identity. Moral categories may not collapse, but no terms appear by which to affirm or apply them, and they thereby effectively disappear. The original "Notice" wryly misleads, then, by implying that poachers might indeed find moral, motive, or plot. For these are categories that can only be imported into, not discovered in, this text. As we have seen, Huck's confused morality depends upon a confused language that allows him to be two things at once—narrator and character, passive and active, morally right yet emotionally satisfied. The book has it two ways to the very end, where Huck escapes from authority only to author his book. Like many another American text, it asserts freedom with the very arguments, in the very tones, that belie the assertion.

NOTES

[1] Laurence B. Holland, "A 'Raft of Trouble': Word and Deed in *Huckleberry Finn,*" in *Glyph 5* (Baltimore: The Johns Hopkins University Press, 1979), pp. 69–87. Holland stands nearly alone in accepting the ending's implications for the novel: ". . . the closing section does not wrench the book from its course; it reveals in sharper light the profound irony that governs the book." For another reading that accepts the ending on quite different terms, see James M. Cox, *Mark Twain: The Fate of Humor* (Princeton, N.J.: Princeton University Press, 1966), pp. 156–84.

[2] This pattern is hardly rare in American literature, reaching back beyond Emerson's and Thoreau's reliance on the authority of the individual "conscience." Yet to take only the example of *Uncle Tom's Cabin,* it forms the major flaw in Harriet Beecher Stowe's "solution" to the problem of antebellum

slavery. Her reliance on voluntary manumission offers no terms, other than "feeling right," by which to persuade others.

[3] Compare Pap's similar self-created reformation, which wins him a jug of "forty-rod."

[4] On only one occasion does Huck reconsider the efficacy of prayer, when loaves of bread float down the river to Jackson's Island: "So there ain't no doubt but there is something in that thing" (Chapter 8).

[5] Alan Trachtenberg has nicely observed that "to be himself Huck must hide himself," and anticipates some points of my argument in pursuing the question, "Who is the controlling comedian of the book, Huck or Mark Twain?" See "The Form of Freedom in *Adventures of Huckleberry Finn,*" *Southern Review* 6, n.s. (Autumn 1970):954–71.

[6] For other examples of such somnolent storytelling, see Chapters 7, 8, and 13.

[7] Huck's loss of voice also occurs in Chapters 4, 8, 13, 29, and 30.

[8] See, for instance, his lexical specifying of "towhead" (Chapter 12) or his claim: "Anybody that don't believe yet ... will believe it now, if they read on" (Chapter 16).

[9] In Chapter 7, he had complained about the inadequacy of his vocabulary: "You know what I mean—I don't know the words to put in." Later, in Chapter 29, he asserts: "the way I lit out ... there ain't nobody can tell."

[10] Richard Bridgman has analyzed the technique of Huck's "self-effacing" style in *The Colloquial Style in America* (New York: Oxford University Press, 1966), pp. 78–130. See also George C. Carrington, Jr., *The Dramatic Unity of* Huckleberry Finn (Columbus: Ohio State University Press, 1976), pp. 111–21.

[11] Janet Holmgren McKay nicely observes Huck's play on such words as "deffersit," and his eye-dialect misspellings of "onkores" for "encores" and "diseased" for "deceased," but these reveal for her only Mark Twain's controlling influence, not Huck's authorial intrusions (p. 177). See also Carrington, *Dramatic Unity,* pp. 115–16.

[12] For another assessment of Huck's "Providence" which assumes from this contradiction that Mark Twain "used" Huck, see J. R. Boggan, "That Slap, Huck, Did It Hurt?" *English Language Notes* 1 (March 1964):212-14.

[13] In this same brief passage, Jim agrees to Tom's plan because he wants " 'no trouble in de house' "—a line that recalls Huck's earlier justification for putting up with the two confidence men: "... what you want, above all things, on a raft, is for everybody to be satisfied."

[14] Although absent from the novel for thirty chapters, Tom is repeatedly invoked by Huck; see Chapters 8, 12, 28, 32, and 34. Louis D. Rubin, Jr., has similarly aligned Tom with Huck, though he finally does not see the two as similarly motivated. See Louis D. Rubin, *The Teller in the Tale* (Seattle: University of Washington Press, 1967), esp. pp. 77–78.

[15] In a curious way, the issues at work in the story resonate through the novel—two accounts vying for authority. And notably, the assumption that the true mother speaks for the child by relinquishing her claim is never tested. This opens the possibility of a somewhat perverse alternative reading that is never excluded: At the last minute, the false testifier rather than the true mother recants, and thereby wins the child. Peter Seitz, in fact, has argued that "the harlot who prevailed in the case shrewdly took the measure of Solomon and decided that he was what would now be called a 'bleeding heart'—that is, a 'pushover' for a clever but insincere ploy. Her ploy was not as disinterested as Solomon assumed but rather was a deceptive stratagem to win the case." See "Strictly Arbitrary: What Do Arbitrators Do?" *American Scholar* 53 (Autumn 1984):514.

Nancy Walker

REFORMERS AND YOUNG MAIDENS: WOMEN AND VIRTUE IN *HUCKLEBERRY FINN*

Mark Twain considered it "another boy's book." The Concord, Massachusetts, public library, in 1885, regarded it as "the veriest trash."[1] Daniel G. Hoffman has called it "the most universal book to have come out of the United States of America."[2] The object of praise, banning, and veneration during the hundred years since its publication, *Adventures of Huckleberry Finn* has not commonly been considered a novel about women in nineteenth-century American society. Men occupy center stage in *Huck Finn;* women stand toward the back and sides of the novel, nagging, providing inspiration, often weeping or hysterical. Indeed, Twain's masterpiece would seem a likely reference point for Judith Fetterley's blunt statement: "American literature is male. To read the canon of what is currently considered classic American literature is perforce to identify as male.... Our literature neither leaves women alone nor allows them to participate."[3]

As one of several novels commonly thought to address the formation of American attitudes and values, and therefore a "classic" part of the American literary tradition, *Huck Finn* is indeed a "male" novel in several senses. The narrative voice, the specific angle of vision from which the events of the novel unfold, is that of a young boy. Moreover, as a deliberate bildungsroman, the novel traces the moral development of Huck Finn: the traditional passage of the young man from youthful innocence to maturity. Most significantly, the thematic core of the novel embodies a dream of escape to freedom that is both peculiarly American and identifiably masculine. Historically, the political and physical experiences of exploring and settling a wilderness have required a power to initiate and lead social movements that has commonly been granted to men rather than to women. In mythic terms, the typical American hero has, like Huck, resisted the "civilizing" efforts of women and has struck out boldly, often iconoclastically, for a new "territory." For Fetterley, as for other recent critics, the exploitation of the land has come to be seen as analogous to the suppression of women, who are traditionally

From *One Hundred Years of* Huckleberry Finn: *The Boy, His Book, and American Culture,* edited by Robert Sattelmeyer and J. Donald Crowley (Columbia: University of Missouri Press, 1985), pp. 171–85.

regarded as both desirable and dangerous. In Fetterley's terms, "America is female; to be American is male; and the quintessential American experience is betrayal by a woman."[4]

Although it would not be accurate to say that Huck Finn is "betrayed" by a woman, Miss Watson's decision to sell Jim down the river—certainly a betrayal of Jim—sets the novel in motion. Were it not for the relationship between the slave and the boy, much of Twain's social commentary would be impossible, and Miss Watson's action allows their relationship to develop, making her a vital element of the plot. Nevertheless, for most readers, the significance of Huck Finn requires the male characters to occupy the foreground, leaving the female characters as part of the scenic backdrop. Virtually all readings of the novel, from Leslie Fiedler's assumption of a homosexual relationship between Huck and Jim[5] to discussions of the novel's roots in Southwestern humor,[6] reflect its origins in a male-dominated culture. Even the controversy about the role Tom Sawyer plays in the last seven chapters of the novel centers on the conflict between Tom's romantic swagger and Huck's tenuous moral supremacy: a boy's games versus adult responsibility.

Without detracting from the central role that Huck Finn plays in the novel that bears his name, it is possible to re-view Huck Finn as embodying a basic tension between male and female values and roles—a tension that bears directly on Huck's moral growth. Most of the female characters are derived from traditional—usually unflattering—stereotypes of women common to nineteenth-century authors and readers; indeed, the novel could serve as an index to common attitudes toward women as reflected in these stereotypical images. Those few women in the novel who are not merely stereotypes, such as Judith Loftus and Mary Jane Wilks, have more to do with Huck's development than is normally acknowledged. Finally, Huck's ambivalence about women—whom he tends to view as either nagging moralists or paragons of virtue—demonstrates the limited nature of his maturity by the end of the novel. The virtues that Huck begins to develop—honesty, compassion, a sense of duty—are identified in the novel as female virtues. Yet Huck's maleness requires that he ultimately emulate men, that he see women as "other"; and in the end he tries to run from the civilizing presence of women, unable to make the distinction between essential humanity and what society incorrectly considers virtue.

Discussions of Twain's male characters' attitudes toward or relationships with women seem inevitably to address the attitudes of Twain—or, rather, Samuel Clemens—toward women in his own life. Clemens's relationships with his mother, Jane Clemens, and with his wife, Olivia, particularly as they appear to be sources for the female characters in his works (and, in the case of Olivia, to be a "censor" of his work), have been the subject of much biographical and critical study. Although such an approach can invite a confusion of character and author, it may be useful to consider briefly Clemens's view of womanhood, since it is likely that, as the creation of a nineteenth-century male imagination, Huck mirrors some of Clemens's conceptions of the nature and role of women.

Mary Ellen Goad has defined the role that Clemens wished women to play in his own life in order to illuminate his creation of female characters. Goad contends that Twain created patterns of female behavior to which even the actual women in his life were expected to adhere, and that his fictional women were designed as models for the real women in his life:

> Twain viewed the role of the female in a particular, and, to the modern mind, strange way. He operated on the theory that the male of the species was rough and crude, and needed the softening and refining influence of a woman, or, if necessary, many women. The primary function of the women was thus the reformation of man.[7]

This view of woman as the reformer of inherently brutish man was not unique to Twain and had been enhanced by the Victorian insistence on female purity. Ann Douglas argues that between 1820 and 1875 middle-class women and Protestant ministers turned simultaneously to the promulgation of "the potentially matriarchal values of nurture, generosity, and acceptance."[8] Both groups felt powerless to exert influence in overt ways—women because of the removal of key economic activities from the household to the factory, and clergymen because of the legal disestablishment of the church—and therefore adopted the moral suasion of others as their sphere of influence. The fact that this position resulted in women remaining in a real sense powerless coincided with society's efforts to oppress them, according to Douglas, who states: "The cruelest aspect of the process of oppression is the logic by which it forces its objects to be oppressive in turn, to do the dirty work of their society in several senses."[9] The Victorian definition of woman's role as moral guide would account for such characters as Miss Watson and Aunt Sally, part of whose function is "civilizing" recalcitrant boys. In addition, the persistence of this figure in Twain's life and art is explained, Goad says, by the habit that Twain and some of his male characters had of not remaining long in a reformed state. "The business of reform became a game in which one made promises, then suffered periodic relapses, as a sort of recreation."[10]

When Goad discusses the female characters in Twain's work, however, she argues, as so many others have done, that they are merely flat and stereotypical—that in fact they represent one of Twain's failures as a writer. "Twain," she says, "was simply unable to create a female character, of whatever age, of whatever time and place, who is other than wooden and unrealistic." She continues:

> He had evolved over the years a narrow, specialized role for women, and although none of the women he knew fit the ideal, Twain continued to hold it in the abstract. Livy refused to become the narrow, moralizing, reforming shrew that Twain seemed to want, and it is no doubt well that she did, for Twain could not have lived with such a woman. When he was creating a female character in a work of fiction, however, Twain was not troubled by either a refusal to fit a role or the problem of living with someone who did

fit the role. He could make a character do exactly what he wanted her to do, and what he wanted was an idealization.[11]

In *Huck Finn*, however, the relationship between Huck and women is more complex and dynamic than a simple response to idealized figures. Changes in our perceptions of the realities of women's lives during the last one hundred years allow us to see that, although Twain may have used idealizations of women as the basis for many of his female characters, those characters play a vital if underrated role in the society of which they are a part; although they may be perceived by the male characters only as occasions for rebellion or opportunities for heroic action, they represent both positive and negative values of that society. For all Twain's mockery of middle-class "respectability," without the real human virtues represented primarily by the women in *Huck Finn* there would be little opportunity for Huck to grow.

With few exceptions, the male characters in the novel are far from admirable by the standards of either conventional or actual morality. They tend to be degenerate, selfish, greedy, and vengeful and are just as stereotypical as are many of the female characters. Pap is an exaggerated version of the "natural man" on the frontier, an illiterate alcoholic such as inspired the temperance movement of the nineteenth century. Though a figure of broad comedy at times, he lives outside society's rules and rejects even its positive values, such as education. Huck's description of Pap in Chapter 5 underscores his subhuman status:

> There warn't no color in his face, where his face showed; it was white; not like another man's white, but a white to make a body sick, a white to make a body's flesh crawl—a tree-toad white, a fish-belly white. (P. [39])

The Duke and the Dauphin are far more human; they are—initially, at least— rogues rather than bestial villains despite their dishonest schemes. Twain clearly admires their rascality; they are vehicles of satire rather than subjects of horror. Also satirically treated are the Grangerfords and the Shepherdsons, to whom a half-forgotten lawsuit and murder are sufficient to maintain a multi-generational feud. Though Huck describes Colonel Grangerford as a "gentleman all over" (p. [143]), we are meant to see the irony of the term "gentle," and Huck is eventually glad to leave his house. Similarly, Colonel Sherburn, for all his insight into the cowardice of a lynch mob, is the cold-blooded killer of the drunken Boggs.

Not all the men in the novel are this recklessly violent, but none except Jim exhibits maturity and virtue. Uncle Silas Phelps is the stereotype of the bumbling, absentminded man married to a woman with a tart tongue; the couple is in the tradition of Rip and Dame Van Winkle and Harriet Beecher Stowe's Sam Lawson and his wife. Tom Sawyer, the classic "bad boy," turns from youthful prankster early in the novel to cunning—if not malicious—torturer during the "freeing" of Jim at the end.

When Huck and Jim lie and steal, they do so to survive, and this behavior seems therefore excusable. Huck's numerous false identities and Jim's posing as a "sick Arab" are ways of avoiding detection and thus contribute to rather than detract from the moral thrust of the novel. The same is true of their habit of stealing, or "borrowing," as Huck prefers to call it:

> Pap always said it warn't no harm to borrow things, if you was meaning to pay them back, sometime; but the widow said it warn't anything but a soft name for stealing, and no decent body would do it. Jim said he reckoned the widow was partly right and Pap was partly right. (P. 95)

Jim's morality thus mediates between the socially unacceptable element, represented by Pap, and the acceptable behavior represented by the widow. Because Jim and Huck steal food and other necessities, rather than the Wilks girls' inheritance, as do the Duke and the Dauphin, this habit, like lying, seems justified to the reader. Huck's most flagrant "sin" is helping a slave to escape, just as Jim's is running away from his owner; ironically, of course, these acts are in Twain's view their greatest moral triumphs, even though they are not sanctioned by the society Twain describes. Only Jim, among the male characters in the novel, exerts a positive influence on Huck. Jim's position outside white society allows him freedom from—if nothing else—both the moralizers and the rascals of that society, and he teaches Huck morality by example rather than by precept.

In contrast to the male characters in the novel, the female characters largely conform to what society—and Mark Twain—expects of them, and this conformity is the source of their often flat, stereotypical presence. Whether stern moralizers, like Miss Watson, or innocent young girls, like Boggs's daughter, the women have been molded by social pressure into representations of several kinds of womanly virtue. As members of the gender responsible for upholding the moral and religious values of civilization, even when those values sanction slaveowning, the women make possible the lawlessness and violence of the men. If we accept the fact that Twain saw men as naturally "rough and crude," then women were either reformers one could tease by temporarily conforming to their rules, or innocent maidens who could restore one's faith in decency and goodness.

Including the deceased Emmeline Grangerford, there are twelve women in *Huck Finn* aged fourteen or older. Of these, some are merely walk-on characters; for example, Emmeline's sisters, Charlotte and Sophia, and Mary Jane Wilks's sisters, Susan and Joanna. Sophia Grangerford, who Huck says is "gentle and sweet, like a dove" (p. 144), is one-half of the Romeo-and-Juliet couple whose elopement triggers a renewal of the feud between the Grangerfords and the Shepherdsons. Twain describes her as the stereotypical young woman in love, blushing and sighing and always "sweet." With Charlotte Grangerford and the younger Wilks sisters Huck has little to do, and Twain seems to use them all merely as parts of his portrait of Southern gentility.

The most obvious "reformers" in *Huck Finn* are the Widow Douglas, Miss Watson, and Aunt Sally Phelps. The widow and Miss Watson are Huck's unofficial guardians at the beginning of the novel; it is their insistence on prayers and clothes that makes Huck feel "all cramped up" (p. 18), and it is from Aunt Sally that Huck runs at the end, with his famous concluding statement, "But I reckon I got to light out for the Territory ahead of the rest, because Aunt Sally she's going to adopt me and sivilize me and I can't stand it. I been there before" (p. 366). Huck's comment that he's "been there before" points to the pattern of reform and backsliding that Goad discusses and suggests that, having escaped the clutches of the Widow Douglas and Miss Watson at the beginning of the novel, Huck has, at the end, endured another period of civilizing at the hands of Aunt Sally. The repetition of the pattern of reform and escape might lead one to believe that all these women are instances of the same stereotype, whereas in fact they represent three different popular images of women in the nineteenth century. There is no doubt that Twain had different models in mind when he created these three characters, and Huck's responses to them emphasize their differences.

The key to the differences among these three female reformers is their marital status. No matter how devoutly some women of the time clung to a state of "single blessedness," marriage was the only widely sanctioned state for an adult woman. American humor in the nineteenth century is filled with satiric portraits of husband-hunting spinsters and widows, and both humorous and serious literature describes the older single woman as straight-laced and narrow-minded. The novelist Marietta Holley, for example, has her persona, Samantha Allen, describe her spinster neighbor, Betsey Bobbet:

> She is awful opposed to wimmin's havein' any right only the right to get married. She holds on to that right as tight as any single woman I ever see which makes it hard and wearin' on the single men round here.[12]

Widows had a somewhat better time of it than spinsters in the public eye, as was pointed out by another female humorist, Helen Rowland: "Even a dead husband gives a widow some advantage over an old maid."[13] The spinster, presumed to be unwanted, is presumed also to have ossified. The image of the widow, at one time a wife and probably a mother, is somewhat softer; even as a "reformer," she has a kinder heart. The married woman, assumed to be in her proper element, provides the most contented image of the three and thus is likely to be the mildest reformer of all. The three principal reformers in *Huck Finn* represent each of these three states.

Walter Blair has suggested that the prototype for Miss Watson might have been a spinster schoolteacher who visited the Clemens family in Hannibal. Twain remembered this woman, Mary Ann Newcomb, as being a thin woman and a strict Calvinist.[14] Miss Watson has both of these qualities. Huck describes her as "a tolerable slim old maid, with goggles on" (p. 19), and she threatens Huck with hellfire for his sins. It is not surprising that when Huck, Tom, and the other boys are forming their gang, and Huck has no family to be killed if he reveals the gang's secrets, he offers to let them kill Miss Watson. Miss Watson is a constant nagging presence who is particularly concerned with Huck's manners and his education. It is she, Huck says, who "took a set at me … with a spelling-book" and "worked me middling hard for about an hour" (p. 19). She is eternally watchful of his demeanor: "Miss Watson would say, 'Dont put your feet up there, Huckleberry;' and 'dont scrunch up like that, Huckleberry—set up straight' " (p. 19). In the matter of religion she seems to Huck prissy and sterile. The heaven she describes to him is unappealing: "She said all a body would have to do there was to go around all day long with a harp and sing, forever and ever. So I didn't think much of it" (pp. 19–20). The subject of heaven is one of several on which Huck distinguishes between the Widow Douglas and Miss Watson:

> Sometimes the widow would take me one side and talk about Providence in a way to make a body's mouth water; but maybe next day Miss Watson would take hold and knock it all down again. I judged I could see that there was two Providences, and a poor chap would stand considerable show with the widow's Providence, but if Miss Watson's got him there warn't no help for him any more. (P. 30)

Dedicated to duty rather than pleasure in a life that apparently has given her little of the latter, Miss Watson imagines an afterlife inspired by her Calvinist background, one ill-suited to the imagination of an adolescent boy.

Although Huck resists Miss Watson's bleak vision, he recognizes that she merely wishes to make him a "good" person according to her definition of that concept, and Twain suggests that Huck understands that Miss Watson is filling a role determined for "old maids" in American society. Huck's offer to let the gang kill her if he betrays them may be read in two ways. On the one hand, she may be an expendable person in his world, but the gang members have specifically required that he have a "family" to kill, and, by naming Miss Watson, Huck suggests that he accepts her as such. More telling is the famous episode in Chapter 31 in which Huck wrestles with his conscience about helping a slave to escape and ultimately decides that he will go to hell. Jim is Miss Watson's property, and the morality he has absorbed—partly from her—tells him he is stealing from her. As his argument with himself gradually builds from practical to humanistic considerations, he fears sending Jim back to Miss Watson because "she'd be mad and disgusted at [Jim's] rascality and ungratefulness for leaving her" (p. 269). When his "conscience" overtakes him, however, he agonizes about "stealing a poor old woman's nigger that hadn't ever done me no harm" (p. 270). Despite the syntax of the sentence, it is clear that Huck means that Miss Watson has "done [him] no harm." Although the reader can easily see the harm done by the spurious morality of people like Miss Watson, Huck merely sees her as a "poor old woman," as indeed she is.

Twain makes a clear distinction between Miss Watson and the Widow Douglas. The widow is a far more gentle reformer than her unmarried sister and often intercedes between Huck and Miss Watson to mitigate the latter's severity. Although Twain based the character of the widow on a popular nineteenth-century conception of widowhood, he omitted several of the least desirable characteristics of that image. The most negative presentation of the widow in American humor is Frances M. Whicher's Widow Bedott, a gossiping husband-hunter who was the pseudonymous author of sketches in *Neal's Saturday Gazette* in the 1840s. Despite her protestations to the contrary, she is always on the lookout for eligible men, whom she smothers with terrible poetry and home remedies.[15] Twain's notes about his immediate prototype for the Widow Douglas, Mrs. Richard Holiday, suggest that he originally regarded her as a target of similar satire:

> Well off. Hospitable. Fond of having young people. Old, but anxious to marry. Always consulting fortune tellers; always managed to make them understand that she had been promised three husbands by the first fraud.[16]

Aside from the fondness for young people, the Widow Douglas is considerably modified from this model.

Huck does not resent or pity the widow as he does Miss Watson. He is quick to excuse her behavior toward him, as he does early in the first chapter: "The widow she cried over me, and called me a poor lost lamb, and she called me a lot of other names, too, but she never meant no harm by it" (p. 18). He finds her attitude toward tobacco hypocritical, but is more amused than angry:

> Pretty soon I wanted to smoke, and asked the widow to let me. But she wouldn't. She said it was a mean practice and wasn't clean, and I must try not to do it any more.... And she took snuff, too; of course that was all right, because she done it herself. (Pp. 18–19)

The widow's method of reforming is to request or explain rather than to scold or nag. Whereas Miss Watson's "pecking" makes Huck feel "tiresome and lonesome" (p. 20), he responds favorably to the widow's kind heart. When Huck stays out all night with Tom and the gang, the two women react quite differently:

> Well, I got a good going-over in the morning, from old Miss Watson, on account of my clothes; but the widow she didn't scold, but only cleaned off the grease and clay and looked so sorry that I thought I would behave a while if I could. (P. [29])

By Chapter 4, Huck has become accustomed to being civilized. When he slips into his old habits, such as playing hooky from school, he welcomes the ensuing punishment: "the hiding I got next day done me good and cheered me up" (p. [34]). He retains a fondness for his old life but is pleased by the widow's praise of his progress:

> I liked the old ways best, but I was getting so I liked the new ones, too, a little bit. The widow said I was coming along slow but sure, and doing very satisfactory. She said she warn't ashamed of me. (P. [34])

Huck's response to the Widow Douglas's kindness is important to understanding his later reaction to Jim's essential humanity. From the first pages of the novel, Twain presents Huck as a basically decent boy who is able to respond to loving discipline, and it seems likely that he altered the stereotype of the widow—removing her more laughable traits—in order to allow her to have a positive influence on Huck's moral development. Before Huck sets out on the raft with Jim, Miss Watson and the Widow Douglas are the only representatives of decency in his world. Despite her implicit approval of slavery, the widow has a coherent view of what Huck needs in order to be a "respectable" citizen—a view involving education, cleanliness, and Christian virtues. Were it not for the events that propel Huck into his trip down the river with Jim, he could grow up in the mold of the Horatio Alger hero. The other two major models for Huck's development at this point are Tom Sawyer and Pap; Tom, as the eternal child, would have Huck remain irresponsible and unrealistic, and Pap, in his complete rejection of society's rules and forms, would have him descend into barbarism. It is, after all, from Pap and not from the Widow Douglas that Huck flees in Chapter 7.

The most important lesson that Huck learns from the widow is that it is possible—even desirable—to place another human being's welfare before one's own. Not only has the widow taken the unpromising Huck into her home; she has also demonstrated that she cares about him, that his escapades make her not so much angry as sad. When Huck responds favorably to the widow's efforts to alter his behavior and values, he does so because he realizes his actions have an effect on others. It is this same principle that motivates Huck's final decision to help Jim escape regardless of the consequences for himself. As he is struggling with his conscience, he recalls first the good times he and Jim have had, then the favors Jim has done for him, and finally "the time I saved him by telling the men we had small-pox aboard, and he was so grateful, and said I was the best friend old Jim ever had in the world, and the *only* one he's got now" (p. 271). In his realization of his responsibility for another human being, Huck builds upon the example the widow has set for him; in fact, he surpasses the widow in moral integrity by recognizing a black man as a fellow human being.

Yet Huck's experiences with the third "reforming woman," Aunt Sally Phelps, show the limits of his maturation. The effectiveness of the final chapters of *Huck Finn* has been debated for decades. Those critics who find Huck's acquiescence to Tom's romantic game-playing disturbing in light of his previous maturation on the river probably have the stronger argument, and this objection is strengthened by the presence of Aunt Sally. If Huck ever needs a reformer, it is during the torture of Jim in these final chapters, but Aunt Sally, because of the particular stereotype upon which she is based, is an ineffectual reformer, though reforming is clearly her function.

Aunt Sally and Uncle Silas are a familiar pair in American humor: the harmless nag and the befuddled husband. Aunt Sally is a warm, gregarious woman who whirls around the still center of Uncle Silas. Hers is far from the strict, staid demeanor of Miss Watson; though Uncle Silas is a part-time preacher, Aunt Sally is untouched by the Calvinist gloom that characterizes Miss Watson's outlook. Apparently happily married to the good-hearted Silas, and the mother of several children, she has a far sunnier disposition than the Widow Douglas and is more likely to be understanding of youthful pranks. When Tom Sawyer kisses her while she still thinks he is the stranger William Thompson, she calls him an "owdacious puppy" and a "born fool," but once she thinks he is Sid Sawyer, she enjoys the joke: "I don't mind the terms—I'd be willing to stand a thousand such jokes to have you here" (p. 289).

But when Huck and Tom—disguised as Tom and Sid—embark on the activities that Tom feels appropriate to freeing a prisoner and begin stealing sheets and spoons and filling the Phelps house with rats and snakes, Aunt Sally shows her temper. Twain's gift for comic exaggeration is nowhere more apparent than in some of these slapstick scenes, and the descriptions of Aunt Sally are strikingly similar to those of Livy, his own "reforming woman," that he included in letters to friends and relatives early in their marriage. In February 1870 he wrote:

> But there is no romance in this existence for Livy. She embodies the Practical, the Hard, the Practical, the Unsentimental. She is lord of all she surveys. She goes around with her bunch of housekeeper's keys (which she don't know how to unlock anything with them because they are mixed,) & is overbearing & perfectly happy, when things don't go right she breaks the furniture & knocks everything endways. You ought to see her charge around. When I hear her war whoop I know it is time to climb out on the roof.[17]

Just as the dignified Livy becomes a comic figure in such descriptions, so Aunt Sally becomes comic and nonthreatening even as she attempts to discipline Huck and Tom. To cover their theft of a spoon, the two boys confuse Aunt Sally as she attempts to count:

> Well, she *was* in a tearing way—just a trembling all over, she was so mad. But she counted and counted, till she got that addled she'd start to count-in the *basket* for a spoon, sometimes; and so, three times they come out right, and three times they come out wrong. Then she grabbed up the basket and slammed it across the house and knocked the cat galley-west; and she said cle'r out and let her have some peace, and if we come bothering around her again betwixt that and dinner, she'd skin us. (Pp. 320–21)

Most of the time Aunt Sally's threats are idle, but even when she punishes the boys it has little effect. When the snakes they have collected to put in Jim's cabin get loose in the house, Aunt Sally takes action:

> We got a licking every time one of our snakes come in her way; and she allowed these lickings warn't nothing to what she would do if we ever loaded up the place again with them. I didn't mind the lickings, because they didn't

amount to nothing; but I minded the trouble we had, to lay in another lot. (P. 334)

Huck's response to Aunt Sally's discipline is to ignore it—it "didn't amount to nothing"—whereas his reaction to the Widow Douglas's disappointment in his backsliding early in the novel had been to try to "behave a while" if he could. The widow touched Huck's humanity; Aunt Sally merely touches his backside with a hickory switch.

It is difficult, therefore, to take seriously Huck's fear of being "sivilized" by Aunt Sally at the end of the novel. Not a true "reformer," she is a harmless comic figure similar to the Livy of Clemens's letters. Given Twain's insistence on the conflict between Huck's innocence and the corruption of civilization, it is important that Huck thinks he can escape at the end and that the reader knows he cannot—knows, that is, that the "Territory" is simply another civilization. But it seems odd to posit Aunt Sally as a major representative of civilization—instead of, say, Miss Watson or the Widow Douglas—unless we understand that Twain's view of women as the reformers of young men was a product of his own youthful fantasy, formed in part by the Victorian culture in which he lived. In attempting to claim legitimate—if ultimately ineffectual—authority and self-esteem in a society that had made them powerless, Victorian women willingly acceded to a "cult of mother-hood," which, as Ann Douglas points out, "was nearly as sacred in mid-nineteenth-century America as the belief in some version of democracy." Douglas quotes Lydia Sigourney, who, writing to young mothers in 1838, urged them to realize their potential influence on their children: "How entire and perfect is this dominion over the unformed character of your infant.... Now you have over a new-born immortal almost that degree of power which the mind exercises over the body."[18] All three of the women who attempt to make Huck conform to society's rules are derived from traditional stereotypes of women who may superficially be seen as mother figures from the same societal mold; but Huck's more complex and ambivalent relationships with them point up the different social realities they represent and his own boyish immaturity at the end of the novel. The fact that Huck can ignore Aunt Sally's female authority testifies to both his own lack of significant maturity and Mark Twain's awareness of the final ineffectuality of women in his society.

What growth Huck does achieve comes largely from his perception of qualities in others that he wishes to assume himself. With the exception of Jim, all of Huck's important models of decent human behavior are female. Though the "goodness" of both the reforming older women and the young girls in the novel is exaggerated for comic or satiric effect, several of the women display qualities that Huck begins to adopt as his character develops before the final chapters. In addition to the Widow Douglas, whose kindness and sincerity are apparent to Huck even as he chafes at the restrictions of his life with her, Mrs. Judith Loftus and Mary Jane Wilks are important influences on his self-definition. Both characters are more than mere stereotypes, and both demonstrate intelligence and courage that Huck does not find in most of the men he knows.

Mrs. Loftus, whom Huck encounters just before he and Jim begin their trip on the raft, is the shrewd, garrulous woman who sees through Huck's disguise as a girl. She shares with common stereotypes of women a love of gossip, but it is her common sense and kindness to which Huck responds. In terms of her age, Mrs. Loftus belongs to the category of "reforming" women; Huck thinks she is "about forty year old" (p. 83). But her advice at this point in the novel (unlike the moralizing of Miss Watson and the Widow Douglas) is the practical sort that Huck needs for survival, and Huck perceives her as strong and intelligent. His clumsy efforts to thread a needle and catch a lump of lead in his lap call forth Mrs. Loftus's scorn, but Twain also emphasizes her kindly attitude toward the boy she assumes to be a runaway apprentice:

> I ain't going to hurt you, and I ain't going to tell on you, nuther. You just tell me your secret, and trust me. I'll keep it; and what's more, I'll help you. . . . Bless you, child, I wouldn't tell on you. (P. 89)

Huck cautiously responds with another lie about his identity, but he is clearly impressed with Mrs. Loftus's perspicacity. When he returns to the raft and reports on his conversation with Judith Loftus, Jim says she is a "smart one" (p. 94).

More importantly, Mrs. Loftus confirms Huck in his maleness early in the novel. Not only does she quickly see through Huck's female disguise; she also outlines for him the male behavior that has betrayed him:

> Bless you, child, when you set out to thread a needle, don't hold the thread still and fetch the needle up to it; hold the needle still and poke the thread at it—that's the way a woman most always does; but a man always does 'tother way. And when you throw at a rat or anything, hitch yourself up a tip-toe, and fetch your hand up over your head as awkward as you can, and miss your rat about six or seven foot. . . . And mind you, when a girl tries to catch anything in her lap, she throws her knees apart; she don't clap them together, the way you did when you catched the lump of lead. (Pp. 90–91)

Instead of following Mrs. Loftus's advice, Huck never again pretends to be a girl. He rejects his female disguise after he leaves the Loftus house by taking off his sunbonnet, "for I didn't want no blinders on" (p. 91). A few paragraphs later, at the end of Chapter 11, he joins his fortunes to those of Jim when he says, "There ain't a minute to lose. They're after us!" (p. 92). The male identification forecasts the American male adventure, at the end of which Huck will assume Tom Sawyer's identity and his behavior.

Later in the novel, in anticipation of Huck's final capitulation to Tom's boyish romanticism, comes Huck's rescue of the "damsel in distress," Mary Jane Wilks. Huck's response to Mary Jane is not merely that of the gallant knight to the damsel, however; he is at this point (Chaps. 24–30) still on his way to the real moral stature he will achieve in Chapter 31, and Mary Jane is more complex than the traditional damsel. Twain makes her simultaneously weak and strong, so that she in some ways embodies the paradox that Ann Douglas points to in Victorian women who "lived out a display of competence while they talked and wrote of the beauties of incompetence."[19] Though Mary Jane in part matches the sentimental stereotype of the pure, innocent young woman, Huck's view of her includes admiration as well as protectiveness. She combines the piety of the older reforming woman with the absolute innocence of the ideal young girl, but it is finally her intelligence and courage that Huck finds most appealing.

Twain was apparently fascinated with young girls, and he idealized them in both his life and his art. His deep attachment to his daughter Susy and his intense interest in Joan of Arc are only two examples among many of this preoccupation, and portraits of young female characters in his fiction are often suffused with reverence for their beauty and spotless virtue. Albert E. Stone, Jr., explores Twain's devotion to "young maidens, hovering on the edge of adult experience," and quotes from a fragment that Twain wrote in 1898, describing a recurrent dream of adolescent love:

> She was always fifteen, and looked it and acted it; and I was always seventeen, and never felt a day older. To me she is a real person not a fiction, and her sweet and innocent society has been one of the prettiest and pleasantest experiences of my life.[20]

Most of the young girls in *Huck Finn* are versions of this romantic ideal, including such minor figures as Boggs's daughter, glimpsed grieving over her father's body: "She was about sixteen, and very sweet and gentle-looking, but awful pale and scared" (p. 187). Here an object of pity, the young girl can also be an object of satire, as in the well-known portrait of Emmeline Grangerford. Apparently modeled on Julia A. Moore, a sentimental poet known as the "Sweet Singer of Michigan,"[21] Emmeline represents the common stereotype of the morbid female poet, and Twain uses her to satirize sentimental art and the execrable taste of the Grangerford family.

However, it is precisely for her *lack* of sentimentality that Huck admires Mary Jane Wilks. At nineteen, she is the oldest of the three Wilks sisters, undoubtedly older than Huck. The only drawback to her beauty is her red hair, but Huck forgives that: "Mary Jane *was* red-headed, but that don't make no difference, she was most awful beautiful, and her face and her eyes was all lit up like glory" (p. [211]). Mary Jane is indeed innocent and trusting. She gives the inheritance money to the Duke and the Dauphin to prove her faith in them and defends Huck when her younger sister accuses him—accurately—of lying:

> "It don't make no difference what he *said*—that ain't the thing. The thing is for you to treat him *kind*, and not be saying things to make him remember he ain't in his own country and amongst his own folks."

> I says to myself, *this* is a girl that I'm letting that old reptile rob her of her money! (P. 225)

Mary Jane's goodness bothers Huck's conscience sufficiently that he decides to foil the Duke and Dauphin's scheme by recovering and hiding the money, but he does not tell her what he has done until he realizes that she is upset about the slave family being broken up. In his effort to comfort her, Huck inadvertently tells her the truth, and in a passage that closely prefigures his later decision to help Jim escape, he wrestles with the necessity for truth, still in Mary Jane's presence:

> she set there, very impatient and excited, and handsome, but looking kind of happy and eased-up, like a person that's had a tooth pulled out. So I went to studying it out. I says to myself, I reckon a body that ups and tells the truth when he is in a tight place, is taking considerable many resks, . . . and yet here's a case where I'm blest if it don't look to me like the truth is better, and actuly *safer,* than a lie. (P. 240)

The passage describing Huck's parting with Mary Jane in Chapter 28 marks the penultimate step in the moral development that culminates in his decision to risk his soul to help Jim. He is impressed by her willingness to go along with his plan to save the girls' inheritance—a plan that, though involving lies and deceptions, is a model of decency compared with Tom's plan to free Jim—and particularly by her offer to pray for him. Contrasting his sinful nature to her goodness, he thinks:

> Pray for me! I reckoned if she knowed me she'd take a job that was more nearer her size. But I bet she done it, just the same—she was just that kind. She had the grit to pray for Judas if she took the notion—there warn't no backdown to her, I judge. (P. 245)

By putting himself in a category with Judas and emphasizing Mary Jane's virtues, Huck is playing a game with his reformer: though drawn to the innocence and purity she represents, he simultaneously insists on his unregenerate nature. Mary Jane represents the female principle of virtue, always coupled with beauty. "And when it comes to beauty," Huck says, "and goodness too—she lays over them all" (p. 245). Huck, on the other hand, is the sinful male, unworthy of but longing for the redeeming power of the woman.

However, Huck is not merely playing a game at this point. His praise of Mary Jane Wilks is couched in terms that show he has an adolescent crush on her. She has, he says, "more sand in her than any girl I ever see," and though she disappears from his life at this point, Huck's memory of her testifies to her effect on his values: "I reckon I've thought of her a many and a many a million times, and of her saying she would pray for me; and if ever I'd a thought it would do any good for me to pray for *her,* blamed if I wouldn't a done it or bust" (p. 245). Twain combines here the terms of a boy's admiration—"grit" and "sand"—and the desire to help another person that marks the maturing human being. Given Huck's uncomfortable relationship with religion, his willingness to pray for Mary Jane Wilks is a true gift of love. Huck's feelings for Mary Jane and Twain's depiction of her strength and determination raise her above the level of stereotype and allow her, like other women in the novel, to be a significant influence on Huck's developing conscience. His offer to pray for her if it "would do any good" suggests that the idea of self-sacrifice is becoming natural to him and prepares for his ultimate "sacrifice" of his own soul to help Jim.

A close look at the part women play in Huck Finn's life thus makes clearer the extent of his moral regression at the end of the novel. In his relationships with his principal female mentors—the Widow Douglas, Judith Loftus, and Mary Jane Wilks—he has achieved an appreciation of those virtues that begin to separate him from the hypocrisy and violence of the society in which he lives. But his contact with these women has also confirmed that he is in fact male and must remove himself from what he perceives as a "female" world of conformity to certain standards of behavior. With the Widow Douglas and Miss Watson he plays the part of the unruly boy; with Judith Loftus he tries to be a girl and fails; and with Mary Jane Wilks he assumes the role of the male protector of female innocence. Finally, with Jim, he arrives at a mature friendship with another man, one for whom he is prepared to risk eternal damnation. But his acquiescence to the adolescent behavior of Tom Sawyer in the final chapters demonstrates just how tenuous and fragile his maturity has been, and his desire to "light out for the Territory" is youthful escapism rather than a mature rejection of a corrupt society.

Twain's use of nineteenth-century stereotypes of women as the basis of his female characters in Huck Finn allows the reader to understand some of the ways a male-dominated culture perceived woman's place and function. Both the men and the women in the novel illustrate the values of a society that has little regard for human dignity, but the female characters also embody virtues that could redeem that society if the women were empowered to do so. The male characters, even the rascals and thieves, are allowed the freedom to accept or reject these values, whereas the women, as members of a subservient group, are obliged to preserve and transmit them. Whether as innocent young girls or as middle-aged reforming women, the female characters are for the most part creations of a male imagination that requires them to inspire men with their goodness or "save" them from their undesirable tendencies. Huck is both inspired and "saved" or "sivilized" in the course of the novel, but finally he exercises the male prerogative of rejection—not of the values of his society, but of the "female" virtues he has struggled so hard to attain. By accepting the limited roles for women that his culture promoted, Twain effectively limits the extent to which Huck Finn can be a moral force in his society. Though they are frequently inspirational or influential, the women in Huck Finn, viewed from the male perspective of the novel, are finally powerless—as Aunt Sally Phelps demonstrates—to change the adolescent dreams of the American male.

NOTES

All citations to *Adventures of Huckleberry Finn* are taken here from the reproduction of the first American edition of 1885 included in *The Art of* Huckleberry Finn: *Text, Sources, Criticism,* edited by Walter Blair and Hamlin Hill (San Francisco: Chandler Publishing Co., 1962).

[1] Reported in the *Boston Transcript,* 17 March 1885, reprinted in Thomas Asa Tenney, *Mark Twain: A Reference Guide* (Boston: G. K. Hall, 1977), p. 14.

[2] *Form and Fable in American Fiction* (Oxford University Press, 1961), p. 317.

[3] *The Resisting Reader: A Feminist Approach to American Fiction* (Bloomington: Indiana University Press, 1978), p. xii.

[4] Ibid., p. xiii.

[5] "Come Back to the Raft Ag'in, Huck Honey!" *Partisan Review* 15 (1948): 664–71.

[6] See especially Walter Blair, *Mark Twain and Huck Finn* (Berkeley: University of California Press, 1960).

[7] "The Image and the Woman in the Life and Writings of Mark Twain," *Emporia State Research Studies* 19:3 (March 1971): 5.

[8] *The Feminization of American Culture* (New York: Alfred A. Knopf, 1977), p. 10.

[9] Ibid., p. 11.

[10] Goad, "Image and Woman," p. 5.

[11] Ibid., p. 56.

[12] *My Opinions and Betsey Bobbet's* (Hartford: American Publishing Co., 1872), p. 27.

[13] *Reflections of a Bachelor Girl* (New York: Dodge, 1909), p. 35.

[14] *Mark Twain and Huck Finn,* p. 106.

[15] *The Widow Bedott Papers* (New York: J. D. Derby, 1856).

[16] Quoted in Blair, *Mark Twain and Huck Finn,* p. 106.

[17] Dixon Wecter, ed., *Mark Twain to Mrs. Fairbanks* (San Marino, Calif.: Huntington Library, 1949), p. 123.

[18] Douglas, *Feminization,* pp. 74–75.

[19] Ibid., p. 93.

[20] *The Innocent Eye: Childhood in Mark Twain's Imagination* (New Haven: Archon Books, 1970), pp. 207–9.

[21] See L. W. Michaelson, "Four Emmeline Grangerfords," *Mark Twain Journal* 11 (1961): 10–12.

John S. Whitley

KID'S STUFF:
MARK TWAIN'S BOYS

In *Tom Sawyer,* the need of the narrator to assert that the world of St. Petersburg is 'fickle' and 'unreasoning' points to a process of telling rather than showing. The society which surrounds Tom is supportive because its adult denizens are children writ large. The repetition of human experience is insisted upon in the first chapter:

> Within two minutes, or even less, he had forgotten all his troubles. Not because his troubles were one wit less heavy and bitter to him than a man's are to a man, but because a new and powerful interest bore them down and drove them out of his mind for the time—just as men's misfortunes are forgotten in the excitement of new enterprises

and it is the concept of similarity between youth and age, rather than dislocation, which governs the novel. Tom's attempts to 'show off' in front of the Thatchers are mirrored by the activities of all the inhabitants of the Sunday School, including the adults.[1] If there is a juvenile pariah, Huckleberry Finn, he is matched by an adult pariah, Muff Potter. Both are forgiven and clasped to the bosom of the community. If Tom's return to life at his own funeral impresses him with its theatricality, that is what also impresses the members of the congregation: 'As the "sold" congregation trooped out they said they would almost be willing to be made ridiculous again to hear Old Hundred sung like that once more' (XVII). When Tom and Huck discover and keep their treasure, their adult fellow-citizens, albeit for rather different motives, replicate the boys' activities:

> Every "haunted" house in St. Petersburg and the neighbouring villages was dissected, plank by plank, and its foundations dug up and ransacked for hidden treasure—and not by boys, but men—pretty grave, unromantic men, too, some of them. (XXXIV)

This replication of experience makes it difficult to take seriously the contention that there is a dark side of St. Petersburg. ⟨. . .⟩

From *Mark Twain: A Sumptuous Variety,* edited by Robert Giddings (New York: Barnes & Noble, 1985), pp. 60–61, 64–76.

Tom Sawyer is, more than anything, a boys' book because its hero can always go home again. In Chapter XXXIII, Tom and Huck discuss the advantages of being robbers: ' "Why, its real bully Tom. I b'lieve its better'n to be a pirate." "Yes, it's better in some ways, because it's close to home and circuses and all that." ' Like the diminutive heroes and heroines of the many books by Enid Blyton, he can enjoy the most outrageous adventures and then go back home to tea and buns. Because both St. Petersburg society and the structure of the novel follow Tom's romantic inclinations he is never in any danger of expulsion from the community. He can turn work into play (the famous whitewashing scene) and death into life (when he attends his own funeral). He can even find his way out of the labyrinth of caves, whereas Injun Joe, once in there, is utterly doomed because he has no home to which he can return:

> Injun Joe lay stretched upon the ground, dead, with his face close to the crock of the door, as if his longing eyes had been fixed, to the latest moment, upon the light and the cheer of the free world outside. (XXXIII)

He dies as he had lived. When Tom goes off to his 'pirate' camp, 'It was but a small strain on his imagination to remove Jackson's Island beyond eyeshot of the village' (XIII); yet the Island is always close to home, so that Tom can nip back to St. Petersburg and hear Aunt Polly bewailing his death. He is like one of those small rubber balls attached, by a length of elastic, to a wooden bat. No matter how hard the ball is hit it still returns. Huck seems to find a home by the end of *Tom Sawyer*, but in *Huckleberry Finn* someone cuts the elastic. In the later novel, Jackson's Island is but a way stage on an inevitable and final journey away from home.

The final chapter of *Tom Sawyer* does serve, in a minor key, as a transition from the world of St. Petersburg to the world of the raft. Tom's own evaluation of himself as a hero, signalled by his emergence from the caves and his acquiring such a large sum of money, is vindicated by Judge Thatcher's comparison of the boy with the young George Washington and his determination to secure a great military/legal career for Tom. Tom's play rebellions are all now comfortably subsumed into the possibility of an Horatio Alger-like 'rags-to-riches' happy ending. Huck, by contrast, is made unhappy by the respectability which wealth has conferred upon him, a respectability defined in terms which playfully echo major social problems of post–Civil War America. Tom's 'freedom' occurs strictly within civilized society; Huck loses his freedom amid the 'bars and shackles of civilization'. He sees the Widow Douglas's protection solely in terms of confinement, a confinement brought about by money and imaged by a regularity like that of recent industrializing processes: 'The widder eats by a bell; she goes to bed by a bell; she gets up by a bell—everything's so awful regular a body can't stand it.' Tom is able to persuade Huck to postpone his true rebellion in favour of a play rebellion: a robber gang in which, significantly, all the members must be respectable because, in romantic literature, robbers are frequently 'dukes and such' and they swear to 'kill anybody and all his family that hurts one of the gang'. Huck cannot join this gang unless he returns home to live with the Widow Douglas. There *Tom Sawyer* ends, but that ending prepares us for its greater sequel where Huck and Jim do constitute a gang headed by a King and a Duke and where the Grangerford family *is* being destroyed by a romantic (that is, non-explainable) feud.

Before that happened, Twain published a novel half-way between enchanted confinement and appallingly difficult freedom, *The Prince and the Pauper*. Tom Sawyer's dreams of power and fame had stopped short of royalty. He dreamed of being an outlaw, a pirate and a treasure-seeker. His last dream, in the manner of much of the novel, comes true when he and Huck discover the huge fortune of 12,000 dollars. One of the heroes of *The Prince and the Pauper* is also called Tom, Tom Canty, and, lying on the floor of his family hovel, he persistently dreams of being a prince. Like Tom Sawyer, he can persuade his playmates of the validity of his dreams and can duly create the central parts:

> Daily the mock prince was received with elaborate ceremonials bor-
> rowed by Tom from his romantic readings; daily the great affairs of the mimic
> kingdom were discussed in the royal council; and daily his mimic highness
> issued decrees to his imaginary armies, navies and viceroyalties. (II)

Very early in the novel Tom Canty transfers from dream to reality when he inadvertently changes places with his lookalike, Edward the Prince of Wales. Both, following this, feel that they are in a dream-state and both are thought by their respective fathers to be mad. Both, like Huck, have bad fathers (there is mutual affection between Henry and Edward but, nationally, the King is known as a 'grim tyrant' (XII)) and both, like Huck, have to move from the confinements of the romantic to a harsher reality. Tom moves from his dream of royalty to the less acceptable realities of power, realities which seem imprisoning: 'And turn where he would, he seemed to see floating in the air the severed head and the remembered face of the great Duke of Norfolk, the eyes fixed on him reproachfully' (V). Edward moves out into the bustling world beyond the palace gates, a world of cruelty and pursuit where he continually feels lost. 'The houseless prince, the homeless heir to the throne of England, still moved on, drifting deeper into the maze of squalid alleys' (IV). The solitariness of both boys is persistently emphasized. Tom is to be crowned head of a nation divided sharply into the overwhelmingly rich few and the miserably poor many; Edward is 'crowned' by the Ruffler and his gang, not now the pirates and banditti of Tom Sawyer's imagination but a miserable band of thieves for whom violence, treachery and licentiousness have become a way of life and whose stories suggest, unlike Injun Joe's, an alternative society forced into existence by the harsh laws of Tudor England. Both boys gain humanity and courage through their experiences, experiences which seem more realistic than those of *Tom Sawyer* because they are given greater social and historical weight.

Both these heroes, therefore, look forward to Huck far more than they look back to Tom, particularly in suggesting a version of the Wordsworthian notion that the child is father to the man. Just as Huck is to show a sensitivity and wisdom beyond both his years and the very limited adults who surround him, so the two boys put most of their elders to shame because they have acquired an experience of the 'two nations' which none of the adults (except Miles Hendon) possesses. Even while thinking them mad, the adults recognize this quality in the boys. Yet the terrible freedom granted to Huck is circumscribed here by Twain's sentimentality and careful use of a romance plot. Although both boys have tyrannical fathers, Tom Canty has a loving mother and sisters:

> the young girls crept to where the prince lay and covered him tenderly from the cold with straw and rags; and their mother crept to him also, and stroked his hair, and cried over him, whispering broken words of comfort and compassion in his ear the while (X)

whom he comes close to renouncing when his love of power and majesty becomes too strong at the coronation. In the end he is reunited with them; he returns 'home'. Edward, too, returns home from the Underworld, but principally because he has a helper, Miles Hendon, who is also trying to return home and prove his identity. Hendon has been correctly described by Albert E. Stone, Jr., as 'a small boy's dream of a father-protector'[2] (though he thinks of himself instinctively as 'his elder brother' (XII)). He is the ideal protector because he is himself in quest for a re-established identity and has all the necessary skills to make his way through the turmoil of Tudor England. He is introduced as '. . . tall, trim-built, muscular . . .' (XI) and, when the mob lays its hands on Edward, '. . . the stranger's long sword was out and the meddler went to the earth under a sounding thump with the flat of it' (XI). In this introduction an interesting comparison is made, for it is said of Hendon that '. . . his swaggering carriage marked him at once as a ruffler of the camp' (XI). According to John Awdeley,

> a ruffler goeth with a weapon to seek service, saying he has been a servitor in the wars, and beggeth for his relief. But his chiefest trade is to rob the poor wayfaring men and market-women . . .[3]

and, according to Thomas Harman, the ruffler '. . . weary of well-doing, shaking off all pain doth choose him this idle life, and wretchedly wanders about the most shires of this realm'.[4] Hendon has seen service abroad, been imprisoned and is wretchedly poor, though far from being criminal. Like some members of the Ruffler's gang, he has been the victim of a gross injustice, occurring within his family rather than the 'family' of England. He is at home in both nations and is therefore an ideal wish fulfilment father/brother/protector. From the moment he enters the novel the reader can foresee everybody going home to a happy ending. No such protector ever appears to aid Huck. His father is worthless; the Grangerfords are being killed off by the Shepherdsons; the King and the Duke use him for their own ends. His one genuine relationship, with Jim, does not provide him with a protector because Jim is a frightened slave whose level of education and knowledge of the world leaves him in need of Huck's protection. The child is, again, father of the man.

Small wonder that Huck, trying desperately to make sense of the bloodshed and mendacity that surround him, should acquiesce in Tom's absurd games at the Phelps Farm. Tom has always been the leader, the initiator of the action, and Huck is relieved to have the burden of his responsibility lightened. Throughout his journey Huck has used Tom as a Yardstick for measuring his actions and plans. Leaving a false trail before starting for Jackson's Island, Huck laments 'I did wish Tom Sawyer was there . . .' (VII) and, urging Jim to help 'rummage' the wrecked steamboat, he argues, 'Do you reckon Tom Sawyer would ever go by this thing?' (XII). Much later, trying to work out the Wilks family problems, he pats himself on the back: '. . . I judged I had done it pretty neat—I reckoned Tom Sawyer couldn't a done it no neater himself' (XXVIII). Now, at Phelps Farm, with consummate irony, Tom appears as Huck's saviour (and Jim's):

> What a head for just a boy to have! If I had Tom Sawyer's head, I wouldn't trade it off to be a duke, nor mate of a steamboat, nor clown in a circus, nor nothing I can think of. (XXXIV)

Huckleberry Finn begins his story surrounded by fictions which have a greater social resonance than those in the earlier novel and so prod the reader at a very early point into a revaluation of the superstition and moral blinkeredness of the Missouri small town. Miss Watson's view of heaven ('She said all a body would have to do there was to go around all day long with a harp and sing, forever and ever' (I)) is matched by Tom's book-learning ('Don't you reckon that the people that made the books knows what's the correct thing to do?' (II)) which transforms a Sunday school picnic into a crowd of Spaniards and A-rabs and leads Huck, at the end of Chapter III, to unite, in his contempt, these two kinds of fiction ('It had all the marks of a Sunday school'). Aunt Polly acts as a proper parent to Tom, a representative of comfort and home. Just as Huck rejects his surrogate parent, the Widow Douglas, he also rejects his real parent whose reality is that of the thing itself, almost primeval in its awfulness, but decidedly and anciently human ('A body would have thought he was Adam, he was just all mud' (VI)) and, seen through the keenly sensitive eyes and sharply accurate descriptive powers of Huck, no longer a type ('. . . not like another man's white, but a white to make a body sick, a white to make a body's flesh crawl—a tree-toad white, a fish-belly white' (V)).

From then on, the reality of Huck's journey is chronicled both by the truth of the innocent vision and by persistently setting that vision against reminders of Tom's adherence to a popular, debased romantic view. The quality of Huck's truth-telling can be illustrated by two comparisons. Here is Huck describing a view along the river:

> The first thing to see, looking away over the water, was a kind of dull line—that was the woods on t'other side—you couldn't make nothing else out; then a pale place in the sky; then more paleness, spreading around; then the river softened up, away off, and waren't black anymore, but gray; you

could see little dark spots drifting along, ever so far away—trading scows, and
such things; and long black streaks—rafts: (XIX)

where the vagueness of the uneducated vocabulary is tempered by a marvellous
sense of the process of the human eye identifying changes in its surroundings; the
whole passage becoming a description of seeing as much as the seen.[5] Against that,
here is a typical passage from *Tom Sawyer:*

It was a cool gray dawn, and there was a delicious sense of repose and
peace in the deep pervading calm and silence of the woods. Not a leaf stirred;
not a sound intruded upon great Nature's meditation. (XIV)

The vagueness of this description has nothing to do with the process of seeing but
is deliberately platitudinous in order to remind the reader of an adult memory
which idealizes and deserts observation. In the social realm, descriptions of people
in *Tom Sawyer* are suitably typological:

The superintendent was a slim creature of thirty-five, with a sandy
goatee and short sandy hair; he wore a stiff standing collar whose upper edge
almost reached his ears and whose sharp points curved forward abreast the
corners of his mouth—a fence that compelled a straight lookout ahead. . . . (IV)

The amusing assumption of exceedingly minor authority is transmitted, in a gently
Dickensian manner, through the stiff pomposity of his dress, a Sunday get-up which
imprisons adults and children alike. Compare this with Huck's description of the
undertaker at the Wilks funeral:

When the place was packed full, the undertaker he slid around in his
black gloves with his softy soothering ways, putting on the last touches, and
getting people and things all shipshape and comfortable, and making no more
sound than a cat. He never spoke; he moved people around, he squeezed in
late ones, he opened up passage-ways, and done it all with nods, and signs with
his hands. Then he took his place over against the wall. He was the softest,
glidingest, stealthiest man I ever see; and there warn't no more smile to him
than there is to a ham. (XXVII)

The sibilant alliteration captures beautifully both the movement and the attitude of
this man and the 'black gloves', instead of being merely a part of the typology of
reification, enforce his activity, where people and things are treated indiscriminately.
The basic lack of compassion, despite the professional silence, is emphasized by the
final flat sound of 'ham' and serves to make the undertaker an emblem of the
society he serves. In other words he exists as an index of the society in which Huck
moves and as an individualized figure caught, however briefly, in the full light of
Huck's honesty.

Romanticism, as many critics have commented, gets exceedingly short shrift in
Huckleberry Finn. On the reality of the river, steamboats sink, especially if they

are called the 'Walter Scott' (whom Twain blamed for the American Civil War) or the 'Lally Rook' (a lengthy exercise in romantic orientalism by Thomas Moore, who had some very disparaging remarks to make about American democracy). The Grangerford's refusal to see the horror of their feud is indicated by the grossly sentimental visions of death painted by their late daughter,[6] visions condemned by both Huck's genuine if brief farewell to Buck and by the relative casualness with which death is discovered and discarded early in the journey:

> He went and bent down and looked, and says: 'It's a dead man. Yes, indeedy; naked, too. He's ben shot in de back. I reckon he's ben dead two er three days. Come in, Huck, but doan' look at his face—it's too gashly.' I didn't look at him at all. Jim throwed some old rags over him, but he needn't done it; I didn't want to see him. (IX)

One measure of the distance we have traveled from *Tom Sawyer* is the astonishing amount of violence and death that occurs in *Huckleberry Finn,* and the grisliness of death is here underlined by its manifestation as a sight which cannot deter Huck and Jim from their looting and by its difference from the nocturnal child's nightmare of death that occurs in the earlier novel. The death in *Tom Sawyer* was that of the grave-robbing Dr. Robinson and a Dr. Robinson appears in *Huckleberry Finn,* but now an upstanding, intelligent citizen who immediately sees through the King and the Duke. Miss Watson's (and the Sunday school's) vision of heaven is counterbalanced by the 'natural' religion which emerges on the raft. Huck kneels to pray, unencumbered by the restrictions of social, sentimental piety and finds, in this one-to-one relationship with God, that, 'You can't pray a lie' (XXXI) and so decides, in the most momentous decision of the book, that he will go to Hell. The power of this decision, vested as it is in the fully-developed relationship between the hero and the runaway slave, is heavily supported by a memory of the St. Petersburg fiction of heaven. Huck never believed in that but he truly believes in the torments of Hell to which he freely decides he will be subjected. As Huck says of one of his adventures on the river; '. . . it wor'nt no time to be sentimentering' (XIII). Finally, of course, the process of Huck's education down river is viciously counterpointed by the return of Tom, still full of Hugo and Dumas, determined to reduce Jim to a comic object of his literary games, to impose his pattern of play on a situation which has grown too complex and serious to be so contained. To the end Tom remains resolutely himself. Not even the misfortune of being shot can stem the babble of his fantasies of control, and in the last paragraph he is shown fetishizing the bullet, hanging it round his neck as a watch-guard and constantly looking to see what the time is, that time which should tick him towards a maturity he can never have. Since Huck, as we have seen, looks plaintively to Tom, throughout the novel, as a measure of his success in dealing with the world, it is ironic that, when mistaken for Tom at Phelps Farm, he at last believes he has an identity: 'But if they was joyful, it wor'nt nothing to what I was; for it was like being born again, I was so glad to find out who I was' (XXXII). The moral divide between Tom and Huck has now become unbridgeable. Tom is a 'flat' character; he cannot surprise us. Huck is 'round' because he has learned and changed; even if, at Phelps Farm, he cannot find the courage to repudiate Tom's games.

Problems of identity bring us back to the theme of 'home'. Huck repudiates any concept of a home in St. Petersburg and succeeds in making a home with Jim, both on Jackson's Island and on the raft. Despite feeling lonely once he has arrived at Jackson's Island, Huck makes himself a 'nice camp' there and, unlike the boys in *Tom Sawyer,* does not continue to think of the life he has left behind. It is no longer a pirates' lair, but his new home: 'I was boss of it; it all belonged to me, so to say, and I wanted to know all about it' (VIII). Even after he meets Jim he remarks, 'I wouldn't want to be nowhere else but here' (IX), and after they see the dead man on the boat, he ends Chapter IX with the words, 'We got home all safe.' After exchanging Jackson's Island for the raft he similarly makes himself comfortable: 'We said there wor'nt no home like a raft, after all' (XVIII). Yet Twain never falls into a simplistic river-versus-land polarization. The raft steadily takes Huck and Jim deeper into slave-holding territory; it is continually threatened by the hidden dangers of the river (which is presented as 'natural', that is to say, both good and bad) and it is not free from the duplicities of adult life. The raft is taken over by the King and the Duke, grotesques who use romantic, aristocratic identities to defraud the gullible river communities. As with the Grangerfords, their moral vacuity is matched by the vacuity of their culture. The Duke's Shakespearian soliloquy is a monstrously funny, magpie affair, without any continuous sense. Huck quickly recognizes the rogues for what they are but, as a realistically timid boy, does not want any trouble:

> It didn't take me long to make up my mind that these liars worn't no kings nor dukes, at all, but just low-down humbugs and frauds. But I never said nothing, never let on; kept it to myself; it's the best way; then you don't have no quarrels, and don't get into no trouble. If they wanted us to call them kings and dukes, I hadn't no objections, 'long as it would keep peace in the family. . . . (XIX)

A 'family' is created on the raft 'home' but it is an utterly bogus one which both points up the frailty of that home and speeds its destruction. The inadequacy of this family is further emphasized by the participation of the King and the Duke, in bogus identities, as mourners at the family funeral of the Wilkses: pretending to be family in order to exploit family.

Huck's frequent changes of identity both spotlight the difficulties of finding a proper family and home, and his abiding wish to do so. The bogus identity he gives himself usually involves him in lying descriptions of his family, but the families, in these sagas, seem destined to suffer disaster, disintegration and death: 'Pa's luck didn't hold out; a steamboat run over the forrard corner of the raft, one night, and we all went overboard and dove under the wheel' (XX). Moreover, his fake identities are never safe because he is such an incompetent liar. His disguise of a young girl is quickly penetrated and his attempted rôle in the Wilks episode is equally untalented: ' "I reckon you ain't used to lying, it don't seem to come handy; what you want is practice. You do it pretty awkward" ' (XXIX). It is Huck's moral salvation and social damnation that he *is* a bad liar. For the novel has shown him arduously working his way to true relationships with God, Jim, the river, Mary Jane, and to true compassion when he sees the tarred and feathered figures of the King and the Duke. Yet his vision of the truth prevents him joining any family permanently or finding more than a temporary home. In the final pages Tom recovers his Aunt Polly, and Huck at last learns that his miserable father is dead. He also learns that Tom's adventure has been one huge lie, for Jim has been a free man all along. Tom wants again to be a hero, but now his heroism is shown to be as bogus as the culture of the South-West which supports his fantasies. Tom is the hero of Twain's Gilded Age, an era which Twain had already described as false and possessing an almost Jonsonian capacity for corrupting the truth. Huck is a mythic, timeless American hero, making that ever-recurrent, endlessly hopeful and desperate move West.

NOTES

[1] I am indebted here, as elsewhere, to James M. Cox, *Mark Twain: The Fate of Humor* (Princeton: Princeton University Press, 1966), pp. 141–49.
[2] Albert E. Stone, Jr., *The Innocent Eye: Childhood in Mark Twain's Imagination* (New Haven: Yale University Press, 1961), p. 121.
[3] G. Salgado (ed.), *Cony-Catchers and Bawdy Baskets* (Harmondsworth: Penguin, 1972), p. 63.
[4] Ibid., p. 89.
[5] Tony Tanner puts the matter well: 'Rather as though he had just taken Whitman's "first step" Huck absorbs the totality of things unsieved'—Tony Tanner, *The Reign of Wonder* (Cambridge: Cambridge University Press, 1965), p. 124.
[6] Not according to Bradley, Beatty and Long, who say: 'The two chapters devoted to the Grangerford episode contrast the idyllic and picturesque description of the family and their home with the hideous and vainglorious inhumanity of the feud, which even Huck's experience has not prepared him to stomach'—Sculley Bradley, Richard Croom Beatty, E. Hudson Long (eds.), *Adventures of Huckleberry Finn* (New York: Norton, 1962), p. 95.

Forrest G. Robinson
THE GRAND EVASION

When the duke insists that it is "blame foolishness" to risk the harsh consequences of being exposed as fraudulent claimants to the estate of Peter Wilks, the king replies: "Hain't we got all the fools in town on our side? and ain't that a big enough majority in any town?" (228)[1] The argument is perfectly plausible, of course; the townspeople in *Huckleberry Finn* are as perpetually ready to be deceived as the residents of St. Petersburg in *Tom Sawyer*. Armed with this knowledge, these comical, utterly unprincipled charlatans enjoyed virtual immunity from detection and great material benefit in the confidence games they play on unsuspecting bumpkins along the Mississippi. It has been noted more than once that Tom Sawyer's possession and exploitation of the same knowledge is a key ingredient in his kinship with this pair of humbugs. When Huck warns that the plans for Jim's escape are much too easily detected, Tom replies that the Phelpses and their neighbors are all "so confiding and mullet-headed they don't take notice of nothing at all" (332). Such self-assurance is well founded in the world of *Huckleberry Finn*, where improbable claims of all kinds earn ready credulity. Citizens in river towns spend money on manifestly bogus entertainments and cures, make large donations toward the conversion of pirates in the Indian Ocean, and settle estates on thinly varnished frauds. Jim believes that he has dreamt when, quite obviously, he has not. Uncle Silas is persuaded that he filled the rat-holes with tallow, though he can't remember when; aunt Sally believes that Huck is Tom, and Tom is Sid; and the boys "let on" endlessly in their play, and in laying their plans for Jim's escape.

This is not to suggest that widespread belief in the unbelievable is simple, wide-eyed gullibility. In both novels, the readiness to be deceived is an integral component of the culture of bad faith, in which credulity is almost always in the service of unacknowledged, often unconscious ends. Prominent exploiters of bad faith, such as the king and the duke, and Tom, and, as we shall see, Huck, are

From *In Bad Faith: The Dynamics of Deception in Mark Twain's America* (Cambridge, MA: Harvard University Press, 1986), pp. 111–22.

enabled in their manipulations by an intuitive penetration into this ulterior dimension of the readiness to believe. They recognize that the tolerance for varieties of deceit is roughly proportional to the benefits that derive from being deceived. As in *Tom Sawyer*, there is a premium on pious falsehoods, and it is evident that the religious and legal establishments accommodate themselves quite readily to a host of social delusions, some harmless, some full of mischief. Those intrepid successors to Sid Sawyer, who perceive the gross deceptions in their midst and attempt to expose them, are characterized as abrasive, physically unattractive killjoys and are either silenced or ignored.

But if the mechanisms of bad faith are virtually identical in the two novels, the contexts in which those mechanisms operate, and the manner of their presentation—and, therefore, of their reception—differ significantly. *Tom Sawyer* explores the dynamics of bad faith within a rather narrowly defined social reality. It verges on the mythic in its deliberate, step-by-step exposition of the hero's education and final initiation into the mysteries and obligations of his calling. At the same time, the narrative is admirably thorough in its implicit analysis of the creation and maintenance of a complex social system. But while the pattern of deception of self and other running through the cultural fabric is everywhere in evidence, and while the training of its master manipulator is centrally dealt with, the novel never engages in or seriously invites an explicit, sustained challenge to the values of the unfolding scheme of things. . . . Such hushed acquiescence is testimony to the cultural authority of bad faith not only with the citizens of St. Petersburg, but with the novel's narrator, Mark Twain, and with generations of readers as well. We may go further in this vein and argue that the potency and continuity of the social scheme are manifest in the very narrowness of the social reality envisioned by the novel. *Tom Sawyer* is a comic novel because of the relative ease with which it overcomes obstacles to the assertion and confirmation of its social order; but this relative ease is in turn inseparable from the readiness of actors and audience to settle for the narrative's construction of reality. In fact, *Tom Sawyer* successfully conveys the illusion that all experience is ultimately reducible to entertainment. Murder, grave-robbing, the withholding of life-saving evidence, impulses to suicide, simulated disasters, numerous close brushes with death, the violation of sanguinary oaths, wrenching fear and guilt, and numberless suppressions of the truth and miscarriages of justice are all transformed, through masterful orchestration and narrative control, into entertainment. The relationship between the principal agent of comic transformation and his audience within the fictive world of the novel is mirrored rather precisely in the relationship between Mark Twain and his audience without. Both function, in parallel spheres of influence, as master gamesmen, heroic artificers, cultural impresarios, to fabricate in language an image of experience that is at once immediately identifiable as our own, warmly gratifying to our cultural prepossessions, proof against the revelation of its essential bad faith, and therefore as bountiful a source of entertainment for us as it is for our kin in St. Petersburg.

In good part, then, we settle for the comic illusion—the entertainment—of

Tom Sawyer because of the novel's complex narrative manner. Quite inevitably, however, our smiling acquiescence is also tied to the matter of the story.... *Tom Sawyer* is notable for its success at turning grave developments to festive ends. Success in this area is the more remarkable for the fact that the novel's endless chronicling of extreme, painful emotions, and its deep drift toward catastrophe, are little or long noticed by most readers. Yet it is also the case, as the example of *Huckleberry Finn* well illustrates, that the apparently resistless comedic thrust of *Tom Sawyer* is hardly invulnerable. For the sequel is cut from the same cultural cloth as its predecessor, and it is no more burdened with violence and suffering; yet it is immeasurably heavier in tone. Differences in narrative point of view notwithstanding, we can begin to account fully for this affective disparity only when we recognize, and properly emphasize, the omission of black people and—what is the same thing, given the time and setting of the story—slavery from *Tom Sawyer*. Once observed, the omission is immediately recognizable as conspicuous; but that recognition in turn draws attention to the paradox that the omission is notable not only because it is conspicuous, but also because it generally goes unnoticed.

Black people and slavery are virtually nonexistent in *Tom Sawyer* because they are utterly incompatible, for Mark Twain and his audience, with a comic perspective on that world. It is the very essence of the bad faith of this omission that it is not experienced as a distortion or a lack—indeed, that it is not consciously experienced at all. Yet the absence of slavery where its presence is properly, if subliminally, anticipated, makes all the difference in the reception of the novel. We happily endure the painful realities of *Tom Sawyer* because of the much greater woe that the fiction implicitly threatens, and then defers. Our readiness to join Mark Twain in submerging this constituent social and historical reality, and our difficulty in recognizing the omission for what it is, are an index to the painful confusion that attaches to this tragic national legacy, and the urgency of our impulse to mitigate its impact on consciousness. It is, as *Tom Sawyer* may serve to suggest, something we are strongly inclined to exclude from our happiest cultural self-portraits, something we would prefer to keep from our children. Slavery and racism are so absolutely counter to America's proudest ideals that the vast majority of attempts to deal with them—whether to justify, explain, repudiate, or ignore—almost perforce involve recourse to varieties of bad faith. And since the deceptions of self and other on this score usually served in some fashion to rationalize or renounce or eclipse from consciousness what has been, by our own standards and admission, a crime against humanity, the bad faith involved may well be integral to the problem.

If *Tom Sawyer* is symptomatic, by its conspicuous omissions, of our culture's bad faith in its most severely pathological form, then *Huckleberry Finn* is a direct, anguished meditation on the affliction itself, the environment through which it spreads, and the tortuous pattern of its operation in the minds of its agents and victims and witnesses. To be sure, the world of the novel is everywhere informed by Huck's way of seeing it; but it is equally the case that Huck's point of view is heavily influenced by the world he surveys. That world is virtually identical to Tom's in its values and social organization, though Huck's marginal point of vantage affords him a wider but culturally much less mediated perspective than his privileged friend's. Thus Huck expresses himself in a blunt, unwashed vernacular that bespeaks a broad but uneven immersion in St. Petersburg culture. He has notions about Providence and propriety and style, but they overlap very imperfectly with accepted views on such matters. His departures from correct form and his intermittent chafing at the manifold contradictions of Christian civilization serve to focus attention, often in an inadvertently humorous light, on the clear if generally unobserved boundaries that separate what is culturally "in" from what is culturally "out." Tom, on the other hand, operates from within a much more correct, and therefore much narrower, range of experience. His culturally mediated point of view takes expression in the carefully modulated voice of an urbane, literate, rather smug adult who has occasional brushes with village bad faith, but quite readily absorbs them into his own. Tom's mobility within the field of respectability seems almost unlimited because attention falls almost exclusively on the apparent freedom of his social play, and not on the sharp boundaries that he at once observes and helps to reinforce.

While Tom experiences a measure of freedom, and looks free to most observers, this is because he conforms, usually without reflection, to a rigid, elaborate, often contradictory social code. In fact, his freedom is largely the lack of abrasion that results from a near perfect "fit" between the contours of his aspirations and their social mold. This snug coextension between personal and cultural boundaries accounts for the visual transparency of the numerous constraints on Tom's consciousness and behavior. By comparison, Huck is much freer from the pressure of social forms, but he is also much more alert to and contained by the bad-faith contradictions of those that he does feel. Paradoxically, then, Tom's relative freedom and contentment are the result of his submission to the heavy informing hand of his culture, while Huck's sense of constricted discontent issues directly from the relatively free play of his restless resistance to the same forces. The paradox begins to unravel when we recognize that the awareness of culture as an aggregation of constraints on individual autonomy diminishes as the process of acculturation advances. The sense of pressure and contradiction grows less acute as surrender to the contradictory deepens. Thus Huck's discomfort with the weight and inconsistency of St. Petersburg respectability decreases as he shapes his behavior to the widow's civilized regimen; and Tom grows less vulnerable to crippling attacks of guilt and fear as the gamesman's mantle settles on his shoulders. But Huck's immersion in village culture is abruptly terminated when Pap takes him forcibly in tow, while his friend's is well advanced by the beginning of *Tom Sawyer,* and complete to perfection when he emerges from McDougal's cave. The numerous and far-reaching implications of this prominent disparity are nowhere more consequential than in the attitudes that the boys bring to slavery. Tom's gathering mastery and equanimity in the local culture of bad faith are inseparable from his blindness to the inhumanity in his midst. As I have noted, the consciousness of *Tom Sawyer* is a virtual blank on the score of slavery; and Tom responds to Jim, when circumstances bring them together in *Huckleberry Finn*, as an object to be purchased for play. In all of this, of course, the young hero conforms to the view, adopted at least consciously by most of the actors in both books, that the institution of slavery is essentially right. Tom's acculturation renders him as insensible to Jim's suffering and peril as he is to the bullet that lodges in his calf when the escape goes awry, and that he wears around his neck in triumph once the strange entertainment is over. Indeed, by the closing chapters of *Huckleberry Finn*, Tom is so exultant in his mastery of the field of play defined and sanctioned by his culture's "authorities" that he is virtually invulnerable to pain, his own or anyone else's.

For Huck, on the other hand, restive, humorless discontent is deeply rooted in an expanding awareness of slavery, and in gathering, agonized intimations of its hypocrisy and cruelty. As incompletely proof against such anguish as he is imperfectly initiated into the dominant culture of bad faith, Huck's mental suffering grows more painfully acute as increased proximity to slavery draws his irreducible ambivalence into bold relief. Huck's references to blacks in *Tom Sawyer* are few, though they indicate that he is much more aware of and sensitive to slaves than mainstream white people in the book. When Tom asks him where he is going to sleep, for example, Huck replies:

> In Ben Rogers's hayloft. He lets me, and so does his pap's nigger man, Uncle Jake. I tote water for Uncle Jake whenever he wants me to, and any time I ask him he gives me a little something to eat if he can spare it. That's a mighty good nigger, Tom. He likes me, becuz I don't ever act as if I was above him. Sometimes I've set right down and eat *with* him. But you needn't tell that. A body's got to do things when he's awful hungry he wouldn't want to do as a steady thing. (193)

Evidently enough, Huck's humble social station and destitution bring him into company with slaves. To be sure, there is a measure of racism in what he has to say, though the final, apologetic appeal to the demands of survival has a false ring to it, both because it implicitly falsifies his enormous resourcefulness, and because it contrasts so sharply with the sentiments that immediately precede it. After all, Huck begins with blandly unqualified deference to Uncle Jake's authority and liberality, and with the unblinking admission that he works for the black man when he is asked to. There may be hunger here, but there is much greater respect. Indeed, the first half of the passage is clear evidence that Huck and Uncle Jake are friends, and that their relationship is as affectionate and reciprocal as any Huck enjoys until the advent of Jim on Jackson's Island. The racist sentiments that follow are also integral to the young speaker's consciousness, though they surface belatedly, as though Huck intuits that his declarations of friendship for a slave have grown too warm, and may threaten to provoke Tom's suspicion or ridicule. Huck is by circumstance and inclination deeply in touch with the humanity of the slaves in St. Petersburg; at the same time, he is attuned to the unthinking racial cruelty of the dominant white culture. That division in his psyche sets him apart from his neighbors, black and white, and forms the center of all his woe.

The wide disparity in the boys' awareness of slavery is faithfully mirrored in the books bearing their names, both as those narratives represent the experience of an American community, and as they have been received by a large American audience. *Tom Sawyer* at once dramatizes and evokes the equanimity that issues from the bad-faith omission of the culture's leading contradiction. *Huckleberry Finn* at once dramatizes and evokes the agonized ambivalence that the consciousness of slavery can provoke, and the varieties of deception of self and other that relief from that consciousness may entail. With the obvious exception of Huck and Jim, the major figures in both novels seem perfectly comfortable with their peculiar institution. In *Tom Sawyer,* the work of bad faith is so complete that slavery rarely intrudes upon consciousness. In *Huckleberry Finn,* on the other hand, the inhumanity of the institution seems to dominate the foreground; yet members of the white community are untroubled by moral questions, and attend to slavery only when it is profitable, or forced by circumstance into their consciousness. Huck is unique, of course, both for the dividedness of his feelings, and for the painful intensity of awareness that his uncertainty gives rise to.

If it gives us pause to reflect that Huck is alone among the citizens of St. Petersburg in his conscious uneasiness over slavery, then we may be quite struck with the fact that the critics in Mark Twain's audience were initially slow to identify Huck's concern, and to allow that they shared it with him. The large majority of early reviewers of *Huckleberry Finn* were hostile to the novel because of its alleged irreligion and vulgarity. The general tone was set by the Concord, Massachusetts, Library Committee, which excluded the book, declaring it "rough, coarse, and inelegant, dealing with a series of experiences not elevating ... It is the veriest trash." In Springfield, Illinois, offended gentility recoiled with the charge that "Mr. Clemens ... has no reliable sense of propriety."[2] The response focused almost entirely on the novel's lapses from accepted standards of morality and taste. Mark Twain's vernacular art was rarely assessed, while Huck was viewed as a bad moral example for the nation's impressionable youth. Nowhere in the reviews, not even in the occasional favorable responses, was there any attention to the novel's conspicuous preoccupation with slavery. Perhaps the reviewers took the institution so for granted that they perceived no necessity to emphasize its prominent place in the novel. Much more likely, the novel's treatment of slavery came as an unwelcome reminder that the Civil War and Reconstruction had failed utterly to ease racial prejudice and to reduce its attendant hatred and violence. Viewed in this light, the contemporary critics' disproportionate attention to alleged lapses from respectable standards may be seen as an indirect acknowledgment that *Huckleberry Finn* was too painfully current for comfort. There was, in short, a measure of bad faith in their righteous outrage.

This is not to suggest that the early reviewers were singular in their myopia, and that we have now completely overcome the inclination to shrink from the novel's racial implications. To the contrary, modern critics have rediscovered the meaning of *Huckleberry Finn* only to partially resubmerge it in debates which focus too narrowly on the propriety or consistency of Huck's, or the novel's, response to the central, admittedly vexing, problem. Such discussions bear the suggestion that the narrative somehow *contains* within itself all that is necessary to its proper comprehension. In fact, of course, we find *Huckleberry Finn* profoundly meaningful, and we readily acknowledge its cultural authority, because it continues to speak directly to our condition. To read it is to be made mindful of the unbroken legacy of racial discord in America; of the persistence and pervasiveness of prejudice; and of our readiness, out of guilt and frustration and fear, to submerge the novel's most challenging implications in a tempest of esthetic dispute.

We are drawn to and fixed by *Huckleberry Finn* because it thrusts our fondest cultural self-image, an innocent—"natural," rootless, unlettered, pre-adolescent—boy, into direct contact with our most crippling cultural contradiction. We suspect, perhaps, that a proper understanding of the relationship between the innocent white boy and the enslaved black man will throw light on our problem. To the extent that Huck and Jim are perceived to love and care for one another, I suppose we are enlightened. But there is abundant trouble between them, too, and it appears that in lighting out Huck is as much in flight from Jim as he is from the civilization that shackles them both. Uncertainty on this vital question may help to account for our disinclination to reflect on the source of our interest in *Huckleberry Finn*. Rather than confront directly the uncompromising cultural lesson held out to us, we have been inclined, quite understandably I believe, to turn the novel back on itself, and to insist that the problem it dramatizes is Huck's, or the ante-bellum South's, or Mark Twain's, or the text's. At the same time, however, it is precisely its ambiguity that has secured *Huckleberry Finn* its place as the leading popular expression of America's self-image when it comes to matters of slavery and race. We return to the novel, and we read it to our children, because it gives us a bearable perspective on what continues to be an almost unbearable but absolutely unavoidable problem. For the critics, ambiguity has seemed to necessitate the retreat to narrow, comfortable manageable "textual" considerations. For the great mass of admiring readers, because Huck and Jim are friends, and because Jim is finally emancipated, the novel's ambiguities are simply dissolved in an overflow of relief and warm fellow-feeling. In either case, *Huckleberry Finn* continues to be our favorite story about slavery and race because it gives us no more of this reality than we can bear.

It remains to add that *Huckleberry Finn* does more than merely facilitate our bad-faith prevarications. Like *Tom Sawyer,* but in more direct and comprehensive ways, it provides us with models for the management of our shrinking disposition to the dilemma that it poses. *Tom Sawyer* demonstrates that contradiction and inhumanity can be wished—by actors and audience alike—out of sight and mind. *Huckleberry Finn* bears the suggestion that, for Mark Twain at least, consciousness could not repose indefinitely in such gross delusions. But at the same time that the sequel surrenders to the irrepressible, it does so with considerable hesitation at a number of levels. Jim first appears in the novel as the unwitting butt of a practical joke conceived by Tom to expose his gullibility and superstition. Huck urges Tom to forgo the prank; he is not amused. Neither are we. Tom's gamesmanship ceases to be funny when it preys on the credulity of a slave. With Jim's arrival on the seemingly enchanted St. Petersburg scene, the illusion that childish deeds yield only childish consequences gives way to a much more ominous tone. The subsequent drift into disenchantment is gradual, and apparently as irresistible as it is unpremeditated. Mark Twain seems to have been baffled and dismayed with the adverse flow of his narrative. The halting rhythm of the composition of *Huckleberry Finn*, clearly echoed in the uncertain movements of the published novel, is marked by major pauses at recurrent crisis points in the relationship between Huck and Jim. These are generally followed by intervals of separation, followed in turn by reunion and renewed drift toward crisis.[3] As the price of deliverance from this melancholy cycle, Mark Twain was obliged to restore Tom Sawyer to the foreground, and to revert to the strangely compromised, furtive comedy that somehow overtook him at the outset. His ambivalence toward his refractory material—the unfinished manuscript of *Huckleberry Finn* was no more easily completed than forgotten—is faithfully mirrored at the level of narration in Huck's final sentiments on the score of authorship. "There ain't nothing more to write about, and I am rotten glad of it, because if I'd a knowed what a trouble it was to make a book I wouldn't a tackled it and ain't agoing to no more" (362). And with that, he announces his imminent departure for the Territory.

This pattern of uncertainty and ambivalent retreat has been a decisive influence on the general contours of audience response. With Mark Twain and Huck Finn, readers have no doubt been subliminally attuned to the incompatibility of slavery with a sustained and plausible comedic perspective on America. We have shared their deep cultural reluctance to directly acknowledge this enormous obstacle to laughter. Instead, we have been inclined to withdraw along paths that the novel opens up to us. We may follow Mark Twain's example and submit to the alternating currents of a blindly irresolute ambivalence. Or we may surrender the novel's management to Tom Sawyer, and settle for nervous laughter at what he aptly calls the "evasion." As a leading element in this approach, we may wish civilization upon Huck, trusting that the proper training will help to settle the trouble in his mind. Alternatively, we may align ourselves more positively with Huck in the immemorial delusion that the return to Nature will somehow heal the wounds of all God's children and restore us to a peaceable kingdom. Of course we may, with Huck, simply close our eyes and run away. Or, finally, in moments of desperation we may be tempted to emulate in spirit the example of Mark Twain at the first terminal of composition in Chapter 16, when man and boy, black and white, raft and all, go down under the sweep of an enormous, avenging Leviathan. To Hell with it!

But even the apocalypse is inconclusive. Nothing is resolved or revealed; the raft turns up in workable repair and the perilous drift southward is resumed. This is, I take it, the novel's deep meaning. Over and over, one way or another, the seemingly inescapable tragic consequences of the journey are glimpsed and then blinked, skirted and then somehow averted, directly encountered only to be wished away. Audience participation in this process is of course vitally constitutive of meaning so construed. The imperishable currency of *Huckleberry Finn* is part and parcel with its almost ritual authority as a rite of passage. It carries us further into our culture's heart of darkness than is compatible with equanimity; far enough so that we will retreat quite willingly from the dark center to one of the bad-faith perspectives that the novel opens up and validates. This passive, ambivalent, malleably complicit relationship to the narrative finds a striking parallel in the Bricksville crowd's reaction to the murder of Boggs. The people are entertained by the old man's drunken rampages, and they take no action to prevent him from endangering himself, or to interfere with Colonel Sherburn's revenge. In effect, the slaughter of Boggs occurs, public laws and codes of honor notwithstanding, because the people of Bricksville permit it. The episode, I will argue, seems to answer a need arising from the circumstances of their lives. The reaction to the murder tends to confirm this view. The putative claims of justice are subordinated entirely to the craving for spectacle when Sherburn retires unchallenged while the crowd, Huck included, turns its attention to the next act in the exhilarating show. "They took Boggs to a little drug store, the crowd pressing around, just the same, and the whole town following, and I rushed and got a good place at the window, where I was close to him and could see in." There is plenty of competition for the good seats, and people grow impatient, "squirming and scrouging and pushing and shoving to get at the window and have a look." When those in front refuse to move aside for others, the mob surges forward amid appeals to human rights and the spirit of fair play. "Say, now, you've looked enough, you fellows; 'taint right and 'taint fair, for you to stay thar all the time, and never give nobody a chance; other folks has their rights as well as you" (187).

The pious resort to principles of equity and fair play is in perfect bad faith, for the absurd clamoring over audience rights serves to draw attention away from the villagers' complicity in the much heavier injustice that has befallen poor Boggs. The large Bible that is placed on the chest of the expiring victim, and that seems to press the last breath out of his failing body, is richly emblematic of the epidemic of paradoxes at large in the village culture. Public professions of piety and righteous-ness are not simply hollow and harmless; rather, they are silent but very substantial contributors to much that is unholy in Bricksville. Cruelty and violence are staples of the local diet, yet the citizens of Bricksville are no more willing or able to acknowledge the reality of their condition than they are to avert the murder of Boggs. To do so would entail a very painful recognition of the contradictions in their lives; and it would mean an end to the fun. Instead, they have contrived to indulge their weakness for spectacles of lawless violence and at the same time to persist in the delusion that they are a just, righteous people.

In the most general terms, the reader response to *Huckleberry Finn* and the Bricksville response to the murder of Boggs are parallel in the sense that both involve an audience and an entertainment. More specifically, in both the spectacle dramatizes the cultural condition of the audience, but in ways that ease ambivalence by enabling bad-faith evasions; and in both the audience settles quite readily for the relatively composed perspectives that the spectacle seems at once to invite and exemplify. In both, moreover, audience and entertainment are integral to each other, all of a piece, so that the meaning of the drama is neither in the spectacle nor in the response taken separately, but in the collaboration of audience and actors in the fabrication of a complex, dynamic cultural self-image. The absolutely indispensable element in this paradoxically short-sighted yet penetrating mimesis is, of course, bad faith. It releases the impulses that give rise to the spectacle and determine its content, but at the same time it accounts for the fact that the yielding to lawless violence is never so narrowly scrutinized as to threaten the audience's self-esteem. The citizens of Bricksville have collaborated in the creation of the show, but they have collaborated as well in turning a blind eye to its leading implications.

Meanwhile, as members of the larger, framing audience of *Huckleberry Finn*, we have ourselves been rather slow to grasp the bad faith dynamics of the Boggs murder. This is so, I believe, because the analysis of the cultural reflexivity of the fictional episode leads almost inevitably to the disclosure of a similar dynamic in the relationship between the reader and the novel. The seeming reluctance to come to critical terms with Bricksville may thus be seen as a manifestation of a prior, deeper reluctance to explore fully the implications of our involvement with *Huckleberry Finn*.

NOTES

[1] *Tom Sawyer* is cited from *The Adventures of Tom Sawyer*, ed. John C. Gerber, Paul Baender, and Terry Firkins, in *The Works of Mark Twain* (Berkeley: University of California Press, 1980). *Huckleberry Finn* is cited from *Adventures of Huckleberry Finn* (Berkeley: University of California Press, 1985). Hereafter references to these editions will be cited parenthetically in the text.

[2] As quoted in Arthur Lawrence Vogelback, "The Publication and Reception of *Huckleberry Finn* in America," *American Literature*, 11 (1939), 269–70. Victor Fischer's "Huck Finn Reviewed: The Reception of *Huckleberry Finn* in the United States, 1885–1897," *American Literary Realism*, 16 (1983), 1–57, very substantially supplements Vogelback's work.

[3] The standard account of the composition of the novel appears in Walter Blair's "When Was *Huckleberry Finn* Written?," *American Literature*, 30 (1958), 1–25.

Harold Beaver

HUCK AND PAP

'Pap always said, take a chicken when you get a chance ...' (ch. 12)

Huck is a chip off the old block. To understand Huck one must begin with Pap. Pap is his one sure model. He often quotes the old man. After committing his own murder, he opts for the only life he knows, which is Pap's:

All right; I can stop anywhere I want to. Jackson's Island is good enough for me; I know that island pretty well, and nobody ever comes there. And then I can paddle over to town, nights, and slink around and pick up things I want.[1]

What prevents this career of petty crime is Jim.

Old Man Finn, Pap Finn, is an Irish soak who has drifted to the frontier. A ragged, illiterate 50-year-old, with the gift of the gab, he boozes and snoozes in his hut on the Illinois shore. There was a wife once, but we do not know how she died.[2] When drunk, though, he feels persecuted by the dead. It seems that Huck is his only child. But he is paranoid about Huck, deliriously calling him the 'Angel of Death' and chasing him with a clasp-knife. He is paranoid about Blacks, too, ranting against mulattos and free 'niggers'. Just one recorded remark made by the real-life Jimmy Finn is among the depositions (made by Sam's father) in the Smarr-Owsley affair. On entering a store, where Sam Smarr (Boggs's prototype) had that moment let off a pistol, Finn remarked: 'That would have made a hole in a man's belly.'[3]

Pap's end is as mysterious as his beginning. Originally he was to have been Injun Joe's companion in grave-robbing. 'He became Muff Potter,' DeVoto thought,

From *Huckleberry Finn* (London: Allen & Unwin, 1987), pp. 79–91.

'no doubt, to prevent Huck's oath from putting his father's life in jeopardy.'[4] His corpse is found drifting on the Mississippi: naked, shot in the back, among sleazy rubbish. The two black masks there suggest he was mixed up with gangsters.[5] But what kind of gangsters? Why was he naked? Why was he shot? Was it strip-poker they were playing? Had the flood-waters surprised them? Was he shot in a drunken brawl for not paying his debts? Or for rashly boasting that he was 'worth six thousand dollars and upards' (26/33)? There is no way of telling. Huck's father died out nigger-hunting, so he claimed, with a $200 reward (for murder) on his head.

That was Huck's pedigree. Such was his heritage. He, too, is slippery as an eel. He, too, is both a scoundrel and a con-man. White 'trash', at a critical point, Jim calls him. He is fatally overreached in the end only by a couple of older, more experienced con-men, whom he instinctively admires. Though neither drunk, nor sexually active, nor a racist exactly, he carries both the paternal imprint (of that neurotic wreck) and social imprint (of a Southern White).

Pap's entry is scary; he had climbed through a window to catch Huck.[6] But Huck views the apparition (pasty face, black greasy hair) with chilly detachment: 'I stood a-looking at him; he set there a-looking at me' (21/23). Two long measured looks. Each is a kind of mirror image of the other. Each, throughout *Huckleberry Finn,* will seem a reverse image of the other. Whereas Old Finn will be officially alive (though actually dead), Young Finn will be officially dead (though actually alive). Whereas Old Finn had begun life as a grave-robber, Young Finn will become an active accomplice of grave-robbers. Whereas Old Finn (the confirmed bigot) rants at Blacks, Young Finn (the sentimental bigot) will accompany and shelter a Black on the run.

But they have much in common. Pap may cuss and get roaring drunk; Huck just smokes. His very trademark in *Tom Sawyer* had been his corncob pipe. Here he smokes cheap chewing tobacco—even cigars when he can lay hands on them—but *never* touches liquor.[7] His superstitions, too, seem largely to derive from Pap. His belief in ghosts and the significance of 'signs' all sound like Pap. Huck entered the world of Tom Sawyer swinging a dead cat. Here he spots the sign of the cross, made with nails in Pap's left boot-heel, to ward off the devil.

But it is not only his superstitions, but also his saws and practices which he picked up from Pap. Take Pap's cautionary tale of the man who boasted that he had looked at the new moon over his left shoulder:

> Old Hank Bunker done it once, and bragged about it; and in less than two years he got drunk and fell off of the shot tower and spread himself out so that he was just a kind of layer, as you may say; and they slid him edgeways between two barn doors for a coffin, and buried him so, so they say, but I didn't see it. Pap told me.[8]

It was from Pap that Huck learnt this aggressive verbal energy as well as his facility for spinning tall yarns. Huck is every inch Pap's son.

He was his apprentice, too, in the fine art of cussing. As Huck is a champion in Tom's eyes, so Pap is in Huck's. Pap is a self-esteemed master-craftsman of vituperation: 'his speech was all the hottest kind of language' (27/34):

> Then the old man got to cussing, and cussed everything and everybody he could think of, and then cussed them all over again to make sure he hadn't skipped any, and after that he polished off with a kind of general cuss all round, including a considerable parcel of people which he didn't know the names of, and so called them what's-his-name, when he got to them, and went right along with his cussing.

Huck glories in these epic demonstrations, as on the night Pap kicked the pork-barrel:

> and the cussing he done then laid over anything he had ever done previous. He said so his own self, afterwards. He had heard old Sowberry Hagan in his best days, and he said it laid over him, too; but I reckon that was sort of piling it on, maybe.[9]

Huck lives in terms of this epic mythology, ruled by awesome champions like Hank Bunker and Sowberry Hagan, lord of oaths.

Huck's use of the term 'borrowing', too, of course, is a family tradition. Like the oaths and superstitions, Huck has assimilated Pap's social prejudices; and, however abusive, Pap knows his place in the hierarchy. He knows how to kowtow to the 'aristocracy' like Judge Thatcher and the Widow. Even in *Tom Sawyer*, when Huck sneaks off to eat meals with a 'nigger', he promptly adds: 'But you needn't tell that. A body's got to do things when he's awful hungry he wouldn't want to do as a steady thing' (ch. 28). That guilty reflex—that twinge of Southern conscience—already evokes the whole wavering drama of *Huckleberry Finn*.

Though not neurotic exactly, Huck is often 'lonesome'. More than just 'lonesome', depressed. For a boy of 14 such severe depressions seem cause for alarm. 'I felt so lonesome I most wished I was dead' (9/14), he sighs. Or 'then I knowed for certain I wished I was dead' (173/277). When a drunk on horseback weaves up to him to jeer, 'Whar'd you come f'm, boy? You prepared to die?' (115/184), we already know the answer. Yes, Huck is prepared to die. He had begun his *Adventures,* after all, with the staging of his own elaborate suicide.

Like father, like son. Pap has naturally had a poor press. But what is the key difference between them? For one thing age, of course. Pap Finn (*fl. c.* 1790–1840) must have been of that same boisterous, hard-drinking Jacksonian generation of Southern roustabouts and gamblers who struck out West after the war of 1812. He might have heard Mike Fink, that legendary keelboatman, roar:

> I can use up Injens by the cord, I can swallow niggers whole, raw or cooked ... Whoop! holler, you varmints ... or I'll jump right straight down yer throats, quicker nor a streak o' greased lightening can down a nigger's!

That was the language of his youth, not mealy-mouthed stuff about 'free niggers' and professors. It also suggests another difference, his illiteracy. Pap, like Jim, cannot read; Huck, like Tom, can. 'Your mother couldn't read,' he declaims,

> 'and she couldn't write, nuther, before she died. None of the family couldn't, before *they* died. *I* can't; and here you're a-swelling yourself up like this. I ain't the man to stand it—you hear? Say—lemme hear you read.'
>
> I took up a book and begun something about General Washington and the wars.[10]

Pap listens for half a minute; then swipes the revolutionary and patriotic text out of Huck's hand. Pap is not drunk. This is not knockabout farce. Twain knew exactly what he was about. Old Finn bears a grudge, a deep grudge. He is a dispossessed White in an embattled stance against the whole bookish establishment. For one thing, the 'Widow Douglas, she took me for her son' (7/1): it is the law which seeks to appropriate his child, backed by the courts. (The case has failed, but it is awaiting retrial.) Pap is up against the whole St. Petersburg establishment, headed by Judge Thatcher. 'Here's the law', he roars, 'a-standing ready to take a man's son away from him—a man's own son' (26/33). Secondly, it is the law which seeks, by devious delay, to appropriate his right in Huck's $6,000 bonanza; that, too, is an affront. Thirdly, it is the law which has misappropriated his *vote,* as he sees it, by registering black voters.

But what makes him rage and roar is his complete helplessness, his total incapacity to defend his legal and financial and civil rights. Because he is illiterate. His performance is—necessarily and fluently and exasperatingly—*oral:*

> 'Yes, and I *told* 'em so; I told old Thatcher so to his face. Lots of 'em heard me, and can tell what I said. Says I . . .'
> 'Them's the very words. I says . . .'
> 'Look at it, says I . . .'
> '. . . they said he was a p'fessor in a college . . .'
> 'I says I'll never vote agin. Them's the very words I said; they all heard me . . .'
> 'I says to the people . . .'
> 'And what do you reckon they said? Why, they said . . .'[11]

That, in a single burst, is how he addresses Huck. But he addresses Judge Thatcher and Mrs. Thatcher, too, like a public meeting: 'Look at it gentlemen, and ladies all . . . You mark them words—don't forget I said them' (23/17). For in Pap's illiterate world, like Jim's, *speech matters.* Therefore the exact recollection and reportage of the spoken word is essential, since speech is testimony, the ultimate personal affidavit. Speech carries within it its own involuted marks of quotation, of ceaseless quotations within quotations. That is one function of speech: the quoting of a quotation. Human speech is transformed to a cento of quotations both for the historical record and for personal vindication. Such quotation is the ultimate proof—the only proof in an illiterate society—of a man's individual worth.

Huck can both read and write; but his role as a writer, too, is ultimately modelled on Pap. His, too, is an oral performance. His text, too, will offer an active collision, or collusion, of quotations. I shall return to this at length. Here it is enough to note that Huck, too, like Pap, is explicitly conscious of his own thought processes. Says Pap: 'And what do you think? ... Thinks I, what is the country a-coming to?' (26–7/33–4). Says Huck to himself: 'Thinks I, this is what comes of my not thinking' (74/124). The very first sentences of *Huckleberry Finn* show something of this. Huck's gesture towards a text (*The Adventures of Tom Sawyer*) is remote and passive: 'That book was made by Mr. Mark Twain'. What he instinctively and actively grasps is the text as spoken: 'and he told the truth, mainly. There was things which he stretched, but mainly he told the truth.'

Pap views this mirror-image, however, as a potential parricide. In a way, he is right. Huck *is* his 'Angel of Death'. Huck's suicide looks more like the symbolic murder of his own father. For it was Pap who slept 'with the hogs in the tanyard' (22/25). It was Pap who debased himself to the level of hogs. 'Look at it,' he declaimed, raising his hand. 'There's a hand that was the hand of a hog' (23/27). So that when Huck actually kills a wild hog, it seems like the most brutal Oedipal act: 'I shot this fellow ... and hacked into his throat with the ax, and laid him down on the ground to bleed' (31/40). It is the first of his many rituals of death and resurrection; and even there, ironically, he remains very much the son of his father. Was not Pap the man who had 'started in on a new life'? Who had claimed to be 'clean' (23/27)? Had not Pap, too, masqueraded just such a moral and spiritual resurrection?

What for Pap, though, had been airy fiction, Huck turns into symbolic drama. He saws an escape-hatch at the back of the prison-cabin. He smashes the door and splashes blood over the floor. At the end of *Huckleberry Finn* the motif recurs in the ritual of Jim's 'escape' through a tunnel at the rear of *his* prison-cabin. The echo is quite deliberate: 'Jim's counterpin' (193/306) matches Pap's 'horse-blanket' (25/31) as screen. In *Tom Sawyer,* too, there had been scenes of rebirth and renewal. Tom, like Huck, too, rises from the dead. First he staged his own death, sneaking back from Jackson's Island to eavesdrop on his funeral, before revealing himself to the astonished congregation. Next he descended with Becky Thatcher deep into McDougal's Cave; lost, trapped, they spend a biblical three days and nights there, before finally crawling up a long tunnel towards the light to be literally 'reborn' (having been given up for dead).[12] This Return-from-the-Dead and the Cave-as-Tomb were permanent fixtures of Twain's imagination.[13]

The whole of *Huckleberry Finn* is a parody of Christian death and resurrection. In this sense it is a secular fable. Huck dies in his old self as Pap's son in Illinois to confront his new self as ... But what self? That is where the real crisis begins. Who is he? His search for identity, through multiple rebirths and baptismal renewals in the Mississippi, is the story of *Huckleberry Finn.* The multiplication of selves itself becomes his resource against loneliness. He assumes nine incarnations: as Sarah Williams, Mary Williams, Sarah Mary Williams and George Peters (at Mrs. Judith Loftus's); as Charles William Albright, alias Aleck James Hopkins (in the Raftsmen's

Passage); as Mary Ann's brother (confronting the two slave-hunters on the river); as George Jackson (on parleying with the Grangerfords); as Adolphus (English valet to the king and duke); and finally as Tom Sawyer.[14] That is his last, absurd apotheosis: 'for it was like being born again, I was so glad to find out who I was' (177/282). Not a 'born again' Christian, but a 'born again' member of Southern society. The parody never slackens. When the real Tom Sawyer reappears, like his namesake Saint Thomas, he views the risen Huck with shocked awe:

> 'I hain't ever done you no harm. You know that. So then, what you want to come back and ha'nt *me* for?'
> I says:
> 'I hain't come back—I hain't been *gone.*'
> When he heard my voice, it righted him up some, but he warn't quite satisfied yet. He says:
> 'Don't you play nothing on me, because I wouldn't on you. Honest injun, now, you ain't a ghost?'
> 'Honest injun, I ain't,' I says.
> 'Well—I—I—well, that ought to settle it, of course; but I can't somehow seem to understand it, no way. Looky here, warn't you ever murdered *at all?*'
> 'No. I warn't ever murdered at all—I played it on them. You come in here and feel of me if you don't believe me."
> So he done it; and it satisfied him.[15]

This is Huck's last 'post-crucifixion' appearance. Up to this point, in a sense, he *had* been a ghost, ineffectively haunting the shores of the Mississippi. That is why 'The Raftsmen's Passage' is so crucial. As Kenneth S. Lynn first realized, it is a text within a text, a kind of parable for the whole of *Huckleberry Finn*. Like Charles William Albright, whose identity Huck promptly adopts, Huck, too, has taken to the river in pursuit of a father:

> Drifting down the river toward a goal he can neither define nor scarcely imagine, Huck is in fact looking for another father to replace the one he has lost. And this quest is also a quest for himself, because once Huck has found his new father he will know at last who he himself really is.[16]

This quest is doomed to failure. Yet at the very point of his first Judas-like betrayal, he presents Jim instead (in the role of smallpox victim) as his father. 'I wish you would', he says to the slave-hunters, 'because it's pap that's there ...' (75/126).

That had been Huck's problem all along. As Ben Rogers put it: 'Here's Huck Finn, he hain't got no family—what you going to do 'bout him?' (12/10) Huck's answer is to assume a series of alibis which he works into elaborate, thumbnail sketches. Twain brooded over these fictions. They are lavish with family names and details. They respond dramatically to the pressure of each occasion: Sarah Williams from Hookerville, seven miles south of St. Petersburg, come to tell Uncle Abner Moore that mother is 'down sick, and out of money' (48/68); George Peters, the 'runaway 'prentice', bound to a mean old farmer, looking for uncle Abner Moore in Goshen (52/73); Aleck James Hopkins, sent by Pap to contact 'a Mr Jonas Turner, in Cairo'; George Jackson, the Arkansas farmboy, fallen overboard off a steamboat, after a catalogue of disasters on the tenant-farm (82/135); and yet another orphan, from Pike County, Missouri, bound 'fourteen hundred mile' on $16 for Uncle Ben (103/166). Or there is his mercy mission at Booth's Landing where he thoroughly confuses the ferryman with his tale of Miss Hooker and her rich Uncle Hornback, contriving three fictitious deaths in the farrago for the robber trio aboard the *Walter Scott* (ch. 13).

For Huck—an only child, it seems—invariably invents tangled and complex family relationships, which are at once doomed to destruction. He is either an apprentice orphan; or a destitute orphan, deserted by his sister and brothers; or sole survivor of a collision. When a whole family, in one instance, does survive, it is down with smallpox aboard a raft. Huck consistently plays, that is, on others' sensibility as an outcast. For he *feels* his condition to be orphaned, even before learning of Pap's death. (Though, of course, some explanation was needed to account for a 14-year-old boy and a slave together on a raft.) These fictions, these hoaxes, these disguises are all masks. Huck is a creature of masks who sustains himself only in continual metamorphoses. It is when he returns to society at the end, 'appropriately trapped in the mask of Tom Sawyer (*the* mask of masks)', that he finally risks domination by the fixed concepts of civilization.[17]

Twain was a contemporary of Nietzsche, whom he went on to read, though well after the completion of *Huckleberry Finn*. In *Beyond Good and Evil* there is a passage that might almost be a commentary on Huck. The mask, Nietzsche argues, appropriates what is foreign; it arbitrarily falsifies certain traits to suit itself. But, just as arbitrarily, it shuts out and ignores other traits. It approves its own ignorance and even, on occasion, allows itself to be deceived with a joy 'in uncertainty and ambiguity'. For masks are capricious:

> Finally there also belongs here that not altogether innocent readiness of the spirit to deceive other spirits and to dissemble before them, that continual pressing and pushing of a creative, formative, changeable force: in this the spirit enjoys the multiplicity and cunning of its masks.[18]

'Larvatus prodeo': Descartes' motto might well be Huck's. But these 'feigned tales', hoaxes and disguises, as Andrew Lang recognized in 1891, are also essentially epic:

> In one point Mark Twain is Homeric, probably without knowing it. In the Odyssey, Odysseus frequently tells a false tale about himself, to account for his appearance and position when disguised on his own island. He shows extraordinary fertility and appropriateness of invention, wherein he is equalled by the feigned tales of Huckleberry Finn.

Their performance is itself part of the oral tradition. What for Jim is just a 'dodge', or for the duke 'another little job', for Huck become 'yarns' or (on two occasions) 'stretchers'. For the yarn is literally *stretched*. The momentum of the narrative invades these fictions-within-the-fiction, inflating them, just as Homeric similes are dramatically indulged. There is no stopping such oral thrust. The narrative impulse extends every nuance, every play of circumstance—whether surrounding Hank Bunker or George Jackson. Huck, in this sense, is the very heir of Odysseus as Cretan liar. With blithe self-confidence he proclaims: 'I'll go and fix up some kind of a yarn . . .' (61/87).

Even Jim is not immune to his hoaxes; or alibis even. But Huck goes unmasked for Jim. Jim accepts the white boy as a fellow-outlaw on the run; Huck learns to accept Jim as a black and loving father:

> Encountering the outcast colored man in hiding on the island, Huck is at first merely amazed and exasperated by the black man's stupidity, but part of the drama of their relationship is Huck's gathering awareness that Jim is 'most always right' about things that really matter, about how certain movements of the birds mean a storm is coming, about the dangers of messing with snakes, and the meaning of dreams. But while Jim's relationship to Huck is fatherly in the sense that he constantly is correcting and admonishing the boy, forever telling him some new truth about the world, he is identified even more unmistakably as Huck's father by the love that he gives him. As Huck is searching for a father, so Jim is attempting to rejoin his family, and he lavishes on the love-starved boy all of his parental affection.[19]

'Never you mind, honey,' he tells him. 'Don't you git too peart' (46/63). He stands his watch for him, and pets him, and picks the corn-shuck bedding while Huck sleeps on straw. But this, too, is a kind of 'evasion'. A white boy cannot ultimately have a black father. Once freed, Jim will have his own little Johnny. Freed from his own past, Huck will have to grow up. The compact is temporary and cannot resolve Huck's deepest needs: it is a compact of affectionate trust, on the open road, not a family tie.

Huck's awareness oi im, moreover, was always limited. There were glimpses, throughout the *Adventures,* of a shrewd, wily, independent, even manipulative Jim. But had Huck noticed? Had he realized? Had he transcended his own desperate need for a lovable, hurt-but-chuckling Sambo (with a heart of gold)? Jim remains a stereotyped and sentimental figure. When Huck, sleeping naked outside the wigwam, is washed overboard, it 'most killed Jim a-laughing. He was the easiest nigger to laugh that ever was, anyway' (104/168). Instead of Tom, Huck now has his 'Uncle Tom' as a companion on the river, who will turn readily, when occasion offers, into a dignified (and humorous) Messiah.

That is the symbolic 'evasion' to which I shall return at length in Chapter 14. Its effect on Jim's role in the narrative, needless to say, is disastrous. For Huck, the outsider, who had betrayed his own community by siding with a slave, can only redeem his social role (as a pseudo-Tom Sawyer) by humiliating him. Jim must be reduced to a black scapegoat. Jim must suffer for white justice; for white renewal, that is, and reintegration. Jim must suffer for that ultimate Judas (Tom), who sells his conscience, like the two slave-hunters and huckster king, 'for forty dirty dollars'. It is Tom Sawyer who stages the second passion. Chained and stapled to his cabin, Jim Crow is transformed, for a bit of 'fun', to Jesus Christ. Not social fun, *aesthetic* fun to indulge Tom's boyish sense of the proprieties.[20]

Something in this already pre-dates Huck's arrival at the Phelps farm. The crux, as everyone acknowledges, occurs in chapter 31. After writing his letter to Miss Watson, Huck drifts into a daydream, a reverie, the only extended interior monologue in the book:

> and I see Jim before me, all the time, in the day, and in the nighttime, sometimes moonlight, sometimes storms, and we a floating along, talking, and singing, and laughing. But somehow I couldn't seem to strike no places to harden me against him, but only the other kind. I'd see him standing my watch on top of his'n, stead of calling me, so I could go on sleeping; and see him how glad he was when I come back out of the fog; and when I come to him again in the swamp, up there where the feud was; and such-like times; and would always call me honey, and pet me, and do everything he could think of for me, and how good he always was; and at last I struck the time I saved him by telling the men we had small-pox aboard, and he was so grateful, and said I was the best friend old Jim ever had in the world, and the *only* one he's got now . . .[21]

It is an uncomfortable passage that Twain worked and reworked, piling on the effects: 'sometimes moonlight, sometimes storms, and we a floating . . .' Stylistically it *sounds* false. Because psychologically it *is* false. For once Huck meditates on the past, and the meaning of the past, with free poetic leaps of association. He calls it 'thinking'. But we know from earlier where such thinking leads. This is fantasy. This is dreaming. This is the decisive dream itself, feeding on itself, gathering momentum in its ecstasy, until desire inverts the facts in the triumphant recollection.

Jim had called Huck 'de bes' fren' Jim's ever had' and 'de *only* fren' ole Jim's got now' and (here suppressed) 'de on'y white genlman dat ever kep' his promise to ole Jim' (74/125) *before* his potential betrayal, not *after* the successful evasion. Huck transposes what had, in part, pre-empted his Judas-like decision. His memory is self-congratulatory and self-protective. As he had just observed: 'everybody naturally despises an ungrateful nigger' (168/268). On the jubilation of that inverted recollection—so flattering to him and his sense of their mutual dependence and intimacy—Huck makes his celebrated decision. It is both lyrical and (like all extended lyricism as a basis for action) a trifle farcical. For it stretches the truth in the way Huck most complacently and adroitly and painfully and longingly desires. Once Huck has made his decision to '*go* to hell', he never looks back.

NOTES

[References to *Adventures of Huckleberry Finn* are taken from, firstly, the Norton Critical Edition, edited by Sculley Bradley, Richmond Croom Beatty, E. Hudson Long and Thomas Cooley (New York: W. W. Norton, 1961; 2nd ed. 1977), and, secondly, the Mark Twain Library edition, edited by Walter Blair and Victor Fischer (Berkeley, Calif.: University of California Press, 1985).]

[1] *Huckleberry Finn*, ch. 7, p. 32/41.

[2] See *Tom Sawyer*, ch. 25: 'Look at pap and my mother. Fight! Why, they used to fight all the time. I remember mighty well.' For a vague mention of a wider family circle (all dead), see *Huckleberry Finn*, ch. 5.

[3] Dixon Wecter, *Sam Clemens of Hannibal* (Boston, Mass.: Houghton Mifflin, 1952), p. 106.

[4] Bernard DeVoto, *Mark Twain at Work* (Cambridge, Mass.: Harvard University Press, 1942), p. 17.

[5] Cf. ch. 11: '. . . that evening he got drunk and was around till after midnight with a couple of mighty hard looking strangers, and then went off with them' (49/69).

[6] Just as Huck had predicted in *Tom Sawyer*. He thought then there was no point in his finding treasure: 'Pap would come back to thish yer town some day and get his claws on it if I didn't hurry up, and I tell you he'd clean it out pretty quick' (ch. 25). DeVoto called this the germ of *Huckleberry Finn*.

[7] Huck makes off with 'Pap's whiskey jug', though, which comes in useful for Jim. Note his scorn for the baccy-chewing Bills and Bucks of Bricksville (ch. 21).

[8] *Huckleberry Finn*, ch. 10, p. 47/65.

[9] Ibid., ch. 6, pp. 25/31 and 27/34.

[10] Ibid., ch. 5, p. 21/24.

[11] Ibid., ch. 6, pp. 26–27/33–4; cf. Old Mrs Hotchkiss in ch. 41: 'I says so to Sister Damrell—didn't I, Sister Damrell?—s'y, he's crazy, s'y—them's the very words I said. You all hearn me: he's crazy, s'y . . ."' (218/345).

[12] The half-caste, Injun Joe, alone is entombed in McDougal's Cave without hope of resurrection: 'When the cave door was unlocked, a sorrowful sight presented itself in the dim twilight of the place. Injun Joe lay stretched upon the ground, dead, with his face close to the crack of the door, as if his longing eyes had been fixed, to the last moment, upon the light and the cheer of the free world outside' (*Tom Sawyer*, ch. 33).

[13] Cf. Twain's famous *bon mot*: 'The report of my death was greatly exaggerated'; or, as originally framed: 'The report of my death was an exaggeration' (June 1897). Already in the *Early Tales & Sketches* (1863) there is a joke about someone reported dead: 'I asked him about it at church this morning. He said there was no truth in the rumor.'

[14] Peter G. Beidler has put the definitive case for the restoration of 'The Raftsmen's Passage' from *Life in the Mississippi* to *Huckleberry Finn* in 'The Raft Episode in *Huckleberry Finn*', *Modern Fiction Studies*, vol. 14 (Spring 1968), pp. 11–20.

[15] *Huckleberry Finn*, ch. 33, pp. 177–8/283.

[16] Kenneth S. Lynn, *Mark Twain and Southwestern Humor* (Boston, Mass.: Little, Brown, 1959), ch. 9, p. 213.

[17] John Carlos Rowe, *Through the Custom-House: Nineteenth-Century American Fiction and Modern Theory* (Baltimore, Md.: Johns Hopkins University Press, 1982), ch. 6, pp. 164–5.

[18] Nietzsche, *Beyond Good and Evil*, trans. R. J. Hollingdale (Harmondsworth: Penguin Books, 1972), pp. 141–2; cf. also Claude Lévi-Strauss in this quasi-paraphrase of Nietzsche: 'Un masque n'existe pas en soi; il suppose, toujours présents à ses côtés, d'autres masques réels ou possibles qu'on aurait pu choisir pour les lui substituer . . . Un masque n'est pas d'abord ce qu'il présente mais ce qu'il transforme, c'est-à-dire choisit de *ne pas* représenter. Comme un mythe, un masque nie autant qu'il affirme; il n'est pas fait seulement de ce qu'il dit ou croit dire, mais de ce qu'il exclut' (*La Voie des masques*, 1975).

[19] Lynn, *Mark Twain and Southwestern Humor*, pp. 214–15.

[20] See Harold Beaver, 'Time on the Cross: White Fiction and Black Messiahs', *Yearbook of English Studies*, vol. 8 (1978), p. 50.

[21] *Huckleberry Finn*, ch. 31, p. 169/270.

CONTRIBUTORS

HAROLD BLOOM is Sterling Professor of the Humanities at Yale University and Professor of English at the New York University Graduate School. He is a 1985 MacArthur Foundation Award recipient, served as the Charles Eliot Norton Professor of Poetry at Harvard University (1987–88), and is the author of eighteen books, the most recent being *Poetics of Influence: New and Selected Criticism* (1988). Currently he is editing the Chelsea House series Modern Critical Views and Modern Critical Interpretations, and other Chelsea House series in literary criticism.

RICHARD POIRIER is Professor of English at Rutgers University. His most recent work is *The Renewal of Literature: Emersonian Reflections* (1987).

ALAN TRACHTENBERG is Professor of English and American Studies at Yale University. His works include *The City: American Experience* (1971; with Peter Neill and Peter C. Bunnell), *Brooklyn Bridge: Fact and Symbol* (1979), *The Incorporation of America: Culture and Society in the Gilded Age* (1982), and many essays on American literature and culture.

WARWICK WADLINGTON is Professor of English at the University of Texas, Austin. He is the author of *Reading Faulknerian Tragedy* (1987).

SUSAN K. HARRIS is Associate Professor of English at Queens College of the City University of New York. Her articles have appeared in *Legacy, Studies in American Fiction*, and *ESQ*.

R. J. FERTEL has published articles on Wordsworth and film in *The Wordsworth Circle* and the *New Orleans Review*. He teaches at the University of New Orleans.

ROGER ASSELINEAU teaches at the University of Paris (Sorbonne). His works include *The Transcendentalist Constant in American Literature* (1980) and *Saint Jean de Crevecoeur: The Life of an American Farmer* (1987; with Gay Wilson Allen).

MILLICENT BELL is Professor of English at Boston University. Her works include *Edith Wharton and Henry James: The Story of Their Friendship* (1965), *Marquand: An American Life* (1979), and many articles on English and American literature.

LEE CLARK MITCHELL is Associate Professor of English at Princeton University. He is editor of *New Essays on* The Red Badge of Courage (1986) and author of *Witnesses to a Vanishing America* (1981).

NANCY WALKER is Chair of the Department of Languages and Literature at Stephens College. She is author of *A Very Serious Thing: Women's Humor and American Culture* (1988).

JOHN S. WHITLEY is Chairman of American Studies at the University of Sussex. He has written books on William Golding and F. Scott Fitzgerald and has edited Dickens's *American Notes*.

FORREST G. ROBINSON has written *The Shape of Things Known: Sidney's Apology in Its Philosophical Tradition* (1972), *Wallace Stegner* (1977; with Margaret G.

Robinson), and articles on American literature. He is Professor of American Literature at the University of California, Santa Cruz.

HAROLD BEAVER has written *A Figure in the Carpet: Irony and the American Novel* (1962) and *The Great American Masquerade* (1985). He teaches at the University of Amsterdam.

BIBLIOGRAPHY

Barnette, Louise K. "Huckleberry Finn: Picaro as Linguistic Outsider." *College Literature* 6 (1979): 221–31.

Bassett, John E. "Tom, Huck and the Young Pilot: Twain's Quest for Authority." *Mississippi Quarterly* 39 (1985–86): 3–19.

Becker, John E. "Twain: The Statements Was Interesting Enough." In *Poetic Prophecy in Western Literature,* edited by Jan Wojcik and Raymond-Jean Frontain. Rutherford, NJ: Fairleigh Dickinson University Press, 1984.

Bennett, Jonathan. "Conscience of Huckleberry Finn." *Philosophy* 49 (1974): 123–34.

Blakemore, Steven. "Huck Finn's Written World." *American Literary Realism* 21 (1988): 21–29.

Budd, Louis J., ed. *Critical Essays on Mark Twain 1867–1910.* Boston: G. K. Hall, 1983.

———, ed. *Critical Essays on Mark Twain 1910–1980.* Boston: G. K. Hall, 1982.

Burg, David F. "Another View of Huckleberry Finn." *Nineteenth-Century Fiction* 29 (1974): 299–319.

Carter, Everett. "The Modernist Ordeal of Huckleberry Finn." *Studies in American Fiction* 13 (1985): 169–83.

Davis, Sara, and Philip Beidler, ed. *The Mythologizing of Mark Twain.* University: University of Alabama Press, 1984.

Eliot, T. S. "Introduction" to *Adventures of Huckleberry Finn.* London: Cresset Press, 1950, pp. vii–xvi.

Fender, Stephen, " 'The Prodigal in a Far Country Chawing of Husks': Mark Twain's Search for a Style in the West." *Modern Language Review* 71 (1976): 737–56.

Fetterley, Judith. "Mark Twain and the Anxiety of Entertainment." *Georgia Review* 71 (1979): 382–91.

Fiedler, Leslie A. "Come Back to the Raft Ag'in, Huck Honey!" *Partisan Review* 15 (1948): 664–71; rpt. in *The Collected Essays of Leslie Fiedler,* Volume 1. New York: Stein & Day, 1971.

Gillman, Susan, and Robert Patten. "Dickens: Doubles::Twain: Twins." *Nineteenth-Century Fiction* 39 (1985): 441–58.

Griffith, Clark. "Merlin's Grin: From 'Tom' to 'Huck' in a Connecticut Yankee." *New England Quarterly* 48 (1975): 28–46.

Hochman, Baruch. *Character in Literature.* Ithaca: Cornell University Press, 1985.

Holland, Laurence. "A 'Raft of Trouble': Word and Deed in *Huckleberry Finn.*" *Glyph* 5 (1979): 69–87.

Inge, M. Thomas, ed. *Huck Finn among the Critics: A Centennial Selection.* Frederick, MD: University Publications of America, 1985.

Johnson, James L. *Mark Twain and the Limits of Power.* Knoxville: University of Tennessee Press, 1982.

Jones, Rhett S. "Nigger and Knowledge: White Double-Consciousness in *Adventures of Huckleberry Finn.*" *Mark Twain Journal* 22 (Fall 1984): 28–37.

Kastely, James L. "The Ethics of Self-Interest: Narrative Logic in *Huckleberry Finn.*" *Nineteenth-Century Fiction* 40 (1986): 412–37.

Krauss, Jennifer. "Playing Double in *Adventures of Huckleberry Finn.*" *Mark Twain Journal* 21 (Fall 1983): 22–24.

Leary, Lewis. *Southern Excursions: Essays on Mark Twain and Others.* Baton Rouge: Louisiana State University Press, 1971.

Lettis, Richard; McDonnell, Robert F.; and Morris, William E., ed. *Huck Finn and His Critics.* New York: Macmillan, 1962.

MacKethan, Lucinda H. "Huckleberry Finn and the Slave Narratives: Lighting Out as Design." *Southern Review* 20 (1984): 247–64.

Martin, Terence. "The Negative Character in American Fiction." In *Toward a New American Literary History,* edited by Louis J. Budd et al. Durham, NC: Duke University Press, 1980, pp. 230–43.

May, Charles E. "Literary Masters and Masturbators: Sexuality, Fantasy, and Reality in *Huckleberry Finn." Literature and Psychology* 28 (1978): 85–92.

Murphy, Kevin. "Illiterate's Progress." *Texas Studies in Literature and Language* 26 (1984): 363–87.

Opdahl, Keith M. "You'll Be Sorry When I'm Dead: Child Adult Relations in *Huck Finn." Modern Fiction Studies* 25 (1979–80): 613–24.

Pinsker, Sanford. "Huckleberry Finn, Modernist Poet." *Midwest Quarterly* 24 (1983): 261–73.

Price, Martin. *Forms of Life: Character and Moral Imagination in the Novel.* New Haven: Yale University Press, 1983.

Ricard, Serge. "Introduction" to *From Rags to Riches: Le Myth du Self-Made Man.* Aix-en-Provence: Publications de l'Université de Provence, 1984.

Robinson, Forrest G. "The Silences in *Huckleberry Finn." Nineteenth-Century Fiction* 37 (1982): 50–74.

Sawicki, Joseph. "Authority/Author-ity: Representation and Fictionality." *Modern Fiction Studies* 31 (1985): 691–702.

Schacht, Paul. "The Lonesomeness of Huckleberry Finn." *American Literature* 53 (1981): 189–201.

Simpson, Claude M., Jr. "Huck Finn after *Huck Finn."* In *American Humor: Essays Presented to John C. Gerber,* edited by O. M. Brack, Jr. Scottsdale, AZ: Arete, 1977.

Skaggs, Merrill M. *The Folk of Southern Fiction.* Athens: University of Georgia Press, 1972.

Sloane, David E. *Mark Twain as a Literary Comedian.* Baton Rouge: Louisiana State University Press, 1979.

Smith, David L. "Huck, Jim and American Racial Discourse." *Mark Twain Journal* 22 (Fall 1984): 4–12.

Smith, Henry Nash. *Mark Twain: The Development of a Writer.* Cambridge, MA: Harvard University Press, 1962.

Spengemann, William C. *Mark Twain and the Backwoods Angel: The Matter of Innocence in the Works of Samuel L. Clemens.* Kent, OH: Kent State University Press, 1966.

Torrance, Robert M. *The Comic Hero.* Cambridge, MA: Harvard University Press, 1978.

Towers, Tom H. "Love and Power in *Huckleberry Finn." Tulane Studies in English* 23 (1978): 17–37.

Welsh, Alexander. *Reflections on the Hero as Quixote.* Princeton: Princeton University Press, 1981.

Wolff, Cynthia Griffin. *"The Adventures of Tom Sawyer:* A Nightmare Vision of American Boyhood." *Massachusetts Review* 21 (1980): 637–52.

ACKNOWLEDGMENTS

Letters to Van Wyck Brooks (early April 1918) by Sherwood Anderson from *Letters of Sherwood Anderson,* edited by Howard Mumford Jones and Walter B. Rideout, © 1953 by Eleanor Anderson. Reprinted by permission of Harold Ober Associates.

"Huckleberry Finn" by Lionel Trilling from *The Liberal Imagination: Essays on Literature and Society* by Lionel Trilling, © 1948 by Lionel Trilling. Reprinted by permission of Diana Trilling.

"Twentieth-Century Fiction and the Black Mask of Humanity" by Ralph Ellison from *Shadow and Act* by Ralph Ellison, © 1953, 1964 by Ralph Ellison. Reprinted by permission of Random House, Inc., and the William Morris Agency.

"Good Good Girls and Good Bad Boys" by Leslie A. Fiedler from *Love and Death in the American Novel* by Leslie A. Fiedler, © 1960 and 1966 by Leslie A. Fiedler. Reprinted by permission.

"Southwestern Vernacular" by James M. Cox from *Mark Twain: The Fate of Humor* by James M. Cox, © 1966 by Princeton University Press. Reprinted by permission.

"Welcome Back from the Raft, Huck Honey!" by Kenneth S. Lynn from *American Scholar* 46, No. 3 (Summer 1977), © 1977 Kenneth Lynn. Reprinted by permission.

" 'Bless You, Chile': Fiedler and 'Huck Honey' a Generation Later" by Jesse Bier from *Mississippi Quarterly* 34, No. 4 (Fall 1981), © 1981 by Mississippi State University. Reprinted by permission of *The Mississippi Quarterly.*

"Interpreting the Passover Dream: Jim in Traditional Hebrew" by Albert Waldinger from *American Notes and Queries* 22, Nos. 3 & 4 (November–December 1983), © 1983 by Erasmus Press. Reprinted by permission.

"Toward a Chaos of Incomprehensibilities" by David R. Sewell from *Mark Twain's Languages* by David R. Sewell, © 1987 by The Regents of the University of California. Reprinted by permission of the University of California Press.

"Transatlantic Configurations: Mark Twain and Jane Austen" by Richard Poirier from *A World Elsewhere: The Place of Style in American Literature* by Richard Poirier, © 1966 by Richard Poirier. Reprinted by permission.

"The Form of Freedom in *The Adventures of Huckleberry Finn*" by Alan Trachtenberg from *Southern Review* n.s. 6, No. 4 (October 1970), © 1975 by Alan Trachtenberg. Reprinted by permission.

"But I Never Said Nothing" (originally titled "But I Never Said Nothing: *The Adventures of Huckleberry Finn*") by Warwick Wadlington from *The Confidence Game in American Literature* by Warwick Wadlington, © 1975 by Princeton University Press. Reprinted by permission.

"Huck Finn" (originally titled *"The Adventures of Huckleberry Finn:* Huck Finn") by Susan K. Harris from *Mark Twain's Escape from Time* by Susan K. Harris, © 1982 by the

Curators of the University of Missouri. Reprinted by permission of the University of Missouri Press.

"Spontaneity and the Quest for Maturity in *Huckleberry Finn*" (originally titled " 'Free and Easy'? Spontaneity and the Quest for Maturity in the *Adventures of Huckleberry Finn*") by R. J. Fertel from *Modern Language Quarterly* 44, No. 2 (June 1983), © 1984 by the University of Washington. Reprinted by permission of *Modern Language Quarterly*.

"A Transcendentalist Poet Named Huckleberry Finn" by Roger Asselineau from *Studies in American Fiction* 13, No. 2 (Autumn 1985), © 1985 by *Studies in American Fiction*. Reprinted by permission.

"*Huckleberry Finn* and the Sleights of the Imagination" by Millicent Bell from *One Hundred Years of* Huckleberry Finn: *The Boy, His Book, and American Culture*, edited by Robert Sattelmeyer and J. Donald Crowley, © 1985 by the Curators of the University of Missouri. Reprinted by permission of the University of Missouri Press.

"The Authority of Language in *Huckleberry Finn*" (originally titled " 'Nobody but Our Gang Warn't Around': The Authority of Language in *Huckleberry Finn*") by Lee Clark Mitchell from *New Essays on* Adventures of Huckleberry Finn, edited by Louis J. Budd, © 1985 by Cambridge University Press. Reprinted by permission.

"Reformers and Young Maidens: Women and Virtue in *Huckleberry Finn*" (originally titled "Reformers and Young Maidens: Women and Virtue in *Adventures of Huckleberry Finn*") by Nancy Walker from *One Hundred Years of* Huckleberry Finn: *The Boy, His Book, and American Culture*, edited by Robert Sattelmeyer and J. Donald Crowley, © 1985 by the Curators of the University of Missouri. Reprinted by permission of the University of Missouri Press.

"Kid's Stuff: Mark Twain's Boys" by John S. Whitley from *Mark Twain: A Sumptuous Variety*, edited by Robert Giddings, © 1985 by Vision Press, Ltd. Reprinted by permission of Vision Press, Ltd. and Barnes & Noble Books.

"The Grand Evasion" by Forrest G. Robinson from *In Bad Faith: The Dynamics of Deception in Mark Twain's America* by Forrest G. Robinson, © 1986 by the President and Fellows of Harvard College. Reprinted by permission of Harvard University Press.

"Huck and Pap" by Harold Beaver from *Huckleberry Finn* by Harold Beaver, © 1987 by Harold Beaver. Reprinted by permission Unwin Hyman Publishers, Ltd.

INDEX